The
EVERYTHING
ONLINE
AUCTIONS
BOOK

Dear Reader,

This book comes to you from the perspective of two experienced online auction enthusiasts.

Steve first became interested in online auctions as a part-time job his then-pregnant wife could do at home. Over the years, they had gathered a large collection of vintage cowboy boots and had some collectible furniture and art sitting unused and unappreciated in a storage unit. In no time, they worked their way through this stuff, selling their "junk" for prices so high they were astonished. Soon, Steve was also working out of the house full-time, and they were earning a very nice income.

For Si, online auctions have long been convenient, dependable, and affordable places to buy items he needs to mend or upgrade the computers and printers in his business. Online auction sites have also been fun places for him to reconnect with nostalgic items from his past and enhance his lifelong hobbies. Recently, he became an online seller, too.

In our book, we hope to help you enter the online auction world as smoothly and enjoyably as possible, while avoiding the common mistakes we both made when we got started.

You are in for a lot of fun. Good luck!

Steve Encell

Si [signature]

The EVERYTHING® Series

Editorial

Publishing Director	Gary M. Krebs
Director of Product Development	Paula Munier
Associate Managing Editor	Laura M. Daly
Associate Copy Chief	Brett Palana-Shanahan
Acquisitions Editor	Gina Chaimanis
Development Editor	Katie McDonough
Associate Production Editor	Casey Ebert

Production

Director of Manufacturing	Susan Beale
Associate Director of Production	Michelle Roy Kelly
Cover Design	Paul Beatrice
	Matt LeBlanc
	Erick DaCosta
Design and Layout	Colleen Cunningham
	Sorae Lee
	Jennifer Oliveira
Series Cover Artist	Barry Littmann

THE
EVERYTHING®
ONLINE
AUCTIONS
BOOK

All you need to buy and sell with success—on eBay® and beyond!

Steve Encell & Si Dunn

Adams Media
Avon, Massachusetts

An Everything® Series Book.
Everything® and everything.com® are registered trademarks of F+W Publications, Inc.

Published by Adams Media, an F+W Publications Company
57 Littlefield Street, Avon, MA 02322 U.S.A.
www.adamsmedia.com

ISBN: 1-59337-582-4
Printed in the United States of America.

J   I   H   G   F   E   D   C   B   A

Library of Congress Cataloging-in-Publication Data
Encell, Steve.
The everything online auctions book / Steve Encell and Si Dunn.
p. cm. -- (Everything series)
ISBN 1-59337-582-4
1. Internet auctions. I. Dunn, Si II. Title. III. Series.

HF5478.E57 2006
381'.177--dc22

2006004163

This publication is designed to provide accurate and authoritative information with regard to the subject matter covered. It is sold with the understanding that the publisher is not engaged in rendering legal, accounting, or other professional advice. If legal advice or other expert assistance is required, the services of a competent professional person should be sought.

—From a *Declaration of Principles* jointly adopted by a Committee of the American Bar Association and a Committee of Publishers and Associations

All online auction sites identified by name within this book are the intellectual property of their respective owners and no claim of any rights thereto is being made herein. In addition, care has been taken to properly identify each of these sites by their accurate designation(s). Neither the author nor the publisher is in any way associated or affiliated with the entity owning the rights to any of the sites referred to herein. This book is not authorized or endorsed by these auction sites.

Many of the designations used by manufacturers and sellers to distinguish their products are claimed as trademarks. Where those designations appear in this book and Adams Media was aware of a trademark claim, the designations have been printed with initial capital letters.

This book is available at quantity discounts for bulk purchases.
For information, please call 1-800-872-5627.

Contents

Acknowledgments

Steve: Thanks to Larry Brody, Si Dunn, and Pace. This book couldn't have been written without all three of you.

Si: Special thanks to Connie Dunn and Erin Dunn, for helping with research and letting me sell off some excess "treasures" after I decided to become an online auction seller, as well as buyer. Thanks, also, to TV writer and producer Larry Brody for his superb guidance and advice during this book's creation. In the shorthand parlance of the entertainment world: LYMI ("Love ya. Mean it").

Top Ten Things You Will Learn in This Book

1. How online auctions can help you get lower prices for the things you buy and higher prices for the things you sell.

2. How online auction selling can be a good source of extra income or an exciting new career.

3. Why you should be a buyer first, before you become a seller on eBay or any other online auction site.

4. Why getting good feedback is extremely important to online auction sellers and buyers.

5. How to use online auction sites to find the items you need to fix something, replace something, expand a collection, bring new pleasures to a hobby, or save money in a small business.

6. The best ways to list, display, and promote the items you want to sell online.

7. How to pack sold items effectively, so you can keep shipping costs down and sales profits up.

8. The best ways to ship the items you sell online to domestic and international customers.

9. The importance of inventory: how to keep finding more items to sell at online auction sites.

10. What the future may hold for online auction sellers and buyers, as well as for online auction sites.

Introduction

▶Auctions are one of humankind's oldest business pursuits, probably dating back to the earliest sales of food and animal hides. Auctions also represent one of the world's simplest business models: an item or service is offered for sale to the highest bidder. Despite the historical vintage and simplicity of auctions, only small numbers of people actually take part in them. A conventional auction typically requires travel to a central site where you can sell goods or examine the items that will be put up for bid. Sellers have no guarantee that interested buyers will show up for the auction, and buyers have no guarantee that they will find something they want or need.

In 1995, the Internet and one man's hobby turned the ancient auction process totally on its head. Now, online auction Web sites make it easy for almost anyone on the planet who has a computer and Net access to buy from, or sell to, almost anyone else who can log on to the same auction site. In the online auction world, corporations and sole-proprietor home businesses can compete for the same buyers. No special training, certifications, franchises, or storefronts are required to become an online auction seller. Indeed, all you really need are a few items to sell, a camera, and a credit card or debit card (necessary to open a seller account or buyer account at online auction sites such as eBay or Amazon). Many people have launched part-time and full-time sales businesses simply by grabbing a few unneeded things from their households and selling them online. Later, they have branched out to items purchased at yard sales, garage sales, estate sales, and other auctions. Then they have learned how to buy certain merchandise at one online auction site and resell it at others. From there, they have opened online stores and built even bigger businesses that use online auctions to help them sell merchandise and buy more things to sell.

In this book, you will discover how easy and fun it can be to bid and win at online auction sites, and how simple and profitable it can be to sell items online. You will learn how online auctions work and why you should always make a few small purchases first at any auction site before you sign up to be one of its sellers. You will also learn how to open buyer and seller accounts at some of the leading online auction venues, such as eBay, Yahoo!, Amazon, and uBid. This book will guide you through the process of creating your first listing, making your first sale, getting paid quickly, and picking the best way to ship the sold item, whether the buyer is in the next county or halfway around the world. These experiences and the tips in this book will give you the insights you need to master the online auction business.

Online auction sites can be fun places to buy useful items for your home, business, or hobby at bargain prices. Online auctions can be a pleasant, convenient, and profitable means of paring down the overabundance of stuff in your life. Online auctions can also be catalysts for a new career that takes you out of a corporate cubicle, puts a stop to commuting, and lets you work at home during the hours you choose.

Reading this book will not ensure success. In the world of business, there are no guaranteed paths to high achievement. Still, in the pages that follow, you can learn the techniques and skills necessary to succeed as an online auction seller. With the right efforts and determination and a willingness to keep learning, you may be able to create an online auction sales business that will grow far beyond your expectations.

The world of online auctions awaits you. Are you ready to start buying and selling?

Chapter 1
Welcome to Online Auctions

The year 1995 marked a major turning point for personal computer users. A perfect storm of progress swirled together, merging the Internet with hypertext, the World Wide Web, Web sites, Web pages, Web browsers—and AuctionWeb, which soon would change its name to eBay. At last, people could do something with their PCs besides search for information, exchange e-mails, or post their thoughts on message boards. In online auctions, they could buy almost anything they needed or wanted, from hundreds or even thousands of miles away.

A Little Web History

Picture a computer so big it weighed 250 tons and consumed more than a million watts of power. Its 55,000 vacuum tubes and countless flashing lights generated fantastic amounts of heat, and the beast had to be kept cool at all times. Otherwise, its magnetic core memories would melt away in just sixty seconds. IBM built nearly sixty of these massive machines for America's first computerized air defense system, starting in the mid-1950s. The system was called SAGE—Semi-Automatic Ground Environment. Each of the computers required more than a hundred people to operate and maintain it, and the systems were kept in service for nearly thirty years. The power-hungry behemoths had just 64 kilobytes of memory space, and could perform about 75,000 instructions per second—tiny fractions of the capabilities now offered in a single, one-pound computer that nestles in the palm of your hand.

FACT

SAGE was designed to detect Soviet bombers and guide American jet fighters to intercept them. Yet, the system also paved the way for the creation of the Internet, the World Wide Web, and global e-commerce. Essentially, SAGE was the first interactive network, with nearly two-dozen radar detection sites sending data over modems and phone lines to a central command-and-control facility.

During the lifespan of SAGE, thousands of computer programmers and technicians had to be trained, and many migrated to commercial computer companies once they left the military. They became the backbone of hardware and software innovations in the United States in the 1980s and 1990s and helped make possible the creation of the Internet, which eventually gave rise to the World Wide Web and virtually everything now available online.

SAGE, however, was not the only computer game in town. Between World War II and the early 1990s, a number of brilliant thinkers independently created concepts that advanced computer science and stirred many other inventive minds. For example, in a 1945 *Atlantic Monthly* article, a leading U.S. weapons scientist, Vannevar Bush, unveiled his concept for a mechanical desk that could serve as a library and private information file. Bush envisioned a personal unit with a viewing screen and the ability to store information that could be consulted "with exceeding speed and flexibility." Two decades later, the author Marshall McLuhan popularized the concept of an interconnected "global village" able to communicate over "an electronic nervous system." In the mid-1960s, computer researcher Douglas Engelbart developed the first computer mouse, followed soon by the first graphical user interface and the first working hypertext system.

Positive Fallout

The U.S. Defense Department and the Cold War both get some credit for the rise of the Internet. In the 1960s, while the Vietnam War was raging, the Cuban Missile Crisis was still fresh on many U.S. leaders' minds. Devices known as "computers" were beginning to play bigger roles in national government and military planning. Nobody yet had these cantankerous machines in their homes. The early devices filled up entire rooms and buildings, gulped electricity by the megawatt, and needed small armies of technicians and operators to keep them going. Planners soon realized that *many* computers would be needed to meet the growing needs of the government and the armed forces. But if the computers were put in one huge computing facility, it would be a very tempting target for the Soviet Union's long-range bombers and missiles.

A new concept soon emerged. If computers could be *distributed* to key scientific research and industrial facilities across the nation and linked with the Pentagon's computers through leased lines, at least some of the government's and military's command-and-control structure would survive a nuclear attack. The idea soon led to a grant from the Advanced Research Projects Agency (ARPA), and ARPANET was born.

A computer at the University of California at Los Angeles (UCLA) was the first one added to the fledgling network in 1969, followed soon afterward by other computers in California and Utah. During the 1970s, ARPANET continued to expand, adding connections to many other universities that were trying to develop better data networks and methods of data processing.

Communications on ARPANET were complicated by the fact that most of the linked computers used different and typically incompatible operating systems. Early in the 1980s, the Defense Department settled on Internet Protocol (IP) as its networking standard. Gradually, it broke away from ARPANET and created its own network, MILNET. As other agencies and facilities adopted the IP standard, ARPANET lost ground, and the Internet expanded and replaced it.

Home Advantage

Desktop personal computers hit the marketplace in the late 1970s and quickly began popping up in homes and businesses. PC buyers initially used their machines to create documents and help manage their finances. But, with help from external and internal modulator-demodulator (modem) boards and telephone lines, PC owners began using the first commercial e-mail service, CompuServe, in 1979, to send messages to each other. They also started joining specialized "newsgroups," where they could read and respond to messages posted by other group members who shared their interests. Articles and information began to be posted that users could read, print out, or download as research materials. Text advertisements sometimes appeared on the dial-up sites, and businesses started sending out e-mail messages to try to sell things. CompuServe also introduced the first online chat service in 1980. By the early 1990s, CompuServe was the home of numerous online moderated forums on a wide range of topics. Several companies also used forums to provide technical support to their customers.

QUESTION?

Who invented the World Wide Web?
Tim Berners-Lee, a software engineer at CERN, the European particle physics laboratory on the Swiss-French border, and a fellow CERN employee, Robert Cailliau, created the first Web server on December 25, 1990, and posted CERN's phonebook on it. In August 1991, Berners-Lee made his Web server software and simple browser software available to all via the Internet. Web servers quickly sprang up across the planet, and the World Wide Web was born.

For computer users, the focus remained on logging on to proprietary sites to find information or people who shared their interests—not merchandise.

Browser Power

At first, the World Wide Web continued to be a special playground for skilled computer users. That quickly changed in 1994, when Marc Andreessen and Netscape brought the first commercial Web browser to the public, followed soon by Microsoft and its Internet Explorer. As a result, computer users could quickly search the Internet for links to information, and they could visit Web sites run by individuals, companies, agencies, and schools almost anywhere on the planet. They weren't limited to the offerings of one source, such as CompuServe, America Online, or Prodigy.

Shopping on the Web

People sold things online well before they had access to the Web. They posted for-sale notices in their favorite user groups or forums. They e-mailed sales pitches to prospective customers. Web sites, however, made it possible for sellers to post rudimentary online catalogs containing descriptions and pictures of what was being offered for sale and to answer potential buyers' questions via e-mail.

As shopping opportunities started expanding on the Web, some economists predicted consumers would quickly flock to the burgeoning convenience of electronic commerce (e-commerce). The opposite happened. Consumers were immediately concerned about the security of using their credit cards online. In addition, they were accustomed to the instant gratification of buying something at a "real" store and taking it home, not waiting a week or two for delivery. Also, Web stores did not offer any employees or fellow shoppers that consumers could ask about the merchandise they were thinking of buying.

Shopping Cart Blues

A new application—"electronic shopping carts" or "e-shopping carts"—gained popularity in the 1990s, as more and more businesses launched Web sites. Shopping cart software enables customers to select several items from an online catalog and pay for them with a credit card or debit card.

Shopping cart software acts as front-end service. It keeps track of the items an online customer decides to buy. When the customer "checks out," the shopping cart software passes the transaction and credit card information over a secure connection to a "backend service," typically a payment gateway. The payment gateway then routes the information through the seller's Internet merchant account and sends approval or denial of the credit card payment back to the shopping cart software. If any one of the services is down, however, the transaction cannot be completed.

Shopping cart software is seldom easy to set up and maintain, especially for merchants who operate small businesses mostly by themselves. Often, they cannot afford to hire competent help to maintain their shopping cart system and database, and they become frustrated trying to do it themselves.

Auctions Move In

The early pioneers of online commerce focused on business-to-consumer and business-to-business sales. Despite the Internet's ongoing growth, many entrepreneurs shunned its vast possibilities. Instead, they tried and failed to develop proprietary shopping networks that they could control and get others to use. Those who used the Internet and succeeded realized the right merchandise could attract buyers from all over the world to a Web site. So, they built their business models right on top of the Internet and the World Wide Web's almost unlimited interconnections.

OnSale Sets the Tone

In 1993, a veteran of online business startups teamed up with a venture capitalist to try a new approach. The two men would offer an interactive shopping service using the Internet and an online auction format. Jerry Kaplan and Alan Fisher created OnSale in 1994 and put a wide array of merchandise up for bid in May of 1995, including watches, wines, and sports memorabilia, as well as computer hardware and electronics devices. Kaplan and Fisher quickly discovered that their business model needed a narrower focus. Many of their customers were technically proficient males who worked with computers and other electronics devices by day and pursued computer and electronics hobbies on the side. OnSale zeroed in on those two categories, and sales took off.

In 1994, Jeff Bezos founded a company called Amazon in a garage in Bellevue, Washington, a suburb of Seattle. His idea was to use the Internet to sell books online. He launched the Amazon.com Web site in July 1995, and soon was getting book orders from all over the world. Amazon was more than just a digital bookstore, however. Bezos also created an innovative online community where readers could post their thoughts about particular books. This feature quickly became popular with computer users who wanted more information and opinions of titles they were considering buying. Now they didn't have to rely simply on advertisements, professional book reviewers, and word of mouth. They could sample an array of opinions from other readers.

Just two months after Amazon's appearance, an upstart called Auction Web was quietly added to the World Wide Web. Its creator, Pierre Omidyar, a French-Iranian computer programmer living in San Jose, California, initially operated Auction Web as a hobby that would help him get more Internet programming experience. When Auction Web started bringing in more money each month than he was paying to have a Web site, Omidyar realized that people-to-people online auctions could be a good business. He renamed his Web site "eBay," and it quickly took off. Within five years, eBay was a giant in e-commerce, and Amazon.com and other e-commerce sites began setting up online auction sites in an effort to keep up and compete.

How Auctions Work

The basics of auctions are very simple and have scarcely changed throughout recorded human history. Someone with something to sell or trade goes to a public place and announces his auction. Buyers who want what he is offering gather and start offering money or goods to trade—they are placing "bids." As long as the bids keep coming and keep getting higher, the auction continues. Finally, one buyer demonstrates that she wants the item more than the other buyers do. She will outbid them. She wins the auction, claims her purchase, and goes home. Or, she goes down the road to another trading site and puts the item up for bids, hoping to make a quick profit on what she has just bought.

ALERT!

Buyers sometimes allow their emotions or ego to be caught up in a bidding frenzy, and they experience *buyer's remorse* after they win. They realize they will have to pay more than the item is worth. The best defense against buyer's remorse is to research an item before bidding, set a maximum price you will pay, and *stick to it*.

Until the Internet and World Wide Web made bidding from afar available twenty-four hours a day, seven days a week, the vast majority of auctions were local and staged for only short periods. Buyers had to travel to the auction site to examine the goods, make offers, pay, and lug the items home.

A Quick History of Auctions

No one knows when or where the first auctions were held. However, the sessions likely involved the buying and selling of slaves. Some scholars believe the Romans set up the first organized auctions of goods several decades before the birth of Christ. In the sixteenth century, the British held auctions for books and artworks. Later, English settlers brought their auction experience to America in the seventeenth and eighteenth centuries, but the concept did not find much favor in the Colonies, where survival was often a daily and individual struggle. When slaves were brought to America, the slave traders used human auctions to get the highest prices from buyers. After the Civil War, military officers traveled the country, auctioning off surplus equipment and seized goods. In the 1920s and 1930s, as the United States struggled to overcome a great drought and the Great Depression, auctions became linked with trouble. When people could no longer make their house and land payments, creditors seized their properties and often sold them to the highest bidders.

Today, auctions have a much better reputation. Indeed, they can be found in many areas of the American economy. Some typical examples include:

- Livestock and horse auctions
- U.S. Treasury auctions of financial securities such as bonds
- Auctions of properties and merchandise seized by the local, state, or federal government agencies for non-payment of taxes or involvement in criminal activities
- Business inventory reduction auctions
- Used-car auctions

One reason auctions are so popular is that they provide benefits to sellers *and* buyers. In a standard sale, a seller might be tempted to price an item low, hoping he can attract the first buyer who comes along and get the item out of his inventory. In an auction, however, several of the bidders may have a very strong need or desire to own the item, so they will keep bidding up the price until one of them emerges as the winner.

Meanwhile, buyers like auctions because (1) they can often get items for prices much lower than they would have to pay at a store; and (2) they can often locate hard-to-find items such as pristine collectibles or repair parts that are no longer available from dealers or factories.

Three other benefits of auctions include:

- Virtually anything can be put up for bid.
- Buyer and seller are not face-to-face. Therefore, neither party is under pressure to negotiate or make a deal.

- The law of supply and demand keeps the playing field somewhat level. Sellers set the opening bid price; buyers decide how much they are willing to pay.

If several similar items are up for auction, and there are few takers, prices will stay low. Someone who happens to need one of the items will get it for a bargain price. If there is strong demand and the desired item is in short supply, bidders may swarm in and bid up the price to a level that amazes and delights the seller.

Auction Drawbacks

In a perfect world, auctions might be the perfect marketplace. Unfortunately, traditional auctions sometimes draw a few opportunists and thieves, as well as well-meaning buyers and sellers. For example, a seller may have a few "associates" sprinkled throughout the auction crowd. Their job is to place some bids and keep pushing up the price the winning bidder will pay. Meanwhile, buyers at an auction sometimes conspire among themselves to hold bidding prices down by agreeing not to outbid each other.

In online auctions, a seller may have one or two friends placing "shill" bids that help drive up the selling price for his items. But conspiracies among bidders are unlikely, since they may be scattered all over the world.

How Online Auctions Work

Online auctions have improved the traditional auction model in several ways. For example, an online auction may run for a week, ten days, or even longer, giving potential buyers plenty of time to find the item, search for similar items, examine the results of previous auctions, and decide if they want to bid. Furthermore, potential bidders can ask the seller for more information about the item.

Another plus is that online auction sites are typically built around relational database software. This enables the site to store seller and buyer identifications and track items, bids, selling prices and other details.

On sites that offer automatic bidding agents, a buyer can place a bid and store the maximum price she is willing to pay. The seller and other bidders do not see this information. The bidder does not have to keep logging on to the Web site to see how she is doing. If there are other bids, the bidding agent will keep raising her bid automatically, up to the limit she has posted.

Types of Online Auctions

Three types of online auctions are in general use. They are:

- Straight (or absolute) auction
- Reserve auction
- Dutch auction

Straight auctions, sometimes known as *absolute auctions*, are the most common. A seller has only one item up for bid, and no reserve price is set. The seller establishes the opening price and then waits for bids. At the end of the auction, the seller has to accept the highest bid, even if it is not a penny higher than the opening price.

In a *reserve auction*, the seller sets a "reserve" price. This is the lowest amount she is willing to accept in return for giving up the item. When a buyer attempts to place a bid that is lower than the reserve price, he will likely receive a response such as "reserve not met" from the auction site, and his bid will not appear. When a bid *higher* than the reserve price is received, a message such as "reserve met" will be displayed in the listing, and the high-bid price will also show up. At this point, from the buyers' perspective, the auction is under way.

In a *Dutch auction*, a seller can list multiple quantities of the same item. Multiple bidders can win, or a few bidders may try to buy more than one quantity. In any case, all bidders pay the lowest successful bid amount, even if they bid higher. (There is also a so-called Yankee auction. It is very similar to a Dutch auction, except that each winning bidder pays his high-bid price.)

Outbid? Maybe Not!

Here is a cautionary tale to keep in mind once you start using online auctions. If you bid on an item, and another bidder pushes the price higher than you wish to pay, you might assume that you have been knocked out of the auction. You might even search for a similar item in another auction or on another auction site and place a bid on it. *Be careful.*

FACT

Auction sites, including eBay, will typically send you an e-mail notification when you have been outbid. Also, a high bidder can sometimes cancel a bid under very restricted circumstances.

"You can end up in a tight pickle," cautions Mark O'Neill, a Germany-based freelance writer, English language consultant, and eBay mentor for members of the Disabled Online Users Association. "Recently, I bid for an expensive DVD set and subsequently got outbid. Then I found a cheaper deal elsewhere and posted a bid. But when I checked my 'My eBay' page again, I discovered that the person who had outbid me in the first auction had had his bid canceled, and I was now the highest bidder again. I was looking at a total bill of over $100 for two identical DVD sets, because the first seller had canceled the highest bid without informing me. After some hasty e-mail tennis, my bid was subsequently canceled by the seller, but it made me realize for the first time about the pitfalls of bid cancellations. As eBay told me later, 'When you are outbid on an item, you haven't necessarily lost the auction, because the higher bidders can be canceled or suspended for any reason at any time.' So don't go looking for an item elsewhere until the auction you were outbid on has ended."

Of course, if two or three others outbid you, you probably can assume you really *are* out of the running, and it will be safe to place bids in other auctions.

Experienced buyers and sellers often keep *two* computers running during the final minutes of an online auction. One computer is used to place or monitor bids. The other computer has an appropriate e-mail account open. A seller will be watching for last-minute questions sent via e-mail by potential bidders. A buyer will be ready to post questions, watch for any outbid messages, and contact the seller if he wins the auction.

Ready to Buy and Sell?

The best-known online auction sites, including eBay, Amazon, Yahoo! and others, make it very easy to open buyer and seller accounts. After all, to stay in business, they need a constant inflow of auction items and new bidders. Once you get involved in online auctions, you may get hooked not only on buying and selling but also on watching the quiet but fascinating process of electronic bidding itself. You may never cease being surprised at what you can buy and sell in online auctions and what new interests you can discover or rediscover. The toys and books you considered magical as a child are still floating around in cyberspace, sometimes still in their original packaging. The tools you need to do a special job; the gearshift knob you thought you might never find for the 1954 Chevrolet you are restoring; the old lunchbox you need as a prop for a community theater play—these are all tucked away in surprising corners of the world. And they may soon be listed for bids at an online auction site.

However, resist the urge to rush off in search of them. First, you should learn more about online auctions and what is required to use the leading sites as a buyer and seller. You will have accounts to set up, payment methods and shipping addresses to select, and some rules and procedures to review. This book will help guide you and shorten the inevitable learning curve.

Don't skip the chapters that follow. The time you invest now in studying and preparing for the auction process will be rewarded many times over in the months and years ahead. You will enjoy better bargains and higher selling prices, the best reasons for joining in the pleasures and profits of online auctions.

Chapter 2
Why Use Auctions?

Online auctions are open and welcoming to almost anyone who has Internet access. The auctions bring buyers and sellers together with wondrous ease, even from thousands of miles apart. With some restrictions, virtually anything anyone can imagine can be bought or sold in an online auction. The popularity of online auctions is soaring worldwide. But anyone seriously addicted to shopping should stay away or at least learn to keep within safe spending limits while clicking around in a seemingly endless world of appealing merchandise.

Who Should Use Online Auctions?

Online auctions are definitely not for everyone. However, they can work very well for buyers with patience, self-control, and specific needs. Online auctions also are effective and enjoyable venues for sellers who hate trying to convince customers face-to-face to stop shopping and buy something. Millions of people suddenly have access to your sales item, and some of them who need it may do an Internet search and find it. No one may bid on it today, but one bidder may show up tomorrow, and thirty more may show up before the seven-day auction ends.

New and experienced sellers alike almost never tire of the process of posting new auction items, and seeing bid prices and the number of bidders magically start climbing. Unless the winning bidder is a repeat customer with a recognizable screen name, there may often be mysteries and surprises in who is buying what. *Why does somebody in midtown Manhattan want an old-fashioned butter churn? Why is a woman in Tennessee buying so many vintage surfboards? And why did that buyer in rural Alaska bid so high on a used bowling ball?*

You may never know the answers, but you may also never cease to be amazed at what can be sold and how much money people are willing to pay for it.

Buying at Online Auctions

Needs happen. One morning you go into your home office and turn on your personal computer. You also fire up your trusty old laser printer—literally. There is a sudden, loud *pop,* followed by a small cloud of stinky smoke curling out of the cooling vents. Unfortunately, the printer hasn't been manufactured since 1990, and repair shops will no longer touch it. But you have money invested in several spare toner cartridges, and your trusty PC is old, and won't work with most of the newer, sleeker laser printers. You *need* your faithful peripheral.

So, you open the printer and try to do the repairs yourself. Very soon, you spot the problem. A small part on one of the printed circuit boards has self-destructed. At this point, you have only one choice: find a replacement on the Web, either from an online store that stockpiles old printer parts or from an online auction. You log onto eBay, Amazon, Yahoo! or some other auction site, and enter the bad circuit board's part number into the search tool. To your relief and pleasure, you find five of the replacement boards are up for bids, and two of the listings are ending within the hour. You click on the descriptions, determine which one is better, and place your bid. An hour later, you confirm your purchase and pay for it, with expedited shipping. Three days later, the board is in your hands. You install it and turn on the printer again. Success! You're back in business.

Selling at Online Auctions

The need to sell also happens. One day, you decide your house is cluttered with too many things. Mentally, you start taking inventory of what can go: an ice-cream maker that no longer fits your diet, an old table radio with vacuum tubes, a vintage juice pitcher gathering dust on a knickknack shelf, a shoebox full old picture postcards lovingly collected by a now-deceased relative.

QUESTION?

What is the main difference between traditional auctions and online auctions?

Traditional auction houses collect payments, distribute auctioned goods, and act as mediators between buyers and sellers. In online auctions, buyers and sellers deal directly with each other for payment, shipping—and disputes.

You could throw away these items, pile them out by the curb beneath a *Free!* sign, donate them to a social services agency, or start stacking them up for a garage sale.

You also could use the items as the starting inventory for a part-time sales business built around online auctions. The search tools on sites such as eBay, Yahoo! Amazon, and others can reveal a surprising truth. Many of the items that seem like junk or clutter in your home are very much wanted and needed by other people on the planet. An ice-cream maker exactly like yours has just been bid up to $50 on eBay. The old table radio turns out to be a collector's item, and one that is not as nice as yours is about to sell for $75 on Amazon. The vintage juice pitcher was made by Fiesta just before World War II. Yours, you discover, could sell for $40 or more on Yahoo! or eBay.

You start to throw away the box of postcards but decide to do one more online search first. Amazed, you discover that many thousands of people collect postcards and flock to online auctions, willingly paying prices ranging from fifty cents to $50 and more for rare and vintage cards. The shoebox full of postcards you almost threw away could generate hundreds of dollars in online sales. In just a matter of minutes, your new enterprise—online auction seller—has been born.

Participating in online auctions does require at least a small leap of faith. You have to be willing to trust that good things will happen most of the time when strangers hundreds or thousands of miles apart swap money for goods. If you are bidding, you have to rely on a few digital images, a short text description of the item and its condition, and the seller's reputation, or feedback score, on the auction site. On the other hand, if you are selling, the potential buyer has to trust *your* photos, descriptions, and online reputation.

Most people, you will discover, *are* inherently good. They want what you are selling, or they are happy you need something they want to sell. Online auctions create a level playing field for buyers and sellers. The two parties are not standing face-to-face, so there is no pressure. An item simply is offered for a starting price, and bidders are free to look at it and make an offer or quietly move on to other auctions.

Online Auctions and Small Business

Online auction sites can provide sales and purchasing channels that are affordable and effective for home-based businesses and small businesses. Some typical ways auction sites can be employed include:

- Selling off excess inventory
- Test-marketing a new product
- Buying office supplies, shipping supplies, spare parts, and manufacturing goods

- Creating a low-budget "Web store" for your business, at a site where the feature is offered
- Getting a home-based business with no marketing budget off the ground quickly
- Providing extra income for a home-based business or small business that offers products or services mostly in its local community

Who Should Not Use Online Auctions?

At least five categories of buyers and sellers should consider minimizing their contact with online auctions or possibly skipping them altogether:

- Compulsive shoppers
- Impatient buyers who want instant gratification
- Buyers who demand perfection in what they buy
- Buyers who are unwilling to do comparison pricing in current and completed auctions
- Sellers who have no qualms about overstating an item's quality when posting it for sale

Online auctions and compulsive shoppers are a dangerous mix. With almost endless merchandise just a few mouse clicks away, it is much too easy to spend hours at a computer, burning up credit cards instead of dealing with other issues in your life.

Online auction sites can be "extremely addictive," cautions April Lane Benson, Ph.D., a psychotherapist and author of *I Shop, Therefore I Am*. Some online buyers try to fill voids in their lives by making compulsive bids and spending much more than they can afford. "It's extremely important to figure out what it is you're really shopping for. Overshopping is just another way of looking for love in all the wrong places," Dr. Benson warns.

If you are prone to impatience and desires for instant gratification, you will likely hate most online auctions. The typical eBay auction runs for seven days; then the seller has several days to respond to your payment and ship the merchandise. On Yahoo! and other sites, an auction may run for ten days. At least two weeks or longer can pass from the time you post a winning bid until you finally get what you bought.

Hard-core perfectionists definitely should avoid most of the buying opportunities offered by online auction sellers. Posted items often are "collectible," or "vintage" or "used" or "surplus" or "incomplete" or "slightly worn." Of course, many new products *can* be found at good prices on online auction sites and through Web stores that they host. But you have to understand that not everyone can write accurate descriptions of their goods. What they consider "very good" may be "very shoddy" in your opinion, and this can lead to angry exchanges of e-mail, demands for a refund, and exchanges of negative feedback.

FACT

After 2005's massively destructive Hurricane Katrina, Oscar-winning actor Morgan Freeman quickly organized an online auction of celebrity memorabilia and donated the sales proceeds to the American Red Cross to help victims in Louisiana, Mississippi, and Alabama. Numerous other entertainers and organizations also used online auctions to help raise cash for disaster relief. Sites such as Amazon and eBay added links so members could make direct donations, or buy or sell items that would benefit relief agencies.

If you hate comparison shopping while wandering through retail stores, you'll absolutely hate comparison shopping in the online auction world. For one thing, you may have to read the descriptions and compare the photographs of several similar items. You may also need to go to two or three other auction sites to be certain you are getting the best deal. And, you'll need to check out completed auctions as well as current auctions to see what the winning bids were. You will need this information to determine when you are about to bid too much.

Finally, if you think it's okay to exaggerate when convincing someone to buy something, don't expect to last long as an online auction seller. The early years of online auctions were rife with rip-offs. Many sellers oversold the quality of their goods or simply took the buyers' money, sent nothing, and told them the merchandise must have gotten lost in the mail. Buyers are much more wary these days, and the auction sites' feedback systems and other security measures can quickly identify and separate the good sellers from the bad.

Research, Research, Research

You *must* be willing to research an item's value before placing a bid, especially if you plan to buy or sell collectibles, antiques, art objects, or jewelry. This means learning how to look at current and previous auctions of the types of items you expect to buy or sell. The Phoenix Police Department's Organized Crime Bureau offers this tip for auction site newcomers: "Don't take quotes, even verifiable ones, as indicators of the real value of an item. Know the current value, and decide for yourself what the item is worth. Remember, you are the market."

Why the Web Makes a Difference

It isn't hard to understand how the World Wide Web keeps making the world a smaller and smaller place. Fifteen minutes after you list an old stopwatch for sale, you may have someone in Indianapolis and someone in India posting bids for it. Somebody in California will e-mail a question about its lap-counter function, and someone in Maine will ask if you could send it by Express Mail if they win it.

The smallest home-based businesses now can reach into the global marketplace at practically no expense at all. You can sell almost anything if you can get the word out, and that is not hard to do at online auction sites where thousands and even millions of people are shopping at the same time. For example, eBay has estimated that an item of clothing sells every three seconds in its auctions. A vintage pair of Levi jeans, purchased for $5 ten years ago and auctioned online by a farm family in the rural Midwest, may end up being worn by an ultra-hip young man in Asia who has just bid more than $200 to buy them.

If you write a good heading for your item's description, someone will find it with a search engine. Then another will find it. And another. If your description also is well written, and you have posted at least one clear photograph of what you are selling, more bidders will show up. You may soon have a bidding war over an item you otherwise might have thrown away.

What's In It for You?

For better and worse, the Internet will keep pulling you deeper into the grasp of the World Wide Web for years to come. Large corporations and small businesses, schools and universities, and public and private agencies are moving more of their initial contact points, information sources, catalogs, and ordering and service options to the Internet. Increasingly, you hear the message: "Check our Web site first; then e-mail us for more information." Less and less, you hear the old invitation: "Just give us a call!"

If you are accustomed to dialing a phone number and getting help from a caring human being, the continuing exodus of customer service to the Web probably has not made you happy. Once you do locate what seems to be a good phone number, your call is often now routed to a voice menu that urges you to go to the company's Web site or "stay on the line for the next available customer service representative. Your estimated wait time is…twenty-three minutes, five seconds."

Not everyone uses online auctions to accumulate goods or money. Some amateur detectives and history hobbyists search eBay and other sites to buy items such as old high school yearbooks. Then they try to track down the yearbooks' owners or surviving relatives and return the treasures to them.

There is a bright side to this trend, especially if you want to start and grow a small business while hanging on to a corporate job that keeps you and your family covered with health insurance and other benefits. Just like the big companies, you can use the Web to advertise your business, describe available products or services, and provide contact information, such as an e-mail address, phone number, and fax number. If most of your business involves online auctions, you can schedule your lists to end at night or on weekends while you are home. You can pack the goods at night and mail them the next morning or have your spouse handle the shipping. Online auction sales can create the second income that enables one spouse to stay home with young children rather than sending them to day care.

Buyer Success Stories

Online auctions have struck a deep chord in American culture. The sheer numbers of sellers now is so huge that it has become possible to buy many things that you need and want. You can also find items from your past, such as favorite toys or games, that you thought were gone forever. You even buy items to resell for profit. The bazaar never closes; the markets never sleep. You can "shop 'til you drop" and not make the slightest ripple in the Web.

Small businesses are increasingly buying at least some of their computer hardware, peripherals, office supplies, and office furniture from online auction sites, including those that sell large lots of overstocked goods. Owners of small and home-based businesses often have to provide their own technical support. Many have discovered that online auction sites can keep them supplied with hard-to-find repair parts and affordable software, so the older systems they have paid for can stay on the job a couple of years longer.

ALERT!

Because of online security concerns, auction buyers and sellers often shun publicity. Also, online auction sites often have policies against associating screen names with the identities and locations of their members. So, it is better to talk about buying trends and general successes than to try to highlight individuals.

Hobbyists and artists have swarmed to online auction sites, because the Internet and the Web have greatly expanded their ability to buy the exact tools, materials, kits, and specialty items they need.

For collectors, the Web is a wonderland, and online auction sites have brought them an amazingly affordable means of covering a lot of ground in a hurry as they search for rare and coveted items.

College students have to buy a lot of books, and many of the ones they need can be found at online auctions for prices much lower than their bookstores charge. Online auctions are especially thrifty for English majors who must read many classic novels and poetry collections. Amazon.com is famous for its book sales where individuals can sell used copies right alongside online book dealers. A college student may literally find dozens of copies of a needed book on Amazon, ranging from very ratty paperback to a treasured collectible hardback. Books are readily available on most other auction sites, as well.

Seller Success Stories

Now, eBay bills itself as "The World's Online Marketplace," and no competitor is positioned to dispute that claim. More than 724,000 Americans are professional eBay sellers, earning all or most of their annual income from auction sales, Web stores, and other activities on eBay. Another 1.5 million people are supplementing their income by selling on eBay. These figures were reported in a 2005 survey conducted for eBay by ACNielsen International Research. According to an eBay news release, "The number of eBay entrepreneurs in the U.S. has increased 68 percent since the last time a comparable study was conducted in 2003. That study indicated that 430,000 Americans at the time were making some or all of their income selling on eBay."

In estimates from other sources, eBay now controls 80 to 85 percent of the online auction market, with Yahoo! and Amazon running distant second and third. In the first six months of 2005, eBay's members sold merchandise worth nearly $11 billion dollars, ranking the Web site ahead of some countries in economic output.

What types of items are the best sellers on eBay? Some observers say computer equipment, networking devices, and consumer electronics are tops, followed by videos and DVDs, video games, and house and garden items. But the fact remains, with tens of millions of active buyers and sellers online at one time, virtually anything can be bought or sold at an online auction.

FACT

According to the ACNielsen survey, 58 percent of Americans have dreamed of starting a business and becoming their own boss. The survey participants cited two key reasons for wanting to have their own business: to make more money and to have more independence. What holds most of them back? Not enough money to take the risk, they admit.

The Human Connection

A stereotypical scene plays out in many cultures, both in real life and comedy. A wife and husband go shopping in a mall, a bazaar, or a big retail store. The wife wants to touch and examine every item on display. The husband just wants to grab something, pay for it, and go home.

Some of us like shopping much more than others do. Fortunately, online shopping is an *individual* action that can occur literally at any time, day or night. As long as there are two or more Internet-connected computers under a roof, the shopping styles of all the people sharing that household may coexist.

Buying and selling on the Internet will bring you into contact with people in places you never knew existed. Most of the contacts will be brief and pleasant, and you may never hear from them again. Yet, you may rediscover an interest in geography and in the history of places as an offshoot of creating mailing labels for your packages.

Sometimes, you will find a favorite seller. Sometimes, a buyer starts counting your auctions as one of their favorite stops. From these encounters, long-term online friendships can develop. Romances and marriages have evolved, as well, from human connections at online auction sites.

The Internet and the World Wide Web may be shrinking the planet, but they are also helping you connect with a much wider world of people, places, pasts, cultures—and things worth having and selling.

Chapter 3
eBay Reigns

It's hard to argue with success, especially huge success. eBay was the first online auction site for person-to-person bidding, and it remains the top site. Some studies have estimated its market share at more than 80 percent of online auction sales in the United States. Now it is expanding overseas and tapping into the increasingly interconnected global economy. It should be a major force in e-commerce for many years to come as other cultures tap into the online auction phenomenon.

In the eBeginning

What a difference a decade makes. In mid-1995, eBay and other online auction sites were on the verge of being created. But they were not yet icons in the public consciousness. If you collected things or needed a hard-to-find part, you didn't sit down at your trusty PC and do a Web search. You scoured advertisements in magazines and newspapers. You went to garage sales, yard sales, going-out-of-business sales, and estate sales. You asked friends if they knew somebody who knew somebody who had solved a similar problem. By mid-2005, more than 150 million people were using home or office PCs and laptop computers to log on to eBay and other auction sites, including Amazon, Yahoo!, uBid, and many others.

eBay Rises

What is now one of the world's most successful companies was launched in 1995 as a hobby by a twenty-seven-year-old computer professional who had no formal background in auction selling. Using a home PC and inspired by his fiancée's desire to find other collectors of PEZ dispensers, Pierre Omidyar created a simple site known as "eBay's Auction Web" over the 1995 Labor Day weekend. Soon after he launched his site, it became known simply as "eBay." Omidyar tirelessly publicized his auction site on newsgroups frequented by technology-savvy computer users. Some of the first items listed for sale included a used Superman lunchbox and other collectibles. As news of eBay spread among computer users, Omidyar added a category for selling used computer items. The number of online auctions grew quickly. It was the perfect place for computer geeks seeking to buy or sell used hardware. But people selling or seeking everything from celebrity photos to real estate also started logging on.

Omidyar's eBay was able to gain traction quickly on the Internet because it was "the first form of commerce that engage(d) the customer," according to an article by Greg Miller in the *Los Angeles Times*. At last, people could do something with the Net besides download and upload information. They could find *things* they wanted or needed and make bids to buy them, in a marketplace much bigger than they could experience in their daily lives.

In the Old Days (Offline)

Before online auctions, if you lived in, say, Phoenix and wanted a copy—new or used—of William Saroyan's novel *The Human Comedy*, you could spend a weekend or longer going to bookstores or stopping by garage sales and estate sales on the off-chance you might stumble onto the book. You could place want ads in the local newspapers. You could call your friends. Or, you could have a bookstore order it for you, and you might get it in a few weeks. But that was the extent of your marketplace.

The creation of eBay was both a magic moment for consumers and a turning point for focused consumerism. At last, you could seek *exactly* what you wanted, when you wanted it, at prices you were willing to pay. From that point, the digital marketplace quickly evolved into the *global* marketplace.

With the advent of online auctions, you suddenly could do an electronic search and locate exactly what you were seeking. You might find *six* pristine paperback copies of *The Human Comedy* offered by a seller in Pocatello, Idaho; an autographed first-edition hardback copy being auctioned by a seller in Tampa, Florida, and a dog-eared copy that once served hard time in a public library in East Lansing, Michigan. You would have never thought to journey to any of these places to find *The Human Comedy*.

Setting the Standard

During the first years after eBay's appearance, several other online auction sites started appearing. Some followed a "business-to-business" approach. Some focused on "business-to-consumer" auctions. But eBay ran away with the "person-to-person" auction market and left its other competitors gaping—and gasping—at its numbers.

On its third anniversary, eBay issued a press release on September 15, 1998, acknowledging the pending emergence of a new competitor, Yahoo! Auctions. The release also noted pointedly that eBay now had more than one million registered users, with some 700,000 available items and about 70,000 new items being listed for auction each day. Meg Whitman, eBay's chief executive officer, cautioned Yahoo! and other would-be competitors that "any company entering this space must understand the level of personalized support and attention the online person-to-person trading community demands."

This was not simply self-defensive posturing by eBay. Almost from its outset, eBay had zeroed in on four key factors that would drive its success: customer support, trust and safety, community, and choice.

Customer Support

By 1998, as its new competitors tried to gain traction, eBay already was running a twenty-four-hour/seven-day-a-week customer support department and hosting two live public forums. There, eBay support personnel fielded questions from eBay users and posted the answers so all other users could learn from them. Ms. Whitman stated, "eBay takes care of its registered users." It was not an overblown boast. It was a warning to would-be competitors that they would have to do better to overtake eBay's huge lead.

FACT

In recent years, eBay has automated more and more of its features for sellers and buyers. But its customer support and online forums remain key factors in the site's remarkable and still-burgeoning success.

Trust and Safety

It takes a leap of faith and trust to buy items sight unseen from distant strangers. Early adopters of the online auction concept were rewarded with a remarkably convenient way to buy and sell. Unfortunately, fraudsters showed up, too, and began taking buyers' money but shipping goods that did not meet the online descriptions. Sometimes, nothing was shipped at all. Buyers could not always trust sellers, and honest sellers sometimes ran into dishonest buyers who schemed ways to get merchandise for free or unwarranted refunds.

To help fight this trend, eBay pioneered the Feedback Forum, where buyers and sellers can post comments—good, bad, or neutral—about their dealings with each other. This feature, along with the ability to block or cancel bids from questionable buyers, quickly leveled the playing field. Today, on eBay and many other online auction sites, a strongly positive feedback score is a precious commodity. Good sellers and buyers work very hard to keep their ratings high. The comments posted for their transactions are available for all to read. Fraud still happens. But the instances are rare.

Community

In 1998, Meg Whitman told *Business Week* magazine that eBay's management did not set the direction of the multibillion-dollar company. The "community" of buyers and sellers on eBay determines where it goes next. She called eBay both a "self-regulating marketplace" and "an economy" where different categories of goods go from hot to cold and back to hot again in constantly changing marketplace cycles, driven by eBay's massive and steadily growing membership.

Choice

Both eBay's creator and its early management team knew that the site's growth would be driven by the number of auction categories it could offer. The more choices eBay could make available, the more buyers and sellers would show up and draw other buyers and sellers. By its third year of operation, 1998, eBay had swelled to more than 700,000 concurrent auctions, and more than 70,000 new items were being added each day.

Seven years later, in mid-2005, eBay was reporting a record 440.1 million auction item listings, just in one quarter, and it had more than 157 million confirmed registered users. Many thousands of new auction listings were being added each *second*, and eBay was expanding its overseas markets to include China's burgeoning economy and massive population.

eBay Features

Newcomers find no shortage of choices on eBay. Logging on to the site for the first time is a bit like driving into a big city you've never visited. No matter how hard you look at it, you can't take it all in. There are too many sights, points of interest, events, details, and distractions. You have to savor it in small doses and keep venturing out a little bit at a time.

Fortunately, there is one guidepost you can keep coming back to, just as you might use the tallest building in a skyline as your reference point when walking around a downtown area for the first time. The double toolbars, found at the top of most pages, can get you back to a familiar starting point in a hurry.

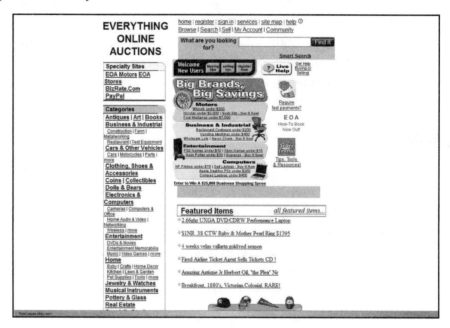

The main toolbar offers five key options in click boxes:

- Buy
- Sell
- My eBay
- Community
- Help

The smaller links above the click boxes are as follows:

- Home
- Pay
- Services
- Site Map

At the screen's far right, you will find the Search button and the Advanced Search link. These two tools are used heavily by almost anyone on who logs on to eBay.

Let's start with the main toolbar.

Buy

Clicking on the Buy link brings up a Search tool and a Browse Categories window. The Search tool can help you find a specific item. Many people are not focused shoppers, however. They like to go inside a store and just wander. Sometimes they don't buy anything, or maybe a small, inexpensive item catches their fancy. Other times, when the shopping mood really hits, they go on a spree, snapping up full bags of new items, sale items, and closeout items.

Another easy way to get to the Browse function on eBay is to click on the main screen's Search button without entering any text in the Start New Search area. This will bring up the All Categories page, which lists all auction categories and subcategories and displays the number of listings currently active in each.

The Browse function is perfect for buyers who are in a mood to buy but "are just looking." However, many eBay sellers also like to use the Browse feature. They scroll through the hundreds of categories and subcategories to get new ideas for items they can sell. Sometimes they also discover that certain items they are holding in storage are suddenly getting hot again.

Sell

The Sell click box will be your entrance portal into the world of auctioning goods on eBay. But don't go there yet, except to satisfy your curiosity. A newcomer to online auctions should be a buyer first, at least for a couple of weeks. The goal is to learn the buying process and start building a good reputation in the eBay community through feedback. You will need positive feedback numbers and a positive feedback percentage to help attract buyers to your first online auctions. The processes for opening buyer and seller accounts are covered later in this book.

My eBay

Once you are signed up as a member, the My eBay button takes you to your My Summary page. If you are a seller, you will first see Selling Reminders, which summarize:

- How many items are awaiting payment.
- How many of your listings will end today.
- How many items are still awaiting your feedback for the buyers.
- How many of your sold items are eligible for Second Chance Offers to runner-up bidders, if the high bidder backs out or disappears.

Farther down the page, you will see Buying Totals, which gives a quick overview of how many items you currently are bidding on and how many you have won and need to acknowledge.

Below that, the Items I've Won display shows the details of your winning bids and the status of payments, shipping, and feedback.

Scrolling down, the Selling Totals window is displayed next. This window gives a quick overview of how many items you are selling and how many have sold, plus the total amount of the winning bids.

Below that, the Items I'm Selling window lists your auction items and shows which ones have bids and which ones do not. Bid prices and the time left in each auction also are displayed, along with # of Watchers. This important count tells you how many potential bidders are watching the progress of your auction. If one of your items has several watchers, you may get a good run of bidders in the final hours and minutes of your listing.

Finally, the Items I've Sold window displays information about each item you have sold, including the winning bid price and the total paid with shipping.

Community

The Community link on eBay's main toolbar opens a Community screen. This screen can take you to:

- Discussion boards open to "any eBay-related topic"
- Online groups for eBay members who share common interests
- An Answer Center, where members can help answer each other's questions
- Chat rooms, where eBay members can talk with other members "in a casual setting"

The Community page also has links to eBay news announcements, calendar events, the official Community newsletter, "The Chatter," and other outlets, centers, and groups.

Help

Whether you are new to eBay or a longtime member, you will use the Help button many times. It will take you to answers for most of your questions. The quality and completeness of the Help screens are one of the key strengths and features of eBay.

The Help screen displays the top five questions about eBay. It also provides the following links as starting points for more focused assistance:

- New to eBay
- Finding What You Are Looking For
- Buying
- Selling
- Paying for an Item
- Feedback
- Using My eBay
- Account Information & Billing

- Rules and Policies
- Online Security and Protection
- Transaction Problems
- Specialty Sites

The links found above the main toolbar can also help you go places in a hurry on eBay.

Home

Click on this link when you are ready to leave the My eBay area or a search area and go back to eBay's main screen.

Pay

This link will take you straight to the Items I've Won page, so you can make payment using PayPal or other means.

Services

This link brings up the Services page, which has links to bidding and buying services, selling services, and general services such as software downloads and creating an About Me page for your eBay account.

Site Map

If you click on this link, it will bring up a text-based display full of links to eBay pages in the following categories:

- Buy
- Sell
- Search
- Help
- Services
- Community

Rules of the Road

The news media and late-night TV comics often latch on to stories about someone selling something strange or outrageous on eBay. Maybe it's a grilled cheese sandwich bearing a likeness of Albert Einstein's hair in the toasted bread. Maybe it's someone auctioning her forehead as advertising space. In reality, many weird things are sold via online auctions. But the vast majority of transactions are for commonplace, useful, and collectible goods.

For example, someone in Missouri has grown weary of the cuckoo clock in her living room, so she decides to list it for auction. Meanwhile, someone who runs a clock shop in Alabama is eager to add a cuckoo clock to his front-window display. He goes online, does a search on eBay, finds the Missouri seller's listing, and submits the winning bid. So, eBay provides the site and the digital features that enable seller and buyer to find each other. After that, the auction is person to person.

Of course, some items cannot and should not be sold on eBay. The site posts a lengthy list of prohibited and restricted items on its eBay Policies page. Once you are ready to sell, you will be responsible for knowing if your items can be legally sold.

The prohibited and restricted items range from academic software, alcohol, and animals to fireworks, tobacco, and knives. Items may be added to or removed from the list periodically. One of the rules of the road for eBay sellers is to review the list often to be sure of compliance.

The Fan Club

Reviewers who rate online auction sites consistently list eBay at or very near the top of their "best" lists. They typically cite eBay's huge number of well-organized auction categories and its steady, user-friendly emphasis on helping people get together to buy and sell. Increasingly, eBay is becoming a major force in the global economy, and it is being credited with helping create thousands of full-time and part-time jobs.

FACT

Finding something to bid on is not a problem on eBay. There are many hundreds of categories and subcategories of items. In some categories, almost a half-million auctions may be under way at this moment. Finding buyers for the things you wish to sell will not be much of a problem, especially if you price your items fairly, prepare good descriptions and photographs, and list the goods in the right categories.

You may find that you feel more comfortable and more at home on a smaller, less-popular auction site; however, in terms of sheer numbers of categories, buyers, sellers, and features, eBay rules.

Chapter 4
The Best of the Rest

For many auction sellers and buyers, eBay is the only digital universe they need or trust. Yet, eBay may be too big and too complicated for some sellers and buyers who may feel more comfortable on some of the other leading sites that operate in eBay's shadow. Options such as Yahoo! Auctions, Amazon .com Auctions, and uBid.com offer fewer features, fewer distractions, and fewer competitors when selling or buying.

Other Auction Worlds

Nobody knows how many auction sites are now online. There may be hundreds or even thousands of small venues trying to take some of the lucrative spotlight away from eBay. Some of the sites specialize in just one type of auction item, such as furniture, while others are general auction venues seeking their competitive edge by taking slightly different approaches to bidding and selling.

You may want to check out a few of the "other" leading online auction sites. Your needs, experiences, and opinions of a site will vary. Do not try selling at any site until you have taken some time to research it. Watch a few auctions and make a couple of small purchases to check the service. If possible, try to get some impressions and opinions from others who have made sales and purchases on a particular site.

Yahoo! Auctions

After wandering through the grand splendors of eBay, you may find the Yahoo! Auctions site a bare-bones arena. Yahoo! provides an online facility where goods can be auctioned. What happens next is mainly up to the sellers and their bidders.

As Yahoo! dryly explains: "Yahoo! Auctions provides the auction service to facilitate exchanges among its users. Items offered for auction through Yahoo! are being sold by other users, not by Yahoo! Sellers and buyers are responsible for all aspects of the transactions in which they participate. All transactions must be consistent with any applicable legal rules and with Yahoo's guidelines, Yahoo! Terms of Service, and the Yahoo! Auctions."

However, in June 2005, Yahoo! Auctions made a competitive move that excited many of its auction participants. It announced the creation of a new pricing model "that is free for all consumers listing items on our Auctions platform. We have eliminated all fees associated with Auctions listings, including listing fees and final value fees." Yahoo! added that the move would "make auctions more cost effective for both large and small sellers who wish to list items on Yahoo!, ultimately improving their margins."

In the Getting Started box, the site's How to Bid and How to Sell links open other pages that explain the basic steps for each function. Also, check out the Safety Tips link in the Resources section of the main page. This link takes you to a page offering Safety Tips for Buyers and Sellers. Read the tips carefully. They present commonsense information that can help protect you on other online auction sites, as well.

ALERT!

Look for cautions and safety tips on other auction sites. Copy them and keep them available for quick reference. Online dealings with strangers are inherently risky. Most auction transactions go smoothly, but be prepared to identify and deal with questionable sellers or bidders who may try to steal your bid money or your auction merchandise.

On the Yahoo! site, pay special attention to the paragraph beneath the bullet heading, "Keep records of all correspondence." According to Yahoo! Auctions, you should: "Keep all e-mail, notes, shipping documents, and payment information. Be sure to print a copy of the auction. This is your responsibility. Yahoo! does not provide user information or copies of old listings." Remember these tips when buying or selling on other sites, as well.

The guidelines for using the Yahoo! Auctions site are not found on the main page, where you might expect them. You have to click on the Help link, and then scroll down the Help page to the Related Links area. There, you will find Guidelines, just below Terms of Service.

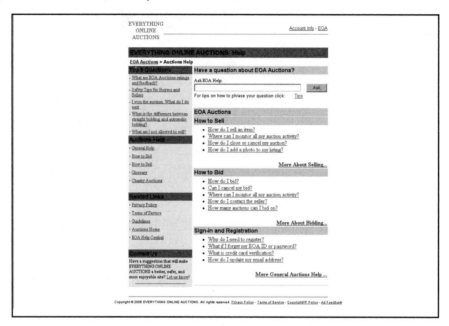

In its guidelines, Yahoo! warns that it "does not screen or control users who may sell or bid on auction items, nor does Yahoo! review or authenticate all auction listings offered for sale." However, if your guiding auction principles are "Buyer, beware" and "Seller, be careful," Yahoo! Auctions' basic approach and its elimination of fees may be well suited for your buying and selling needs.

Amazon.com Auctions

The Amazon.com Auctions site promises "the most secure buying and selling environment on the Web" and offers "several ways to sell your items to our millions of customers." The auction categories range from art and antiques to cars, tools, jewelry, real estate, and games.

However, the auction site's link is not readily visible when you log on to the main Amazon.com site. You have to hunt for it while trying to avoid being distracted by Amazon's numerous links to online stores, bargains, and specials.

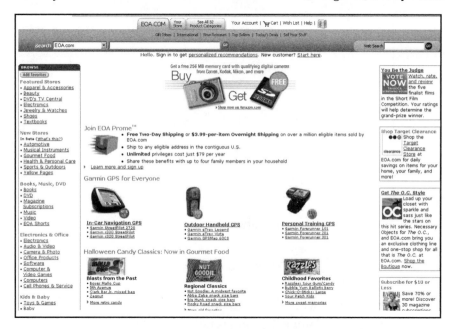

Scroll down toward the bottom of this page, looking on the left for the Bargains heading. Beneath that heading, click on the Auctions link. This will open the Auctions main page.

To find the site's tutorial for newcomers, scroll down the page, again looking on the left side. In the *Do you have questions?* box, click on the *See our tutorial* link.

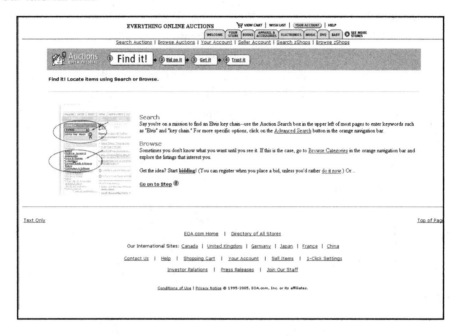

The tutorial describes how to:

- Search for a particular auction item
- Bid on it
- Pay for it and have it shipped
- File a claim if the item is not shipped or is significantly different than described in the auction listing

Features and Transaction Limits

When bidding, you can place your maximum high bid into Amazon's Bid-Click feature. Bid-Click then acts as your automatic bidding proxy. It conceals your maximum bid and raises your current bid at the smallest amount possible when you are competing against other bidders.

All sellers, meanwhile, must offer the Amazon Payments choice to buyers. The Amazon Payments program "is first and foremost a credit card service," according to Amazon. Because of this, Amazon imposes "selling limits" on auction transactions. The selling limits, also known as "velocity limits," are applied to both buyers and sellers. The limits can apply to both the size of individual transactions and the total dollar amount processed.

Amazon's "buyer velocity limit" is $2,475 worth of transactions over a twenty-eight-day rolling period. If you spend the maximum $2,475 in one day, you have to wait another twenty-eight days to bid again. Sellers have the same $2,475 maximum transaction limit. But the amount that a seller can receive in a given period will depend on Amazon's evaluation of the seller's application. Amazon.com Auctions charges its sellers twenty-five cents per item purchased using Amazon Payments, plus 2.5 percent of the transaction amount.

The Amazon Payments plan offers an advantage for sellers who hate hassling with buyer payments. According to Amazon: "When you're paid via Amazon Payments, there's no need for you to do anything but ship your item. Amazon.com deposits the buyer's money into your account and notifies you via e-mail. Funds in your account are deposited directly into your bank account every two weeks."

Not everyone can pay a seller through Amazon Payments. In mid-2005, the payment program was recognized in the United States and U.S. protectorates, plus twenty-eight other countries listed on the Amazon.com Auctions site.

Dollar Deals

In a variation on the popular "dollar stores" found in many cities, Amazon.com Auctions offers a Dollar Deals auction site where bidding starts at one dollar for items ranging from antiques and collectibles to beanbag toys, books, music, and videos.

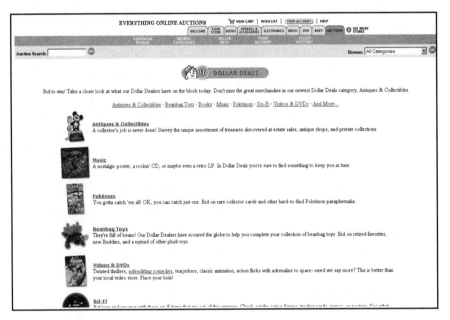

uBid

The online auction site uBid.com turned eight years old in 2005. It bills itself as "the largest online business (only) to consumer marketplace." The site specializes in closeout, refurbished, and end-of-life products, as well as new products.

Thanks in part to some defections from eBay, uBid now has more than 3,000 business partners auctioning a wide array of merchandise that ranges from tile saws and jewelry to pet supplies and refurbished computers.

On uBid, most bidding starts at a dollar, and often, no reserve prices have to be met before the item can be won. It also posts shipping charges up front.

The New uBid

Late in 2002, when fraud was running rampant in the online auction industry, uBid "discontinued the ability for everyday consumers to sell on uBid due to counterfeit, stolen and generally untrusted offerings." The uBid site announced: "Even though we agree with the basic premise that all humans are fundamentally good, a few can ruin it for everyone."

Now uBid lets only Certified Merchants post merchandise for auction. To become a Certified Merchant, a manufacturer, distributor, or reseller must apply to uBid and prove that they have been in business for at least a year. There is also a $99 application fee, and the approval process includes a Dun & Bradstreet report, credit checks, and verification of trade references.

Merchandise specialists procure most of uBid's auction items, and the company is an authorized dealer of many of the products it posts for auction. It offers manufacturer's warranties, optional extended protection plans, and a return policy on certain brand-name merchandise. Site personnel occasionally make random purchases from uBid auctions to help monitor service quality. The company does not ship to addresses outside the United States, and it accepts only two types of payment: credit cards and debit cards.

FACT

Interestingly, uBid operates a million-square-foot warehouse and a call center with more than 200 operators. The call-center operators support customer needs "for all sales, whether shipped from one of our approved suppliers or directly from our warehouse in Naperville, Illinois," according to uBid. All payments are handled in-house, to minimize the chances of fraud and identity theft. "Your payment information never goes outside of uBid," the auction site promises.

Getting Started

To learn more about buying and selling on uBid, click on the Help link on the site's main page. This will open the Welcome to uBid Help page.

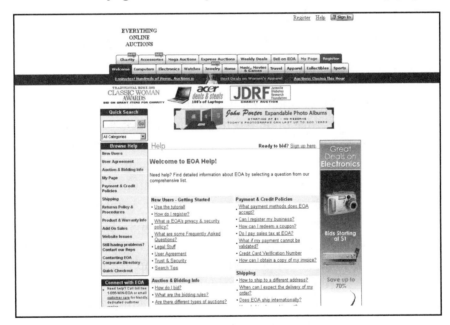

Going, Going, Gone

The Going, Going, Gone feature guards against a practice known as "bid sniping." Some buyers love to bid snipe, while others absolutely hate the practice and consider it unfair.

QUESTION?

What is "bid sniping"?
Bid sniper software lets buyers watch an auction until its final seconds. Then the software places their bid at the last moment, when no time is left to top it.

The Going, Going, Gone feature automatically extends an auction's closing time if there are bids received within the final ten minutes. The auction continues until no more bids are received in a ten-minute period.

Bid sniping aficionados hate uBid, of course, but potential winning bidders often aren't happy with Going, Gone, Gone, either. They have to watch the end of the auction closely and decide whether to bid higher or bail out if the listing is pushed into overtime. There are no limits on how many times the ten-minute ending period can be restarted by new bids.

Overstock.com Auctions

Overstock.com Auctions happily bills itself as "the easier, cheaper, friendlier auction site!" Easier, cheaper, and friendlier than whom? Why, eBay, of course. After eBay raised the prices it charges sellers early in 2005, Overstock.com Auctions' own In the News page quickly blossomed with links to news articles about sellers abandoning eBay in search of cheaper pastures. Many of them were migrating to Overstock, where listing fees were being sharply reduced instead of raised.

Overstock.com uses networking to bring buyers and sellers closer together. A buyer can view a seller's business and personal ratings (the scale is zero to five stars) on the Overstock site, and then follow a link to the seller's home page. At the home page, the buyer can typically see a picture of the seller and read comments the seller has posted about herself and the other items she is selling. Buyers can also contact sellers if they have any questions. The buyer has two options in an auction: place a bid or buy an item outright at its Make It Mine price, when that choice is available.

You won't always gain a bigger profit if you use a new or small auction site to save on seller fees. Experience shows that you may have a better chance of selling at a higher price on big sites such as eBay, where there are more potential buyers to push up the bidding.

Like uBid.com, Overstock.com Auctions keeps the bidding open beyond a listing's scheduled ending time, if there is a bid within the final ten minutes. The bidding will continue until no bid is posted in a ten-minute period.

Getting Started on Overstock.com Auctions

At the Overstock main page, click on the Auctions tab at the top of the page. This will take you to the Auctions site.

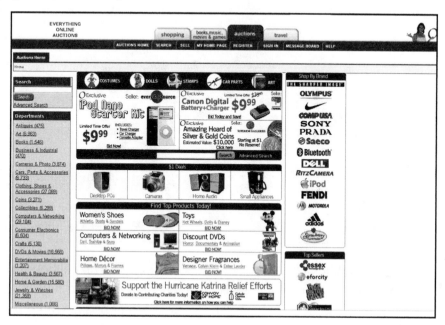

Scroll down to the bottom of the Auctions page and look for the How to Buy and How to Sell tutorials. To buy or sell on the Overstock.com Auctions site, you first must become a Verified Registered User. Registering on Overstock and other top auction sites is covered in Chapter 6.

Click on the Site Policies link at the bottom of a page to pull up the Frequently Asked Questions page. Read the restrictions and disclaimers in the Auction Site Agreement.

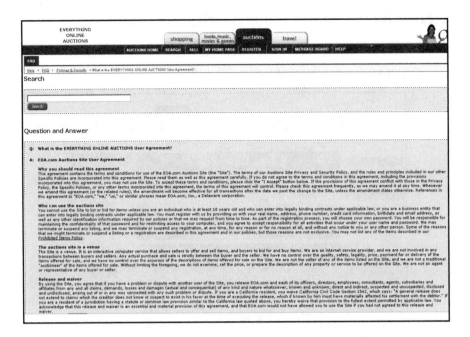

Like Yahoo!, Overstock.com Auctions provides an auction venue. Virtually everything that happens is between the sellers and buyers, as long as the site's restrictions and regulations are met and no laws are broken.

QXL

QXL.com proclaims that it has hosted "UK auctions since 1997." The site actually has a much wider reach. It is a pan-European auction community serving ten countries with sites in several languages. QXL's stated mission is "to provide the essential e-marketplace for buyers and sellers across Europe." Only users with a European shipping address and credit card information can register to buy and sell. The QXL sites are as follows:

- Denmark: *www.qxl.dk*
- France: *www.aucland.fr*
- Germany: *www.ricardo24.de*
- Holland: *www.ricardo.nl*
- Italy: *http://it.qxl.it*
- Norway: *http://no.qxl.no*

- Poland: ✎*www.Aukcje24.pl*
- Sweden: ✎*http://se.qxl.se*
- Switzerland: ✎*www.ricardo.ch*
- UK: ✎*http://qxl.co.uk*

If a buyer and a seller have difficulty understanding each other's language, QXL will help translate.

Like Yahoo!, Overstock, and many others, QXL provides auction venues and leaves the interactions and transactions mostly to the buyers and sellers. QXL collects fees when an item is listed for sale and when it is sold. To get a quick overview of what is on the QXL site, click on the Helpdesk tab on the main screen. This will take you to the QXL Customer Service Help Center page.

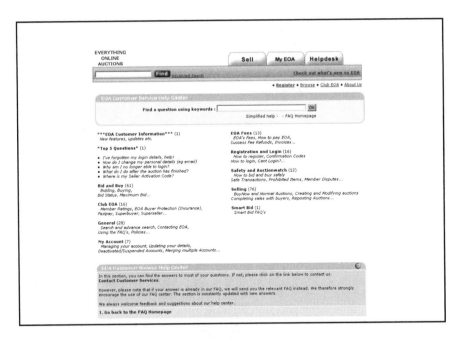

Registration supposedly takes "less than a minute," and it really does—at least on the first registration page. To start the process, click on the Register button on the QXL site.

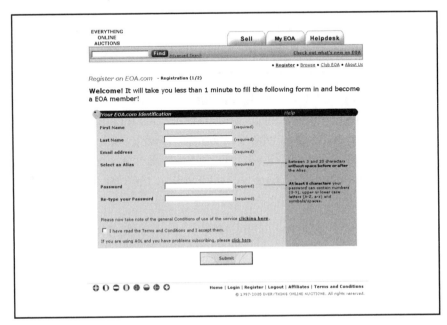

The promised "less than a minute" can stretch into several minutes on the second registration page. Here, you are required to enter some personal information and an e-mail address and also create a password and an alias to use on the QXL auction sites. Once you are registered, other users will be able to click on your alias to find out some information about you.

Verified Sellers

QXL advertises that it "verifies" each seller. How does the verification process work? According to QXL: "We dispatch a special letter with an activation code, which must be entered within 30 days. If the activation code is not entered within this period, the selling account is closed. To become a seller on QXL.com the activation code must be requested and entered." Sellers pay listing fees that vary by auction price, and if an item sells, QXL deducts a "success fee" from money paid to the seller. The costs to sell are specified on the site's How much does it cost? page.

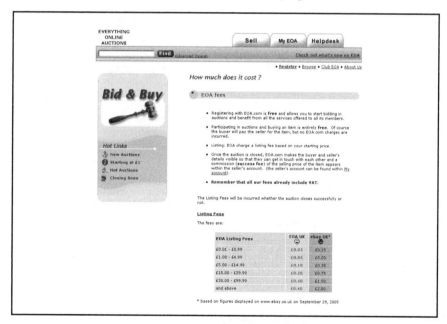

Free Buyer Insurance

The site's free buyer insurance is subject to some restrictions that may sound a bit odd at first: "Any member that has overall positive ratings, who transacts with a seller that has eleven or more positive ratings and has four or more stars at the time of transaction, is covered by the QXL guarantee."

Fortunately, an illustration provides a helpful translation on the QXL Buyer guarantee page:

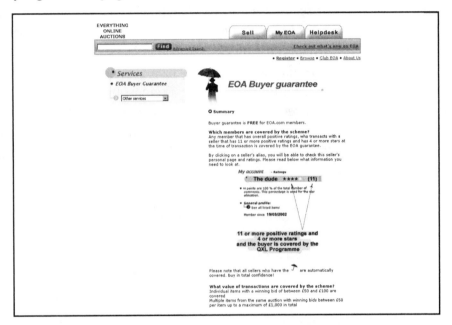

QXL's insurance covers individual items that had winning bids of between £50 and £100 and are (a) not delivered or are (b) substantially different from what was described in the listing. Multiple items from the same auction, with winning bids between £50 per item up to a maximum of £1,000 in total, also are covered. The insurance does not cover damage caused during shipping, QXL points out.

Cross-Cultural Sales Restrictions

Because it operates in several different countries, QXL faces more restrictions than most online auction sites encounter. The following types of items cannot be sold on QXL:

- Items that may infringe on local laws
- Items that are subject to surveillance
- Items that have to be approved for sale in each country

For more detailed listings of the banned items, contact QXL and its auction sites in other countries.

Up-and-Coming Sites

New auction sites rise and old sites fall. What is up-and-coming this week may be gone and forgotten next year. Or, if it has attracted a following, it may have been taken over and assimilated into another, bigger auction site. One way to find new sites is to watch for news articles in online publications such as AuctionBytes.com or in articles from major online news organizations.

Bidz.com

If you yearn to experience live auctions online, check out Bidz.com. This site caters to "anxious bidders with little time to wait." It posts live, three-minute auctions twenty-four hours a day, seven days a week. It also offers "an exclusive line of Extremely Expensive items for the discerning bidders," such as a diamond engagement ring originally priced at nearly $18,000. During a three-minute auction, if a bid is received within the final thirty seconds, the countdown clock automatically resets to thirty seconds, and the bidding keeps going.

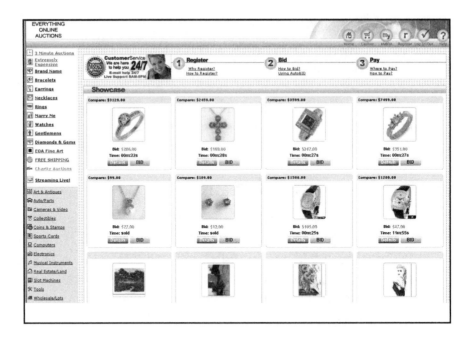

LiveDeal.com

LiveDeal.com calls itself "the Internet's leading marketplace for buying and selling goods locally." It is not a classic online auction site, but it may be a useful tool for finding certain types of items in your own town or region.

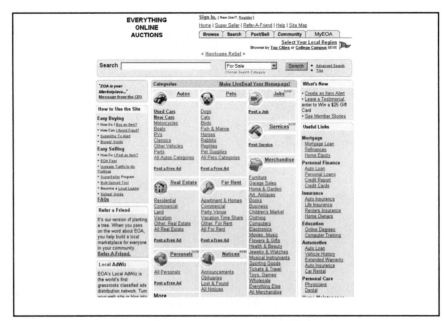

Buying an item through LiveDeal is intended to be like buying something at a neighborhood yard sale or local boutique. You start by entering your Zip Code or city, and then searching the categories that interest you. When an item catches your eye, you can click on it to get more details, including price and availability.

To buy, you may have several options. You can contact the seller by e-mail. You can ask to meet with the seller so you can view the item. Or, you may be able to select the Buy Now option, pay for the item via PayPal, and have it shipped to you, just as you do with online auctions. Some sellers may list their prices as "fixed" or "negotiable." If a price can be negotiated, you can offer a lower bid and see if the seller will take it.

Auction Fire

Auction Fire (*www.auctionfire.com*) offers two appealing features for online auction sellers and buyers. The site charges no listing fees, even for automobiles, and its basic service is free, even for image hosting. Auction Fire, based in Las Vegas, takes a 2.5 percent commission on the sale price for each successful transaction in which the seller receives payment from the buyer. The auction site acts as a trading venue and does not get involved in the buyers' and sellers' monetary transactions. Buyers and sellers must make their own payment and shipping arrangements.

Thirty major categories of items are auctioned, ranging from art and antiques to computers, electronics, jewelry, sports memorabilia, and motor vehicles. While larger auction sites typically promise "investigations" of reported questionable activity by sellers or buyers, Auction Fire states that it has "zero tolerance for abuse or fraud in our community" and promptly reports illegal activity to the Internet Fraud Complaint Center, operated by the Federal Bureau of Investigation.

Whenever a new online auction site catches your eye, watch it carefully and try a few small transactions to test its suitability as a venue for your business or your buying needs.

Chapter 5
Niche Auction Sites

Human beings are curious about everything. In the realm of online auctions, however, individual buyers and sellers often specialize in just one or two types of items. Increasingly, these focused auction participants are drawn to niche sites where nothing is put up for bid unless it fits within one category, such as sports memorabilia or art or stamps. It's harder to get distracted or go off on browsing tangents while bidding at a niche auction site.

Sports Auction Sites

Sports fans often are avid—if not rabid—collectors of memorabilia celebrating their favorite teams and players. Millions of these superfans are also online, actively buying and selling sports-related goods. They can be found on any of the major sites, such as eBay and Yahoo! but they also surge into their favorite niche auction sites much the same way they push into a stadium on the day of a big game—pumped up and ready to play. Here are some of the leading sports online auction sites.

Heritage Sports Collectibles

Dallas-based Heritage Sports Collectibles (*www.heritagesportscollectibles.com*) plays both sides of the auction field. It stages live auctions of rare sports cards and memorabilia at major sports conventions, and it hosts its monthly Amazing Sports Auctions online. Membership is required to bid. In late 2005, its membership totaled about 15,000. Heritage Sports Collectibles is a subsidiary of Heritage Galleries & Auctioneers, which bills itself as "the world's largest collectibles auctioneer."

Lelands

Lelands.com modestly claims to be "the largest and most respected Sports Auction House in the world." It has handled some of America's most famous—and, some would say, infamous—sports memorabilia transactions. One of these was the sale of major-league baseball's famous "Mookie Ball" to actor Charlie Sheen for more than $93,000. This was a baseball hit between the legs of a Boston Red Sox first baseman during the 1986 World Series. Many fans believe the error caused the New York Mets to win the World Series and continue the Red Sox's long-running curse of not winning the Series. (The 2004 Red Sox finally ended the curse that had lingered since 1918.)

Based in Seaford, New York, Lelands.com also handles Americana memorabilia and uses the five-minute rule in its online auctions. Bidding can continue past the scheduled closing time until there are no more bids during a five-minute period. Winning bidders pay a 17.5 percent premium, as well as all shipping and handling costs.

To register to bid at Lelands, you must be able to list at least one reference, such as a valid eBay account with a positive feedback score or a verifiable account with at least one other auction house.

bid4sport

It seems as if every major sports auction site calls itself "number one" in some category. In the case of Great Britain's bid4sport.com, the claim is "the world's number 1 site for 100% authentic, autographed memorabilia." Only registered members can receive information about upcoming online auctions. However, bids can be placed from anywhere in the world. Interestingly, bids can also be placed by telephone if you can't get to a computer on a day when an auction ends. A representative will place the bid for you. However, the telephone bidding service must be scheduled at least twenty-four hours in advance of the auction's end.

NHL.com Auction Network

Hockey fans who like memorabilia and hockey equipment can bid on everything from pro stars' signed jerseys to hockey sticks, pucks, and face masks at auctions.nhl.com, the National Hockey League's online auction site. Other items include posters, autographed caps, and Olympic gold coins.

Entertainment Auction Sites

Entertainment items are hot sellers on many online auction sites, including eBay, Amazon, Yahoo! and others, as well as niche sites that have the entertainment industry as their central focus. Online, you can bid on or sell a vast array of entertainment goods ranging from old records and new posters to props and costumes from recent movies that were smash hits—or smash flops.

eRock.net

This music online auction site features auctions in twenty categories of rock-and-roll memorabilia ranging from the Beatles, Elvis Presley, and the Rolling Stones to guitar picks and vinyl record albums. The site charges no listing fees to sellers and is aimed at "serious diehard fans, collectors and dealers of Rock-n-Roll memorabilia."

Internet Movie Poster Auction

The Internet Movie Poster Auctions are hosted by Heritage Galleries & Auctioneers (*www.heritagegalleries.com*). New items are added each week. Listings are posted for thirty days, and bids can be placed online until 10 PM Central Standard Time (CST) Sunday nights. More than 7,000 members are registered to participate in the auctions.

Overstock.com

Entertainment memorabilia is one of the featured online auction departments at Overstock.com. From the main page, click on the Auctions tab, and then scroll down the left side of the Auctions Home page to the Departments listings. The entertainment memorabilia categories include:

- Autographs
- Celebrity memorabilia
- Movie memorabilia
- Music memorabilia
- Television memorabilia
- Videogame memorabilia
- Other memorabilia

Available items can be sorted by lowest bid, lowest starting price, fewest bids, as well as which ones are ending first, are highest priced, or are newly listed.

New Line Cinema Auction

New Line Cinema holds online auctions for items from its movies, such as *Monster-in-Law* and *Wedding Crashers*, at auction.newline.com. The items up for bid include costumes worn by some of the stars, props from some of the scenes, and movie promotional materials. Each winning bidder gets the auctioned item and a letter of authenticity signed by a New

Line Cinema executive. At the site's Upcoming Auctions link, future auctions are promoted, and initial bids can be placed before the auction officially begins. The bids will place bidders on an e-mail list to be notified when the auction starts.

Nauck's Vintage Records

The auctions at Nauck's Vintage Records (*www.78rpm.com*) are posted online but bidding takes place by e-mail, fax, mail, or telephone. Bid forms can be printed out online, and bids must be submitted by midnight CST of the closing date. New bidders who will be bidding over $500 must first offer two references from major record dealers or post a deposit. Some of the items up for bid range from old acoustic recordings to comedy records, radio transcriptions and wax cylinder recordings that must be played on an old Victrola.

Art Sites

Art, like beauty, is in the eye and mind of the beholder. The quality, emotional impact, and investment value of a work of art often cannot be determined without seeing it in person. Nonetheless, online auctions for artworks are growing in popularity, and safeguards are usually in place to help bidders and sellers have successful transactions. A small sampling of sites follows.

ArtByUs

ArtByUs (*www.artbyus.com*) calls itself "the premiere online auction market exclusively for real art by real artists." ArtByUs does not allow sellers to list mass-produced artworks "unless the artist is selling their own high-quality, fine art prints." It promises works of art within any collector's budget and opportunities to connect with the artist. The listings can range from classical landscapes to pottery, mixed media, and studio supplies. The site does not charge buyers a fee, and sellers do not pay listing or final value fees when a high bidder purchases their artwork.

Heritage Galleries

Along with works of art, Heritage Galleries (*www.heritagegalleries. com*) offers collectible antiques such as Tiffany lamps, works of ceramic and porcelain, silver flatware, and vintage clocks in its online and live auctions. There are six different ways to place a bid:

- Over the Internet: If the auction has a live floor session, Internet bids are accepted until 10 P.M. CST the night before the live auction.
- By e-mail: Bids are accepted up to twenty-four hours before the start of a live auction.
- By postal mail: If your mailed bid is the highest, Heritage Galleries will act as your representative and buy the lot as "as cheaply as competition permits."
- By fax: Bids sent by fax are accepted until 3 P.M. the day before the live auction.
- By phone: Call at least twenty-four hours in advance of the auction and ask for bidding assistance.
- In person: At Heritage Galleries in Dallas, Texas.

Art Brokerage.com

The Art Brokerage.com (*www.artbrokerage.com*) online auction site claims that it buys and sells more works by Andy Warhol than any other outlet. It also boasts getting more than 2 million hits per month from Web searchers. Buyers do not have to register at the site. Once a price is agreed upon, the seller ships the art to Art Brokerage.com for inspection. After it passes inspection, it is sent to the buyer. Sellers can list artworks free. If an artwork sells, the seller pays a 20 percent commission to Art Brokerage.com.

Antiques Sites

Antiques usually are best judged in person, not with a few pictures posted online. Many antique auction houses use the World Wide Web to post details of upcoming live auctions and present photographs of some of the items to be auctioned. Sometimes, to show the quality of their merchandise, they display photographs of items recently sold. Then they post long lists of items, without photos, that will be sold in their next auction. Many antiques sellers will take absentee bids by telephone, e-mail, or other means, but the bids usually must be received no later than a certain deadline before the live auction begins. Here are a few examples.

Apple Tree Auction Center

Located in Newark, Ohio, the Apple Tree Auction Center (*www.apple-treeauction.com*) auctions everything from old Ohio license plates to World War I bayonets, 1940s tractors, and nineteenth-century Royal Worchester jugs, as well as art antiques. Apple Tree accepts absentee bids by e-mail, fax, or postal mail. Absentee bidders must bid at least $25. No buyer fees are added when winning bids are paid with cash or a check. A 5 percent charge is added to credit card payments. At Apple Tree, live telephone bidding can be arranged. An extra fee is charged for winning telephone bids.

whybidmore

The online site whybidmore.com describes itself as a "no fees" antique and collectibles auction that also offers a shopping directory and an interactive community focused on collectibles and antiques. Whybidmore is headquartered in Thorndale, Pennsylvania. Its shopping directory lists nearly 4,000 Web sites that auction or sell a wide range of collectibles. In its online forum, members can post messages, questions, and answers under headings such as Antiques; Arts, Crafts, Pottery, Ceramics; and Postcards and Paper Collectibles.

Donated Treasures

Social relief agencies receive tons of donated items each year. Some of the items are sold in the agencies' thrift stores to help fund their operations and pay employees. Some of the items cannot be used and are discarded. But some of the items that donors considered giveaways actually have tangible value to many collectors and Web shoppers.

Goodwill Industries International helps hundreds of thousands of handi-capped workers overcome employment barriers. In 1999, Goodwill became the first nonprofit agency to launch an online auction site. Today, *shop*good-will.com sells antiques, collectibles, and other auction-worthy items pulled from Goodwill's huge inventory of goods donated to its 184 local, autonomous member organizations in the United States and Canada. The site offers eighteen auction categories including cameras and electronics, clothing, tableware and kitchenware, jewelry and gemstones, toys and dolls, and books, movies, and music. The Goodwill site is operated by Goodwill Industries of Orange County, California. It now lists an average of 11,000 items per day and draws bidders from all over the world. Here is one other measure of its popularity: *shop*good-will.com gets about 500,000 hits per day from Internet users.

Memorabilia and Collectibles Sites

Online auctions offering memorabilia and collectibles are often part of larger sites that feature several categories of auctions. Memorabilia and collectibles are also active categories on the "big" sites that include eBay, Yahoo! and Amazon.

AutographAuction.com

AutographAuction.com has been selling celebrity autographs online since 1997. All autographs auctioned at this site "were obtained in-person by our company. No items were bought or traded for." The auction categories are as follows:

- Female celebrities
- Male celebrities
- Music
- Animation
- NASCAR
- Multi-signed

According to the company, a letter of authenticity and a lifetime money-back guarantee accompany all autographs.

Hake's Americana & Collectibles

Hake's (*www.hakes.com*) is based in Timonium, Maryland, and has been in the Americana and collectibles auction business since 1967. Its online auctions feature objects ranging from *GI Joe* action figures to *Captain Marvel* Rocket Raider compass rings, *Lone Ranger* radios, and *Wizard of Oz* soap figures.

Oh-So-Esoteric Sites

Your first reaction may be: "What? People actually collect this stuff?" The answer is, yes, they do. People around the world like to gather examples of—and place value on—almost anything under the sun. Online auctions provide a practical and popular way for collectors of odd and esoteric items to meet other like-minded collectors and buy or sell collectible items. Here are three examples.

American Matchcover Collecting Club

Many people collect old matchcovers. The American Matchcover Collecting Club (AMCC) was founded in 1986, and its *www.matchcovers.com* site includes a link to an eBay store that sells collectible matchcovers at Buy It Now prices. Its members-only section also includes a link to its online auction site. Memberships are $10 a year. Matchcover auctions can be found online at a few other sites, as well, including whybidmore and eBay.

Postcard Collecting

Some people still think collecting postcards is esoteric. Yet, according to the Shiloh Postcards Web site (*www.shilohpostcards.com*), it is now the third-largest collectible hobby in the world, behind coins and stamps. Indeed, the act of gathering postcards is so popular that it has gained its own word: *deltiology*. There are plenty of postcards to collect. Since its invention in Hungary in 1869, the lowly postcard has pictured many different things, places, and people.

Much of the deltiology trading action happens on eBay, Amazon, and Yahoo! Playle's Online Auctions (✐*www.playle.com*) is one of the other prominent players, with more than 90,000 postcards up for bid. Unlike many auction sites for collectibles, Playle's only accepts bids online—no e-mail, fax, or phone bids. Playle's is a member of the Postcard Traders Association and the International Federation of Postcard Dealers and provides online links to several postcard collectors' clubs in the United States.

The Trade Card Place

Small, illustrated cards were used to advertise American goods in the late 1800s, and even then, adults and children loved to collect them. Contemporary collectors call them "Victorian trade cards," and there is a small but active market for these vintage advertisements. The cards first became plentiful in the 1870s, after the invention of color lithography, touting tobacco products, medicines, sewing notions, and other items. They remained popular for about twenty years, until other forms of advertising started replacing them.

The Trade Card Place (✐*www.tradecards.com*) conducts monthly online auctions for buyers and sellers of the cards. An auction begins on the first Thursday of the month and closes thirteen days later on a Wednesday evening. The site protects bidders against last-second bid snipers by running a fifteen-minute countdown clock. If an increased bid is received within the fifteen-minute countdown, the clock resets to fifteen minutes and keeps resetting until there are no more bids.

The Best of Both Worlds

Active buyers and sellers who love niche auction sites often have the best of both worlds. They can check out the action on the major sites, then jump to their favorite niche sites, and bounce back and forth as the listing clocks tick down. Sometimes, they can buy on one site, sell on another, score a new bargain on one of the big auction sites, and then bring it to the niche site and make a nice profit, all in a matter of days.

Once you are ready to become an online seller, check the back corners of your closets, shelves, and attic very carefully. You may have items stashed away that could make you very popular on a niche auction site.

Chapter 6
Buying Online

Online shopping keeps expanding worldwide, and so does the popularity of buying at online auctions. From your computer, you can now roam from site to site, seeking collectibles, toys, hobby goods, nostalgia items from your past, rare books, musical recordings—the list is almost endless. Virtually anything you can imagine is up for bid, and so are countless items you have probably never imagined. Buying at online auctions can be a journey of delightful discovery and a constantly surprising view of what humanity values.

Doing Your Homework

"Have you done your homework?" You likely dreaded that question as a child. Yet, as a new online auction buyer, you should be happy when you hear that query echoing in your mind. Once you register to buy at an auction site, you will be eager to place your first bids immediately. Resist this temptation. Take some time to learn a few things about the site itself. Each online auction venue is different. The features, rules, and restrictions on what you can buy will vary from one site to another. Be sure you understand what you can do—and cannot do—on a particular auction site, before you place your first bid.

On eBay, for example, you should go to the eBay Policies page. This page provides important details in nine general areas of buying and selling policy:

- The eBay user agreement
- Site rules affecting everyone, including buyers, sellers, and eBay employees
- Rules for buyers
- Items that are prohibited or restricted
- Buyer and seller feedback
- Privacy protection
- Identity protection
- Rules for sellers
- Intellectual property protection

Not So Fast

Learn to slow down and temper any impatience when you log on to online auction sites. These are no places to be in a hurry. The world will not run out of things to buy before you can get online and bid. Indeed, haste can make the proverbial waste if you impulsively bid on an item, and then wish you hadn't.

On each auction site that interests you, take the time to study its features and determine which ones are right for your buying needs. The best way to check out an auction site for the first time is to view a few auctions for things you have absolutely no desire to buy. For example, pick an auction that has several bidders and will be ending soon. The auction may have been running for seven or ten days or longer, but most of the real action will occur within the final two days and especially in the final hour. As the minutes count down, the serious bidders will start maneuvering to post the winning offer. The bid prices may suddenly start jumping several dollars or more at a time as one buyer tops another buyer's maximum bid price, then the outbid buyer counters with a higher bid, and so on.

Registering to Buy

Online auction sites try to make it as easy as possible for new buyers to register. After all, auction sellers need as many potential bidders as possible. The registration process usually requires supplying some personal information, such as:

- Name
- Billing address
- Shipping address (if different from billing address)
- Telephone number
- Occupation
- E-mail address
- Credit or debit card account number and expiration date

Generally, you will also be asked to set up a user name and password for your buyer account. You should pick a user name—a so-called screen name or alias—that is easy to remember but doesn't reveal your identity. Don't use your real name, and don't be surprised if you have to try several aliases. Other buyers may already have taken your first choices. After all, there are many millions of auction buyers now online and thousands more sign up everyday.

Password Tips

Setting up your password can be a bit tricky. The auction site likely will impose restrictions on minimum or maximum password lengths. You may be required to use or avoid using certain characters or symbols.

ALERT!

Never leave your user names and passwords stored together near your computer, where a friend, relative, or thief can discover them. They could log on to one of your auction accounts, on your computer or another, and fraudulently buy or sell something. And you could be investigated for the crime.

Computer users with several online accounts often have several screen names and passwords to remember—sometimes, dozens of them. You may have to write down your auction site screen names and passwords or store them in text files on your computer, so you can remember them. But be very careful how you do this. For example, don't use file names such as *auction_site_user_names.txt* or *auction_site_passwords.doc*. Pick something a bit more cryptic and less enticing to computer hackers, such as *old_broccoli_recipes.txt* and *kidney_stones_info.doc*.

Some auction sites will let you pick a secret question and enter an answer that will help you recall a forgotten password. The question may be "Where were you born?" or "What was your mother's maiden name?" or something similar that a person trying to break into your account might not know.

If you forget a password, you may be able to click on a sign-in link and request the auction site to send it to you via e-mail. You may receive your existing password or a temporary password, plus a link where you can set up a new password.

On eBay, if you forget your user ID, you can click on a link on the eBay Sign In page, right below where you would type your account name. This will bring up the Forgot User ID page. After you enter your e-mail address (the one recognized by eBay if you have multiple e-mail accounts), eBay will send you your user name via e-mail.

If you forget your eBay password, click on *Forgot your password?* just above the Sign in Securely screen button.

Yahoo! Auctions and most other online auction venues also provide online forms or links to help you regain access to your account. The Yahoo! form is accessed from the My Auctions page.

Click on the small *Forgot your Yahoo! ID or password?* link. This will display the Yahoo! Sign-in Problems screen. You will be asked to confirm your identity by entering your birthday, Zip Code, and country. Once you do this, you can choose between getting a new password and finding your Yahoo! account name.

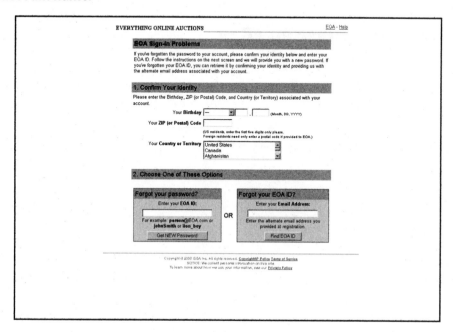

Name, Rank, Serial Number

From one auction site to another, there are a few differences in the registration process and how much information you must supply. You may be given the option to supply or omit certain identifying details, such as your fax number, or your gender or your age. Generally, you must be at least eighteen years old and have a credit card or debit card to set up a buyer's account.

ALERT!

If you are uncomfortable with how much detail one particular auction site requires, you can cancel the registration process before you finish and go to another venue to check out its signup requirements.

Becoming a Buyer on eBay

Most new buyers start by signing up with the planetary leader in online auctions: eBay. At eBay's main page, click on the Buy tab just to the right of the multicolored eBay logo. This opens the Buy page.

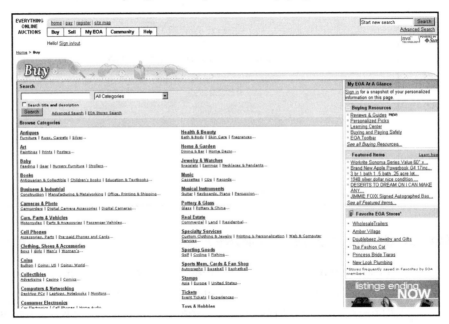

Just below the blue-highlighted word *Buy,* look for the *Hello! Sign in or register* message. Click on the Register link.

The Register: Enter Information page will open. This is where you begin the process of becoming approved as a buyer on eBay.

Enter the required information and read the User Agreement and Privacy Policy. You should also print out a copy of the agreement and policy for your records. To do this, click on the *Printer-friendly version* link just to the right of the heading.

If you click on the Continue button without answering all of the questions, a new screen will pop up with a red warning message: "The following must be corrected before continuing." The uncompleted items will be listed, and new information boxes with red headings will be displayed. Enter the correct information in the appropriate boxes before continuing.

Buying on Overstock.Com

To buy from Overstock.com Auctions, your first step is to become a Verified Registered User. The process is similar to signing up as a buyer on eBay and other sites but requires a few extra steps. First, at Overstock.com's main page, click on the Auctions tab at the top of the screen, near the center.

Clicking on the tab will open the Auctions page.

Scroll down to the very bottom of the Auctions page and click on the small How to Buy Tutorial. That link will open the How to Buy on Overstock. com Auctions page.

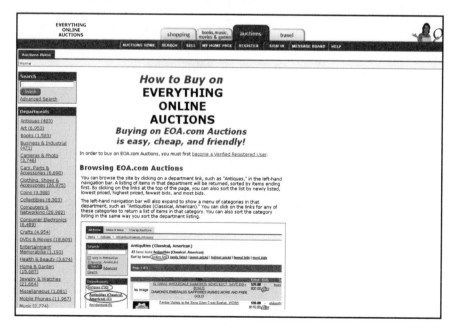

Read the tutorial completely. It covers:

- How to browse auctions
- How to search auctions
- How to bid and receive bid confirmations
- How to monitor an auction
- How to close an auction successfully with a winning bid
- How to leave a "business rating"—feedback about the seller

After you complete the tutorial, return to the top of the page and click on the Become a Verified Registered User link just above the Browsing Overstock.com Auctions heading. This will take you to another tutorial page: How to Become a Verified Registered User on Overstock.com Auctions.

The tutorial points out that you must create an Overstock.com Shopping account and an Overstock.com Auctions account and become a Verified Registered User. Read the tutorial on how to perform these three steps, and then follow the links in each section to set up the appropriate accounts.

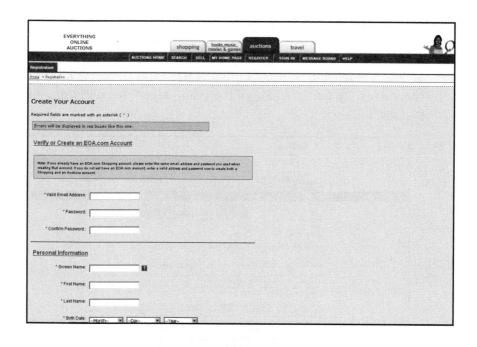

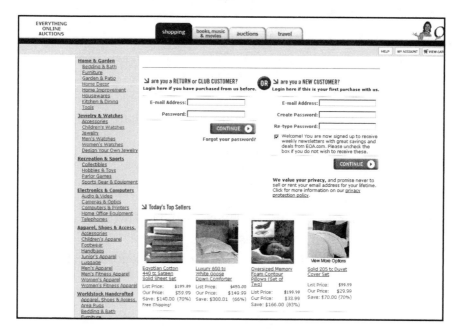

Buying on uBid

On uBid.com, you can place bids on auction goods listed by businesses only, not individual sellers. Starting at the main page, click on the red Register tab at the far right side of the main page. This will bring up the uBid Registration screen.

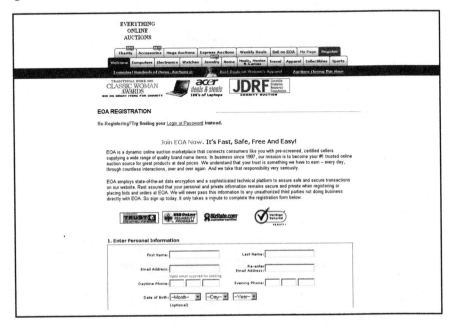

Setting up a buyer's account requires filling in just a few on-screen boxes:

- Name
- E-mail address
- Your desired uBid login name and password
- Your shipping address
- Your credit card or debit card information, including your mailing address

Signing Up for Amazon.com Auctions

On the Amazon.com main page, look on the left side for a frame labeled Browse. Scroll down the column to the Bargains heading and click on Auctions directly beneath it.

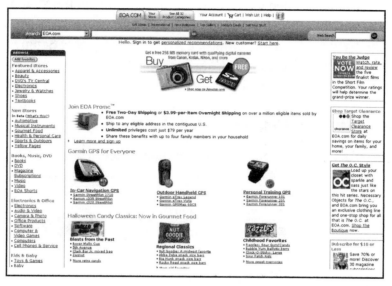

The Amazon.com Auctions page will open. Look for the message: "Hello, first-time visitor. Sign in." Click on the Sign In link. This will bring up the Sign In page.

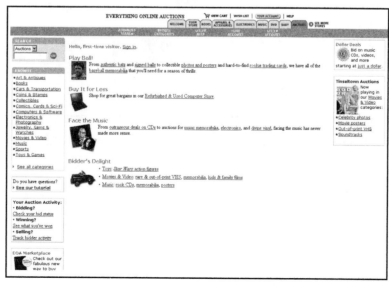

You will start by entering your e-mail address and selecting the option: "I do not have an Amazon.com password." On the next page, you will enter your first and last name, create your Amazon password, and verify it by entering it again. At that point, you are registered on the site and will be taken to the Recommended for [your name] page. Click on the Your Account link at the top of the page. This will open the Your Account page. Scroll down to the heading Account Settings. Look for the Payment Settings heading and the Edit or Delete a Credit Card link. This is where you can enter credit card information that will enable you to buy on Amazon.com Auctions.

Registering to Buy on Yahoo! Auctions

First, open the Yahoo! Auctions main page.

Click on the small New User? Sign Up link right next to the word *Auctions,* directly beneath the Yahoo! Shopping logo.

You will be asked to enter your name, preferred Yahoo! content (such as Yahoo! U.S.), and gender. You will set up a Yahoo! ID and password and be given the option to create a Yahoo! e-mail account. To help identify you if you forget your password, you will be asked to pick a security question, such as "What was the name of your first school?" and enter your answer. You must also enter your birth date and Zip Code. Before completing the registration process, you must read and agree to the Yahoo! terms of service and privacy policy.

Registering to Buy on QXL.com

The QXL.com Register link is easy to find. Look on the right side of the main page for the big, bright-orange Register button. Clicking this will bring up the Register on QXL.com page. (You must have a European address and credit card information to register.)

On the Register page, you will enter your first and last name and select a screen name, or alias. You will also create a password and type it again to verify it. Finally, you must click on a link that opens the general conditions of use. After you read and agree to the conditions, click the box labeled: "I have read the Terms and Conditions and I accept them." When you click on the Submit button, you will go to the second page, where credit card information and other information must be entered.

The Truth about Privacy

Online auction sites typically have a privacy policy, and they post a link to its text on their main page. Yet, there is no such thing as guaranteed privacy in the online world. You can cloak your identity to some degree behind a screen name, a nondescript e-mail address, and a shipping address that is different than your home address. But even on so-called secure Web sites, such as those used by major auction venues, your personal and financial information is definitely not private.

FACT

A 2005 survey by the University of Pennsylvania's Annenberg Public Policy Center found that three out of four Americans who use the Internet mistakenly believe Web site privacy policies are assurances that a site will not share information about its users with other Web sites.

Indeed, a Web site's privacy policy often spells out exactly how that site will share your information with other companies. For example, in agreeing to eBay's lengthy privacy policy during registration, you "expressly consent" to eBay's "use and disclosure of your personal information in accordance with this Privacy Policy." Digging into the fine print, you will find that eBay shares information about you with subsidiaries and joint ventures all over the world. Information about you may be given to advertisers with your "express consent." Also, your bidding and selling activities, feedback postings, and related comments will be visible on the site and accessible to anyone who uses eBay. Those who sell to you also will have your e-mail address, name, shipping address, and credit card information or bank account number, eBay notes.

The privacy policy for eBay is located on its Policies Page, accessed from the Policies link at the bottom of the eBay main page.

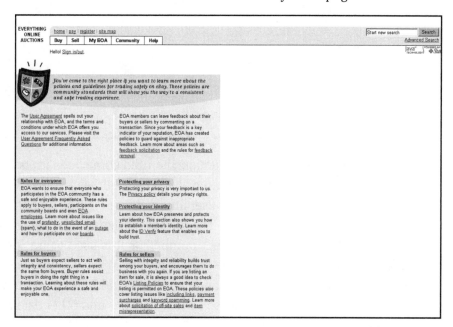

The eBay Privacy Policy page is accessed from the Protecting Your Privacy link on the Policies page.

According to eBay, people may browse the eBay site without identifying themselves or giving any personal information. However, certain types of information must be supplied before the buying and selling features can be used. Also, eBay automatically tracks certain types of information related to the behaviors of registered users on the site.

After reading eBay's privacy statements, if you still have questions, the Privacy page contains a link to eBay's Privacy Central. This page contains more discussions of eBay's privacy practices, plus information about third-party verification Web sites.

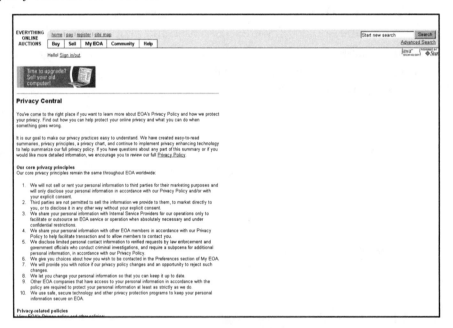

The business-to-consumer auction site uBid.com states in its Privacy & Security policy that products ordered at uBid sometimes are shipped directly from uBid's vendors, and certain user information is shared with the vendors to help them fill and ship orders. The site also assigns each new registrant "a random and anonymous customer number" that is used to track customer orders. The number also may be passed to third-party vendors and may be used "to measure traffic and visiting patterns on uBid and on other websites on the Internet." It may also be used when statistics and other data regarding customer patterns are compiled.

Yahoo! cautions on its Yahoo! Privacy Center page: "Once you register with Yahoo! and sign in to our services, you are not anonymous to us."

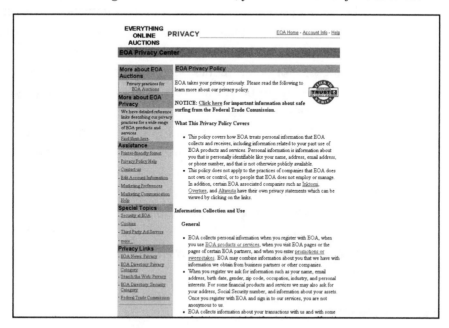

Take as many personal measures as possible to protect your privacy and the security of your financial information, and remain especially vigilant while using online auction sites. The sites' privacy policies will not guarantee anything except that they will try to protect your information—while making at least some of it available to others.

Finding What You Want

Online auctions try to make it very easy for you to find the types of items you are seeking. Three search tools typically are supported on each site: browsing, find or search, and advanced search.

Browsing

Browsing on an online site is a bit like wandering around inside a busy department store and stopping to touch and ponder whenever something new or on sale catches your eye.

Once you click onto an online auction site, you will be bombarded with an array of links, advertisements, announcements, tips, and news flashes. You may be seeking something specific, but the chances are very high that you can get distracted and go off on tangents once you start browsing.

Fortunately, most sites help you stay focused by offering browsing links for major categories or departments, such as Antiques or Cameras or Toys. For example, at the main page for Overstock.com Auctions, you can click on a department link in the left-hand navigation bar. Then you can browse the site by clicking on a department link, such as Antiquities, in the navigation bar on the left side of the page. A listing of auctions in that department will be displayed, sorted by the items that end first. If you use other sorting tools, you can rearrange the list by newly posted items, those with the lowest prices, those with the highest bids, and so on.

On many sites, a major category or department will have additional links to specific subcategories, such as Early-American Furniture or First-Edition Books or Baseball Cards.

Find or Search

Virtually any online auction site will have a Find or Search tool prominently displayed on its main page and probably on other pages as well. As a buyer, you should become very familiar with these useful and timesaving features. They usually will be your starting point for finding desired items and comparing bid prices.

As an example, the uBid.com auction site has a Quick Search tool that is visible on many of its pages. Entering a search term such as "gold jewelry" brings up lists of matching categories and matching brands. You can also narrow your search by entering another keyword or a bidding price range.

The Yahoo! Auctions Search tool lets you select All of Auctions or specific categories such as Electronics & Cameras or Home & Garden before clicking on the Search button.

One of eBay's most powerful tools for buyers and sellers is accessed from the deceptively simple *Start New Search* box in the upper-right corner of most pages. Here, you can enter a keyword, such as "wrenches," or a longer description, such as "19th-century coins," and click on the gray Search button. This will display current auctions, if any are found, and provide links to one or more related auctions, as well.

The wise buyer makes frequent use of an auction site's advanced search tools. These tools can help you quickly find auctions for very specific items within certain price ranges or from specific sellers. You can also find recently completed auctions and see how much other bidders paid for particular items that interest you.

On eBay, the Advanced Search link is right below the Start New Search box.

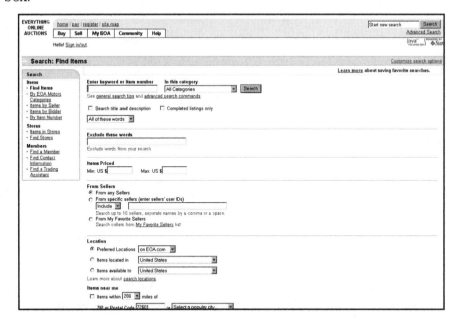

Clicking on the link will open a page labeled Search: Find Items, with boxes you can fill in with search terms. There also are drop-down lists of categories and locations, and checkboxes with certain qualifiers to help narrow your search. As an example, you could list auctions closing within one hour for first-edition hardback books from sellers in your own state who only accept PayPal. You could restrict the search even more by specifying a minimum or maximum price.

Yahoo! Auctions' Advanced Search link provides the option to search by:

- Keyword
- Closed auction
- Yahoo! ID
- Item number

Each choice brings up another page with additional options to focus the search.

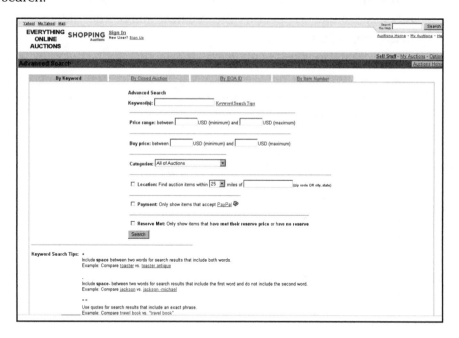

To being an advanced search on the Overstock.com Auctions site, start with the Refine Your Search box on the search page. There are several ways to get to Overstock.com's search page. The main ones include:

- Click on Search in the tabs in the site's top navigation bar.
- Click on the Advanced Search link in the Search box portion of the left-hand navigation bar.

- Click on the Advanced Search link next to the Search box beneath the banner on the Overstock homepage.

To perform an advanced search in the Refine Your Search box, enter one of the following terms:

- A keyword or series of keywords
- An item number
- A minimum price
- A maximum price
- An auction department, such as Books, Music & Videos
- Seller
- Results per page (10–100)

Each time you find a new online auction site that grabs your interest check out its search and advanced search tools before registering to buy. Be sure they offer the types of helpful, timesaving search options that you want.

Know What Is Really Being Sold

Before you place a bid, always ask yourself: How much do I really know about this item? Always be wary of words such as rare, vintage, valuable, and collector's item in online auction listings. In many cases, the words will be true. But there are several other possibilities, as well. For example:

- An inexperienced auction seller may not know enough about what she is selling. Perhaps a friend or relative has convinced her an item is "rare," so that is how she has posted it. She has trusted the judgment of someone who is not an expert.
- An experienced auction seller has posted the item knowing that some buyers will bid on almost anything labeled "collector's item." The item indeed may be collectible right now, but it may go down sharply in value in just a few weeks, not up, as public interest in the item's category fades.

- A new auction seller has purchased some "rare" items from someone who seemed to need money to pay medical bills. Unfortunately, the items were stolen, and the new seller has listed them for auction without knowing this.

Before bidding, be sure you have reviewed an auction site's list of items that must not be sold or are subject to certain sales restrictions. You may want to print the list for each site where you have registered and keep it handy in a reference binder. On Yahoo! Auctions, for example, the prohibited items cover a broad range, from switchblades to fireworks and from counterfeit stamps to stalactites and stalagmites from caves on federal land.

Someone may post a prohibited item for bid and not be discovered by auction site personnel until the item has been sold or someone has complained. Honest buyers are encouraged to help control auction sites by contacting site personnel and reporting any illegal merchandise that they have found up for bid.

Buying Guides

eBay has simplified the auction research process for new buyers, at least in several major product categories. The auction giant has posted a series of buying guides, covering popular topics such as art, digital cameras, jewelry, and sports memorabilia. The buying guides discuss what to look for in particular items, and they provide quick links to the appropriate auction areas. For example, if your interest is radio-controlled model airplanes, and you are seeking a Cox engine, the Radio Control Buying Guide contains a Shop by Brand section, with a link to all current auctions for Cox engines.

Other auction sites have buying guides. For example, the Web site eSmarts.com publishes an "Auctions Buying Guide" that gives basic auction buying tips, links to several Best Auctions sites, and reviews of a few online auction sites. As another example, About.com's Stamps/Coins page presents a collection of online resources for buying stamps and coins at auction sites and has articles that describe how to determine the value of stamps and coins.

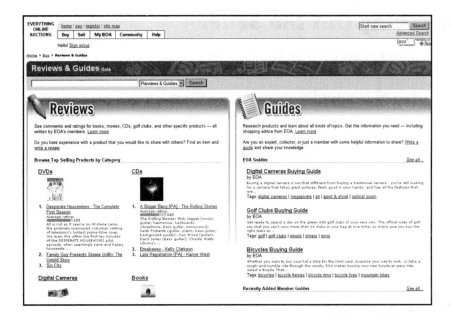

Searching Closed Auctions

One of the most valuable tools for buyers on eBay and other auction sites is the ability to search items in closed auction listings. If you are thinking of bidding on a particular item, you can look for similar items auctioned within the recent past and see their selling prices and who posted the winning bids. Knowing the price ranges in completed auctions can help you stick to an upper limit when you enter the bidding for a similar item in a new auction.

You may also be able to read questions posted by potential bidders and the seller's responses to the questions. The information in these may help you learn more about the item you are watching.

Checking Out the Seller

The number one-rule for all online auction buyers: Never post a bid or send money to any online seller until you are comfortable with the seller, the terms of the deal, and the likelihood that you will receive your purchase.

Always try to check out a seller's reputation before placing a bid on one of his items. Typically, you can do this by reading the seller's feedback or the seller's ratings posted by others who have bought from him on the auction site. Read all of the comments, if you can, and keep in mind that almost no seller can maintain a perfect score for very long. Sometimes, a transaction or shipment goes awry, and negative feedback is posted. Sometimes, a buyer may respond angrily to some matter and post a bad rating for something the seller probably could not control.

Before you bid, you can e-mail a question to the seller and see what kind of response you get. If a seller is new to the auction site, e-mail them to get information that can be verified, such as an address or a home phone number or work phone number. Also, be sure you know what you are bidding on, and be sure you understand the terms of the sale, before you bid.

On eBay, some sellers choose to have their identities verified through the eBay ID Verify process. A third-party company contracted by eBay confirms the seller's identity by checking it against a number of consumer and business databases. After a seller is verified, a special symbol can be displayed in his member profile, indicating his special status.

Many auction sites simply encourage buyers and sellers to check each other out before going ahead with bids and other transactions. However, a few auction sites investigate sellers to be sure they are legitimate, and some of the auction sellers may be eligible for special bonded merchant designations. For example, Overstock.com Auctions' Trusted Merchant program protects buyers before and after a purchase. Trusted Merchants are sellers who have been bonded by buySAFE, Inc., an e-commerce and auction bonding service. This service verifies their identities and confirms that they are financially stable and able to meet their obligations. Any purchase from a merchant with a buySAFE seal was guaranteed up to $25,000 with a Liberty Mutual surety bond, when Overstock.com launched its Trusted Merchant program in mid-2005.

The Careful Buyer

New buyers often go on a spirited registration spree, setting up buying accounts on as many as a dozen or more online auction sites. What frequently happens, however, is that they soon settle on using two or three—or perhaps just one favorite site. The other accounts sit dormant for weeks, months, or even years. Instances have occurred where computer hackers have gotten into unwatched accounts and used them to make fraudulent sales or purchases. You could lose your buyer privileges on an auction site and your credit and reputation could be threatened by the actions of others, if unauthorized users get into one of your auction accounts.

Buying at online auctions can be entertaining, and it can be a quick way to get the things you want or need—and probably thought you might never find again. It can also be the basis for an auction reselling business.

No matter how you approach buying, take it slow and easy at first. Learn to use all the relevant tools at one auction site before signing up for another. Check out items carefully. Check out sellers carefully. Watch auctions patiently. And take a good look at your own buying habits. Online auctions are no place for impulsive shopping.

Chapter 7
Bidding to Win

Online auctions can bring unexpected circumstances into action. Without knowing it, you may compete against bidders who have strong attachments to a particular item. You may encounter bidders driven by ego or by an urgent need to win a particular item. You may bid against buyers who have money to burn and care little for how they spend it. The online auction world can seem like a chess game played in the dark. But common sense and a few simple strategies are what you need to emerge consistently as a winning bidder.

Know the Value

When you need something in a hurry, you likely rush into a twenty-four-hour convenience store and pay premium price for it, so you can solve your situation quickly. The product's immediate availability makes it more valuable to you, and you pay a higher price without hesitation. On a normal shopping day, of course, with more time and choices at hand, you would likely push that same product aside and go for a cheaper generic brand.

The price levels for objects can be driven to eye-opening heights in online auctions for reasons you may never understand. You won't be able to see into the minds or read the body language of the competing bidders. You will probably never learn what has motivated them to place such a high value on a particular object. At the same time, you will encounter many situations in which you will find desirable items listed and no one—or almost no one—bidding on them. These are prime moments for alert buyers who are seeking the items. Some days, you will catch amazing bargains, and some days you will run away from an overheated listing, fearing that people's credit cards are about to burst into flames.

Your strongest defense against getting in over your head is to know the real value of any item that catches your eye. You may be an expert or at least a knowledgeable hobbyist in one or two fields. But online auction bidding can lead you into many unexpected and unfamiliar subject areas.

At one time or another, you may find yourself in unfamiliar territory. A spouse may suddenly ask you to find a certain type of power saw or sewing machine accessory. A child may ask for help in getting an old video game. You may remember a favorite toy from your childhood and wonder if anything like it is still around. A parent may want a telephoto lens for a beloved camera that went out of production in 1975. You may develop a fascination for antique radios or decide to start a home business and need used office furnishings. The possibilities are almost endless. So, you must learn how to search for the information you need.

Dare to Compare

The best way to win consistently in online auctions is to be an unwavering comparison shopper. You may see something you crave in an auction that's ending in two minutes. But unless the price is low and you know it, let it go. A similar object, maybe one in better condition, will be available in another auction soon or may have just been posted on another auction site. Your job is to find it, and that won't require much work if you take the right approach.

Any auction site worth its digital salt has (1) search tools to help you locate what you want, and (2) advanced search tools to help you narrow your search to special qualifiers such as color, size, vintage, price range, and brand.

Another very useful auction site tool is the ability to display the closed listings for particular items that have recently sold. For instance, winning bids in recent auctions can be viewed on eBay by using the Search: Find Items page. Enter a keyword or item number, and then check the Completed Listings Only box.

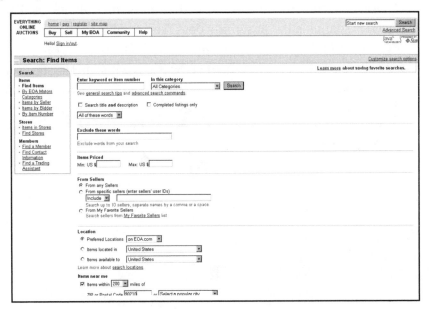

The displayed listings will cover auctions completed within the past fifteen days for the particular type of item you are researching.

Yahoo! Auctions' Advanced Search screen allows searching closed auctions by keyword and by Zip Code, city, state, or radius as small as twenty-five miles.

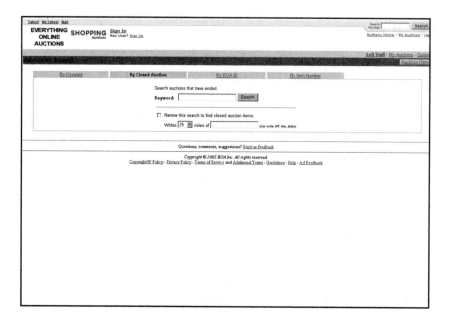

Amazon.com Auctions' Advanced Search screen allows displaying closed auctions spanning the past thirty days. The resulting lists can be a bit daunting, unless further refinements are entered. One search of closed auctions for Computers & Software turned up 32,000 items spanning 640 screens.

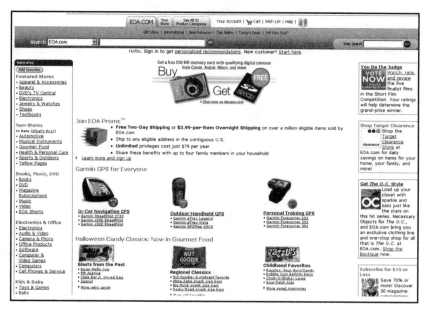

Not all online auction sites offer the ability to prowl through closed listings. For example, some business-to-consumer sites want you to stay focused on what is up for bid right now in their auctions.

Keeping Track

As a new auction buyer, you may spend a lot of time sitting at your computer, actually watching the bidding for items you want to win. As you become more experienced, you will learn to worry less and rely more on the auction sites' automatic (proxy) bidding features and e-mail notifications.

The automatic bidding feature, also known as proxy bidding, lets you enter the top amount you are willing to pay for an item that is being auctioned. Your maximum bid cannot be seen by the seller, or by any of the other bidders.

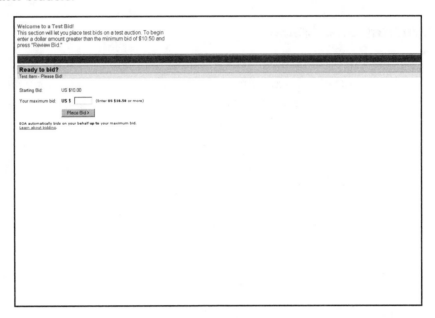

If you set your maximum bid too low, the auction site will respond with an Outbid warning screen and give you the opportunity to increase your bid. You may also receive an e-mail alert.

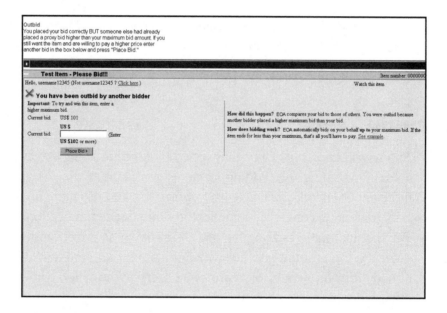

Regaining the Lead

If your opening bid makes you the leader and then someone posts a bid higher than your maximum, you will receive an "outbid" notification via e-mail. The message will describe the item you are bidding on, and it will contain a link to click on if you wish to increase your maximum bid.

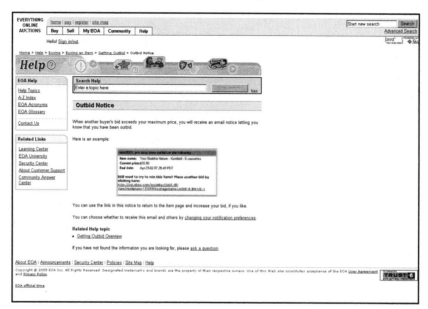

If no one posts a higher bid, the proxy will hold your bid at the minimum amount necessary to keep you at the top. You might have set your maximum bid at $50.99, but your nearest competitor has only bid $30. In this case, your automatic bid will be $31, or whatever the minimum bid increment is, and you will win at this price if no one else bids.

In its tutorials for new buyers, eBay recommends using automatic bidding as a defense against "sniping." This is the practice of trying to post a high bid at the very last moment, when other bidders don't have time to react. If you have set your automatic bid above the price that the bid sniper is offering, you will win by a nose in the final millisecond.

And the Winner Is ... You!

When you win an auction, you should receive a "congratulations" e-mail message with information that will help you get in touch with the seller. On some auction sites, you and the seller may have to communicate by e-mail or telephone and make your own payment and shipping arrangements. On other sites, such as eBay, much of the process is automated and simplified for both the buyer and the seller. The auction-winner e-mail message may also contain links to a payment service such as PayPal, so you can pay for the item and its shipping charges on the spot.

No Bluffing!

An online auction is nothing like poker. In poker, when you are dealt a bad hand, you can still raise the ante and try to bluff the other players into folding. If they take the bluff, you get the pot, and you get back the money you bet. If they call your bluff, you lose everything. In an online auction, if you bid a very high price, trying to bluff the other bidders into quitting, you may indeed succeed. But you will have to pay the full amount of your winning bid.

In some auctions, being the first bidder as well as the high bidder can earn a discount on what you will pay for the item. In some other auctions, holding first-bidder honors may ensure that you will be the winner if you and another bidder get into a last-second tie as the auction ends.

Decide the absolute maximum amount you are willing to pay before you start bidding, and stick to that maximum. If you are outbid, walk away. Search for a similar item up for bid in another auction or on another site. Don't try to battle or bluff a bidder who seems determined to win the item at (almost) all costs. You may emerge victorious—but at a price well above what the merchandise is worth. All you may really win is a case of the blues, better known as "buyer's remorse."

Timing Is Everything

You will hear many different opinions on the "right" time to bid for an item that you really want. The right time to jump in can depend on whether you are bidding (1) in a timed auction that will stick to its predetermined closing deadline or (2) in a "soft close" auction.

Soft-close auctions have a posted closing date and closing time, but if there is a bid within the final ten minutes, the closing time will be extended for another ten minutes, and so on, until there is a high bidder and no additional bid for ten minutes. If you want to win an item in a soft-close auction, you have to be at your computer, ready to offer a counter-bid, as the posted deadline draws near.

Bidding Strategies

If you ask veteran buyers for the "right" bidding strategy, you may get several different pieces of advice, such as:

- Bid early and set your maximum bid at the item's market value or the most you are willing to pay.

- Bid early and keep bidding in small increments, just enough to stay ahead of your competitors.
- Bid in the middle, after you have watched the early bidding trends.
- Jump in just before the auction closes and try to post the final bid.

These approaches all have merit, and one of them may be better suited to your buying temperament than the others. Some auction strategists, however, contend that the sooner you place a bid, the less you may have to pay at the end to win the item. By their reasoning, if you bid early and set your automatic upper-bid limit at the most you are willing to pay, others who try to bid against you will be outbid immediately, each time they bump up their offer. When this happens, they may become discouraged and quit, leaving you free to win. Or, they may push the bidding beyond the true value of the item. When that happens, they may win, but you won't lose. You will still have your money and can soon find another auction for a similar item. With a strong competitor now out of the way, you may even stand a better chance of winning the item, possibly at a lower price than you expected.

The second approach—bidding in small, steady increments—requires more direct involvement in the flow of the auction. In this method, you start early, try to keep your bidding low, and keep pushing your offers by just enough pennies to stay ahead of any other bidders. The strategy here is gradually to wear down your opponents, until they start dropping out, and then try to be the last bidder standing as time expires. In this hands-on process, you will get many outbid notices, and you will spend a lot of time raising your automatic maximum high bid in small increments. But just when another bidder thinks she has taken the lead, you'll pop up again with a new high bid.

ALERT!

The drawback to the slow-and-steady approach is that others may use it, too, resulting in a steady stream of small, lead-changing bids. Ultimately, someone may become frustrated with the seesawing battle and decide to end it by setting a maximum bid that is much higher than you or the other bidders want to pay.

The third approach—waiting until an auction's midway point to post a bid—will give you some time to lurk and size up the other competitors by reading the feedback for each new high bidder. You will also have time to research the item so you can set a good maximum bid once you enter the competition. Some of the other bidders will drop out when you suddenly show up and take the lead. But some of them may become more determined to win. If they raise their bids above the top price you are willing to pay, don't go there. Bail out and seek other auctions.

The fourth approach—bidding during the final minute—may work well if you have a fast computer and a speedy network. Last-minute bidding is very common for hot items, and several bidders may try it at the same time. But if your computer hesitates for some reason or your Internet access suddenly slows down, your one-shot bid can miss the deadline.

Astute buyers of all persuasions typically make heavy use of an auction site's Watch This Auction link. The link displays a list of items they are following and shows the current bid price, how many bids are posted, how much time remains, and other details. Sellers like this feature, too, because each "watcher" activates a counter, such as the "# of Watchers" display that eBay sellers can view on their Items I'm Selling listings. When sellers see several watchers start tracking an item, they know they may have a successful sale.

FACT

Not everyone who watches an auction will click on its Watch This Auction reminder link. There can be dozens of buyers simply lurking and watching the bidding. They may wait until the auction's final minutes, and then jump in. You may think you are the high bidder as the auction clock runs out, but several more bids may arrive literally at the last second from these stealthy watchers.

Endgame Secrets

Experience shows that it is best to be sitting at your computer, ready to respond, when a very important auction is ending. Some experienced buyers like to have two computers running: one to watch the auction site and the other to keep e-mail open and ready for quick action. As the bidding price inches toward your maximum bid, you may suddenly think of a question to ask the seller. Or you may get cold feet and let the other bidders march ahead without you. Or, you may decide the item is really worth another ten dollars to you and raise your maximum bid.

For most items, however, you can enter your absolute maximum bid and rely on your trusty digital proxy to fight the battles for you while you run errands, watch a movie, go grocery shopping, or do a million other things in life. Later, you can check your e-mail and the auction site to see which auctions you won and which ones exceeded your cutoff price. Then you can make your payments and start searches for other examples of the items you didn't win but still want.

Returns

This is essential: Before you place a bid for any item, examine the seller's listing very carefully and read her return policy. Some sellers sell everything "as is" and will allow almost nothing to be returned if the buyer is not satisfied. Some sellers will refund the bid amount if the merchandise is returned, at the buyer's expense, in the same condition as when it was shipped. A few sellers will refund the bid price and the shipping costs, especially if it will help them avoid being the subject of some negative feedback.

Agreeing to a return can be an uncomfortable situation for both a seller and a buyer. The best way to avoid the necessity for a return is to research the item thoroughly before bidding. Examine the seller's pictures and text descriptions very carefully. Read the details of closed auctions for the same type of object. Don't be afraid to ask the seller for more descriptive details or if any more pictures are available that can be sent via e-mail. Read the seller's feedback with a fine-tooth comb. See if anyone has complained about the seller's attitude toward returns.

FACT

Experienced sellers periodically encounter buyers who fail to pay attention to the written descriptions and disclaimers in their auction listings. They see pictures for something they want, and they impulsively bid, hoping the item will turn out to be a lot more valuable than the price they will pay. Then, when they get the item and realize that it really is not perfect, they get mad, demand to return it, and attack the seller's reputation.

Also examine your own needs. Why do you want this object? Are you letting desire override common sense? If you are seeking a perfect collectible plate, for example, and the seller has stated that his plate is not perfect, do not convince yourself that maybe the seller is simply downplaying the quality of his treasure. If he says it has a couple of chips, no amount of imaginings on your part will make it whole again.

Bidding with a calm attitude, a level head, and good information can add up to sheer pleasure, particularly when you win. In the online auction world, these are the real keys to ongoing success as a buyer.

Chapter 8
Best Ways to Pay

Convenience is vital to buyers in online auctions. No one likes to bother with complicated payment arrangements. Buyers on eBay and other online auctions must be comfortable that their payments will be received and processed promptly so their purchases can be shipped with minimum delay. Buyers and sellers alike now have a wide array of online and traditional payment options. Knowing and using the best ways to pay can enhance your enjoyment and excitement of being the winning bidder.

Checking Account Pros and Cons

Despite the spreading use of credit and debit cards online, personal checks remain a convenient and popular choice when paying for auction purchases. Many people feel comfortable with the time-honored process of writing and mailing a check. After all, that is how they have paid their grocers, doctors, utility providers, and credit card companies for decades.

QUESTION?

Will personal checks always be accepted as a form of payment?
Some eBay sellers will not take a check from a new buyer until the newcomer has won a few bids and gotten some positive feedback posted.

Checks provide a paper trail if there is a question or dispute. Unfortunately, the cost of that paper trail keeps getting steeper, as banks continue to hike their service fees and check printing fees.

If you plan to be a frequent buyer on eBay and other online auctions, you will probably need to consider some of the other payment options that are faster and cheaper than mailing a check.

Check, Please

Buyers have several good reasons to pay eBay sellers and other auction sellers with personal checks:

- Checks provide a record of purchase.
- Checks can be traced to a particular mailing address.
- Banks typically offer a stop-payment service (for a fee), if a problem arises before a check is cashed.
- The auction site may offer certain degrees of buyer protection when a winning bid is paid with a check.

ALERT!

Some online auctions offer no protections to buyers, except a reminder of *Caveat emptor*—Let the buyer beware. Some sites employ buyer feedback postings to help newcomers spot the good sellers and suspect sellers. Both eBay and Yahoo! Auctions have limited purchase protection programs that can reimburse buyers up to a certain amount if an item is not shipped or is not what the auction listing described.

Delay of Game

Time delays, both for the buyer and the seller, are a major drawback to paying by check. Consider these typical transaction bottlenecks:

- Your check can be lost in the mail, stolen from the mail, or damaged by a mail-processing machine.
- A seller typically will wait until your check has cleared before sending your merchandise. Count on a shipping delay of two weeks, possibly longer, after you mail your check.
- Some auction sellers will not accept personal checks, because they prefer the faster transaction completions available through other payment means, such as credit cards or online payment services.

Recovering a bad check can be time-consuming and difficult, especially across state lines or international boundaries. So, don't be surprised if you encounter auction sellers who have had negative experiences with personal-check payments and no longer accept checks, period.

Even if you rush a check to a seller by Express Mail or an overnight delivery service, the seller will likely still want to ensure that your payment has cleared before shipping your merchandise. And you will have paid double-digit postage or delivery charges for flying a wisp of paper hundreds or even thousands of miles to the seller.

If you are in a hurry to get your auction purchases, definitely use a faster and cheaper way to pay, such as a check card.

Check Cards

Most banks now issue check cards. These are debit cards tied directly to customers' checking accounts. When you pay with a check card, the purchase amount is automatically deducted from your checking account. The transaction is detailed by merchant name, date, and amount in your monthly bank statement. In online auction transactions, you typically receive a detailed receipt via e-mail after you pay.

If you pay with a check card instead of a check, you don't have to give sensitive personal information, such as your address, phone number, and driver's license number, to a stranger. Also, check cards usually have protections that limit your liability if your card is lost or stolen and used without your permission.

Check cards often are branded with Visa, MasterCard, or other credit card company logos. Typically, where credit cards are accepted, you can use a check card, but it will have to be one of the brands honored by the merchant. For example, if an online auction seller states that payment by Visa or MasterCard is accepted, a check card bearing the appropriate "brand" can almost always be used to pay.

Cashier's Check Pros and Cons

Many, but not all, sellers on eBay and other online auction sites will accept a cashier's check from a winning bidder. Cashier's checks are checks that have been issued and certified by a bank. A cashier's check cannot bounce, because the money already has been deducted from your account and placed in an escrow account. When the seller cashes the check, the money is paid from the escrow account.

The Plus Sides of Cashier's Checks

Historically, cashier's checks have had a "good as gold" reputation. In the online auction world, cashier's checks have often been regarded as one of the safest ways to send a payment from Buyer A to Seller B because:

- Cashier's checks can provide a record of purchase.
- Cashier's checks can be traced to a particular mailing address.
- Payments by cashier's check can be covered for up to $200 (minus a $25 processing fee) through eBay's Standard Protection Program.

Cashier's Check Cons

Unfortunately, there also can be some significant drawbacks to paying with cashier's checks.

- You have to go to a bank to get a cashier's check.
- You may be required to open an account at the bank, if you don't already have one.
- You will likely have to pay a service fee to get the cashier's check issued.
- Cashier's checks are very slow to clear.

Paying with a cashier's check will typically provide no time advantage over paying with a personal check. Federal Reserve Regulation CC requires that the money from a cashier's check must be made available to the recipient within two banking days of deposit. Unfortunately, after the payment is made to the seller, the cashier's check still may require at least two weeks, and possibly a month or longer, to complete the clearance process. Your purchase may not be shipped until the seller is certain the cashier's check is good. And there is a very good reason he may stall: counterfeit cashier's checks.

Hocus Bogus

Counterfeiters have learned how to take advantage of the long gap between when a cashier's check is paid and when it actually clears, and online auction sellers have been some of their prime victims. The crooks bid up the price on an auction item so they can win it. Then they pay the delighted but unsuspecting seller with a counterfeit cashier's check. The counterfeit often is so convincing that it may not be unmasked in the banking system until weeks after the seller has deposited the money and spent it. Suddenly, she will get a demand from the victimized bank to pay them back. And the seller likely will find herself caught up in a police investigation.

ALERT!

The use of counterfeit cashier's checks is on the rise, according to law enforcement agencies. Buy cashier's checks only from financial institutions that you personally know are reputable. In recent years, criminals using counterfeit cashier's checks and fake bank Web sites have scammed many online auction sellers. The bad checks can be "verified" online by the unsuspecting recipient.

The ongoing problem with counterfeit cashier's checks may cause you to encounter an increasing number of online auction sellers who will refuse to accept these once-trustworthy payments—and it would be difficult to blame them. Trained personnel at banks often have a hard time identifying a bad cashier's check. How can an individual auction seller be expected to do better?

Money Order Pros and Cons

A money order is a non–interest bearing financial instrument that is usually issued by a bank, a post office, or certain businesses such as Western Union or MoneyGram. A money order allows the person named to receive a specific amount of money on demand from the issuing bank or postal service.

Money orders can be sent overseas and are sometimes used as a means of transferring funds across international borders.

Secure Payments

A money order can be used to pay for anything that you might normally pay for with cash, a cashier's check, or a personal check. For many years, postal money orders and money orders issued by well-known financial institutions have been considered yet another "gold standard" for safe payments.

"Postal money orders are as secure, if not more so, than any other financial instrument," according to the U.S. Postal Inspection Service, the law enforcement arm of the United States Postal System. "Genuine postal money orders contain design features that maximize their security."

The key word in that news release is *genuine*. Yet again, counterfeiters have struck at the heart of a once secure payment method.

Money Order Scams

In recent years, sophisticated counterfeiters have learned how to create high-quality fake money orders, including U.S. Postal Service money orders, and they have used the bogus instruments in scams that have victimized many online auction sellers. One scam involves sending a fake money order to pay the seller for the auction item and its shipping. In a more brazen version, the seller receives a money order that exceeds the total for the winning bid and shipping. The "buyer" insists an honest mistake has occurred, and asks the seller to refund the "difference." Unsuspecting sellers have sent the money and paid dearly for a crime that also cost them the value of the merchandise and shipping.

FACT

Postal inspectors seized more than 3,700 counterfeit postal money orders, representing potential losses of millions of dollars, in the final three months of 2004, and they were expecting even larger seizures during 2005. According to the U.S. Postal Service, skilled criminals in Eastern Europe and West Africa printed many of the bogus money orders.

Don't be surprised if you encounter an increasing number of online auction sellers who refuse to accept money orders, including "secure" U.S. postal money orders. Publications from the U.S. Post Office show merchants and auction sellers how to spot bogus postal money orders. But using these tips requires time, effort, and attention to detail. A harried seller who earns her living from online auctions may simply prefer to avoid dealing with money orders.

Similarly, money orders also can eat up a buyer's time. First, you have to go to a financial institution or post office to buy one. Then you have to mail it or use a delivery service such as UPS, Federal Express, or DHL. If you become a frequent buyer in online auctions, this process can consume too much time and expense.

Western Union

In spite of the counterfeit money order crisis, Western Union money orders are popular instruments for fast payment in the online auction world. Western Union has been in the money transfer business for more than 150 years and has more than 212,000 agent locations in nearly 200 countries. Western Union operates BidPay.com, an online site specifically tailored for making fast auction payments.

When an auction is over, the winning bidder can visit *www.bidpay .com* and enter the auction details and payment information. Western Union then sends payment to the seller either by mailing a Western Union–branded money order or, if the seller is located in the United States, by sending a payment directly to the seller's U.S. checking account.

Unfortunately, once a money order is sent, there is no way to cancel it. As the buyer, you will need to confirm the seller's legitimacy before completing the transaction.

MoneyGram

A MoneyGram is another convenient way to send money quickly to someone you know in about 170 countries. But, as MoneyGram concedes on its Web site, "its ability to protect you is limited and … you are much better situated to protect yourself." In other words, if you send a MoneyGram to a stranger you only "know" through an online auction site, good luck.

ALERT!

Even eBay recommends not doing business with auction sellers who insist on receiving payments only through "instant money transfer services such as Western Union and MoneyGram that send cash instantly from storefront locations, by telephone and over the Internet." They could take the money and run—and never ship the auction item you thought you won.

Credit Card Pros and Cons

Most online shoppers prefer to use credit cards when paying for purchases on the Internet. Corey Rudl, e-Business columnist for Entrepreneur.com and author of Insider Secrets to Marketing Your Business on the Internet, has called credit cards "the 900-pound gorilla of the online payment world." However, on eBay and other online auction sites, many sellers are not set up to accept credit cards directly. Payments to them via credit card have to be made through online payment services such as PayPal, discussed later in this chapter.

Plastic Positives

There are three key reasons using a credit card can make good sense on eBay and other auction sites:

- Paying online with a credit card is almost as convenient and easy as paying in person at a retail store.
- A payment can be traced in the event a seller claims it was not received.
- Your credit card account may provide you with certain protections against fraudulent transactions.

Plastic Downsides

Despite plastic's popularity, many people remain nervous about using credit cards online. To pay an auction seller directly with plastic, you have to provide your credit card information to someone you've probably never met nor likely will ever see face-to-face.

There are at least two other potentially serious downsides. First, a credit card's monthly interest charges can quickly turn your auction "bargain" into a cash cow—for the financial institution that issued the card. To avoid these costs, you must pay off your credit card balance each month. Second, you must control your buying urges very carefully when paying with credit cards. If available credit is burning a hole in your pocket, as the old saying goes, you may be tempted to buy more items at auction or to bid higher amounts than you can realistically afford. Suddenly, you will find yourself owing thousands of dollars to a credit card company and having to make big monthly payments on a balance that will take years to pay off. To raise needed money, you might even have to auction off—and take a loss on— the items that put you into hock in the first place.

Online Payment Services

An online payment service enables a buyer to use a credit card or electronic bank transfer to pay for a purchase from a seller who otherwise would not be able to accept such transactions.

Some online payment services, such as PayPal, offer convenient means for transferring money from buyer to seller. They also offer degrees of protection on both ends of a transaction. For a small monthly fee, Microsoft's MSN Bill Pay lets a user pay recurring bills and send one-time payments to virtually anyone with a street address. Unfortunately, some online payment services provide little more than links to services that send money orders. Some online services have stopped supporting buyer-to-seller transactions altogether. Instead, they have settled on being online bill-paying services that collect a fee for helping you manage monthly payments, such as car payments, mortgage payments, utility payments, and credit card bills.

Not surprisingly, cyber-thieves have also set up a few online payment "services" that did little more than gather unsuspecting victims' personal and financial information.

Research an online payment service very carefully before using it.

All about PayPal

PayPal, eBay's online payment service, was founded in 1998 and quickly became a useful and popular tool for online auction participants. PayPal enables any person or business with an e-mail address to securely send and receive payments immediately, online. The site acquired PayPal in 2002. By mid-2005, the online payment service had grown to 71 million members in forty-five countries and was signing up roughly 50,000 new members per day. Part of the growth surge was attributed to the 2005 elimination of a long-standing PayPal policy. Now, payments can be made through PayPal without opening a PayPal account first.

The sellers of more than 90 percent of the items listed on eBay accept PayPal as a payment method. Not surprisingly, PayPal now touts itself as "the global leader in online payments."

How PayPal Works

PayPal's free Send Money feature enables a buyer to use a bankcard to pay any seller with an e-mail address in the countries that accept PayPal. The recipient does not have to have a PayPal account. You simply enter the seller's e-mail address and the amount you wish to pay. PayPal then e-mails the seller with information on how to get his or her money.

PayPal's Request Money feature follows a similar format. It can be used to request money from an auction's winning bidder, or to invoice a customer or to send someone a personal bill. PayPal sends the recipient an e-mail message that contains instructions on how to pay via PayPal.

Many eBay sellers now choose PayPal as their primary choice for receiving payments because of its convenience and widespread acceptance. This means a new eBay auction buyer should consider establishing a PayPal account as well. With a PayPal account, you do not give the seller any of your financial information, such as credit card or debit card numbers. "When you make a payment using PayPal," the Web site promises, "the recipient never learns your financial information. All PayPal transactions are based on the buyer's and seller's e-mail addresses."

FACT

You can open a PayPal account without giving PayPal any credit card information. However, you can't pay for an online purchase until the information is provided.

PayPal and eBay came to the rescue of Si Dunn during the writing of this book. One day, while he was typing away on one of the chapters, there was a sudden, loud *pop!* inside his computer monitor. The screen went dark and could not be revived. Using his emergency backup computer, he got online, went to eBay, did a quick search using the monitor's model number, and found an auction listing, ending quickly, for the same device. The seller accepted PayPal and had a convenient shipping arrangement with UPS. A Calculate Shipping Rates link on the seller's site enabled Si to enter his Zip Code and immediately see how much would be required for shipping. The shipping seemed reasonable, so Si entered the bidding and won. When he clicked on a link to pay with PayPal, his shipping information was sent to the seller as well. The monitor was picked up by UPS that same day and was on his desk, working, four days later.

As of mid-2005, PayPal payments could be made in the following currencies:

- Australian dollar
- Canadian dollar
- Euro
- Japanese yen
- Pound sterling
- U.S. dollar

A PayPal payment in one currency, such as the U.S. dollar, is automatically converted to the currency desired by the seller, as long as it is on PayPal's list of supported currencies. The buyer no longer has to know currency exchange rates, or have a balance in a foreign currency, to make payments.

PayPal's Buyer Protection plan is another reason the online payment service is increasingly popular. Buyer Protection offers "free coverage up to

$1000.00 USD at no additional cost on qualified eBay purchases." The "qualified" purchases are those "significantly not as described or never received." PayPal first tries to help settle a dispute between an eBay buyer and a seller. But if a satisfactory solution cannot be found, Buyer Protection may be invoked.

FACT

But eBay is not the only place where PayPal can be used. Any buyer and any seller with an e-mail address can use it. As of mid-2005, PayPal was also accepted at more than 42,000 online shops and at a number of charitable organizations seeking donations, such as Doctors Without Borders.

Account Options

When you sign up for PayPal, you have a choice of three types of user accounts: personal, premier, and business.

Personal Account

A personal account allows you to send money via PayPal and to receive money with certain restrictions. This type of account is adequate for personal online shopping, bidding in online auctions, and selling an occasional item on eBay. You can pay for auction purchases using a credit card, a debit card, or your bank account. No fees are assessed. However, personal account holders cannot receive payments funded by credit cards. They also may not receive more than $500 per month in payments for eBay items, non-eBay auction items, and other payment types specified in the account agreement.

Premier Account

A premier account allows you to buy and sell online under your own name. The account is free, and you can send payments without charge. There is no limit on how much money you can receive through a PayPal premier account. But you will be charged a small fee each time you receive money. The fees are spelled out in the PayPal account application pages.

Business Account

A business account enables your online business to accept payments via credit cards, debit cards, and bank accounts. Sending money is free, and there is no limit on how much money can be received. But your account is charged a small fee each time you receive a payment via PayPal. A business account also allows multiuser access. This feature lets you establish separate logins and give others in your business varying levels of access to your PayPal account.

If you enjoy buying items for personal use on eBay, then decide you also want to buy and sell other types of items and run an online business, there is an option for you. PayPal will let a member set up one personal account and one premier or business account. Each account must have a different e-mail address and separate financial information, but accounts can be upgraded as needed, at any time.

Beware of Spoof Pal

Many PayPal users receive frequent e-mails from "spoof" PayPal Web sites. The messages often contain telltale misspellings or punctuation errors and warn darkly that there has been some "suspicious" activity in our accounts recently. Or, they warn that our accounts are about to be canceled if we don't update our personal information and credit card information immediately. The "spoof" messages always include convenient links, such as "Please click here to update your account records." The links will take you to Web sites that look a lot like the real PayPal, but aren't.

"Spoof Pal" Web sites have only one purpose: to steal your personal information and credit card information. Many PayPal newcomers have fallen into these digital traps. Should you become a victim, PayPal offers the following advice: "If you have surrendered any personal or financial information to this fraudulent Web site, you should immediately log into your PayPal Account and change your password and secret question and answer information. Any compromised financial information should be reported to the appropriate parties."

What are the two worst ways to pay for an online auction purchase?

Cash and instant wire transfers, according to eBay. If you pay with cash and there is a dispute, you cannot prove that the payment was made, nor can your cash payment be traced and verified. Instant cash wire transfers also are not traceable, and locating the recipient could be difficult or impossible if a paid-for auction item is not shipped.

Be suspicious of any Dear PayPal User or Dear PayPal Member e-mails that appear to be from PayPal. If the message does not address you by first and last name, it likely is not from PayPal. If you have any doubts, forward the message to *spoof@paypal.com* and ask PayPal—the real PayPal—to verify its authenticity.

Buyer Power

As a buyer, you have many different ways to pay for online auction purchases. Sellers, however, may limit your payment options or refuse to accept certain payment methods, for honest or sinister reasons. Before placing an online bid, carefully read the payment options posted by the seller. Also, keep a record of those options, in case the seller tries to change them after you have posted your bid. On eBay, for example, you are only obliged to pay a seller using one of the payment methods specified in the eBay listing. If the seller tries to change the payment methods after you have won the bidding, you may insist on paying through one of the methods previously stated in the listing.

When you have questions or are confused about any payment choices posted (or not posted) in a seller's auction listing, be direct. Contact the seller by e-mail or other means and ask for clarification.

If you don't get a satisfactory answer, don't post a bid. The online auction world is a very big place. You can quickly find other sellers with similar items and the payment choices you prefer.

Chapter 9
Protecting Yourself as a Buyer

In an online auction, you must rely only on descriptions, photographs, the seller's reputation with other buyers, and your own finely tuned senses. If something seems slightly amiss or feels flat-out wrong, you must have the self-discipline not to bid, which may mean passing up an item you have craved for months, even years. Go with your instincts; the Internet is alive with many hundreds of online auctions. You will find the item again, maybe tomorrow, maybe at a lower price, from a seller you can trust.

Potential Problems

Most sellers and buyers in online auctions are honest. They believe in fair transactions. Unfortunately, the Internet is also wide open to the worst elements of humanity, including technology-savvy opportunists who spend their working hours trying to steal as much money and merchandise as they can from as many victims as they can find. Without even realizing it, you can become a victim of an Internet crime committed from almost anywhere on the planet.

A long list of potential problems can be associated with buying from online auctions. Yet, with some common sense, patience, and a few digital tools, you can avoid almost every bad situation. When trouble does occur, buyers and sellers often can resolve it via e-mail or other contact, without intervention from auction-site officials or neutral arbiters.

These days, a seller typically cannot be held responsible for the quality of an item he or she sells you, unless the quality has been specifically guaranteed in a warranty. Items sold through online auctions seldom have warranties, so you must learn how to quickly size up sellers and their auction items before you can become the winning bidder. You also must understand what recourse is available if you become a victim of seller fraud, one of the most common complaints against online auctions.

QUESTION?

What are the main buyer complaints against online auction sellers?
According to the Federal Trade Commission (FTC), complaints include: (1) late shipment of purchase, (2) no shipment of purchase, (3) shipped products that are not the same quality as advertised, (4) bogus online payment services or escrow services, and (5) fraudulent dealers who lure bidders from legitimate auction sites with seemingly better deals.

Certain types of online auction listings pose greater risks to bidders simply because a lot of money is at stake. You will seldom run across computer thieves who are trying to auction nonexistent pocket screwdriver sets or "new, still in original box" radio tubes that actually were used in combat in World War II. Computer crooks generally subscribe to the teachings of a

Depression-era criminal named Willie Sutton who famously admitted that he robbed banks because "that's where the money is." For example, several online automobile auctions were hit hard by a rash of fraudulent buyers who "overpaid" sellers with fake money orders or cashier's checks, and then asked for refunds of the balance. In some cases, the thieves got away with the cash and the cars before the phony payment instruments bounced.

In the high-dollar world of online auctions for antiques, collectibles, and fine art, for example, you will encounter inexperienced sellers who make honest mistakes in their descriptions of "rare" art objects. Likewise, you may encounter sellers who knowingly traffic in fakes and forgeries but do their best to appear legitimate. They may respond to questions quickly, pack items with great care, and ship them promptly. But once the questions and negative feedback start hitting, they disappear into the digital wilderness with their loot. Later, they may re-emerge and start selling on a different auction site under a different seller name. Other fraudulent sellers use this similar pattern of operation. They may even make a few legitimate sales, earn some very positive feedback, and then draw in a few victims, take their money, and run.

Always proceed with caution and a healthy sense of skepticism on any online auction site, whether you hunt for common bargains or rare, expensive collectibles. More than once, cyber-thieves have set up elaborate fake auction sites and used them to steal money, credit card numbers, and bank account information from gullible buyers whose eagerness to bid far outweighed their common sense.

FACT

Nearly 10 million consumers were victims of identity fraud in 2004, and it cost them more than $5 billion, according to the U.S. Postal Inspection Service. Businesses and financial institutions took an even steeper hit: $48 billion. If crooks get your Social Security number, they can gain access to your medical, financial, credit, and educational records.

Anything can be made to appear genuine on the Internet. Yet, it may be just a well-crafted, sinister mirage. What seems like a friendly new bank in Michigan eager for online customers could be a pair of cyber-thieves working from a hotel room in Bolivia, stealing information. "Buyer beware" takes on new depths of meaning when you suddenly find yourself logged onto a fake eBay, PayPal, or Yahoo! site and realistic-looking prompts ask you to "update" your personal and credit card information and to enter your password. EBay has responded to the rash of spoof eBay Web sites by offering a special toolbar with an Account Guard symbol. The symbol changes colors to warn you when you are on a fake eBay site.

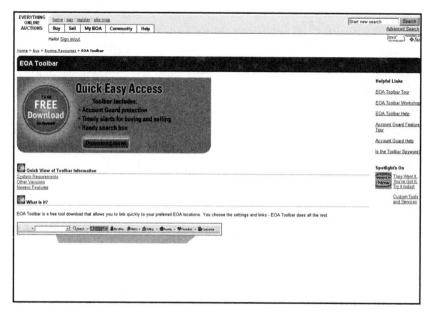

Bid Low, Win Low

Many new buyers become excited when they find a long-desired object for auction. Their typical reaction is to bid well above the current leader to show their determination to win. Unfortunately, their inexperience can get them into a shill game. A shill is a friend or associate of a seller. The shill's job is to push auction novices and overeager collectors into a bidding war. The shill carefully ups the ante by a dollar; the novice bidder reacts by pumping the price a lot higher. As the auction nears its end, the shill again bids a dollar higher, and the novice, desperate to win, counters with another fat bid. Now the price for the object is so high that the novice bidder begins to have second thoughts, or bidder's remorse. He hopes his "competition" will bid higher and get him off the hook, but it's too late. The shill suddenly drops out of the bidding and lets the novice or overeager collector win the overpriced object. After the seller collects her fattened fee, she pays the shill a percentage for his services.

Pick the maximum price you will pay for an auction item and stick to it. On eBay and some other sites, you can set the upper limit when you place your opening bid. Sellers and other bidders can't see it. As long as other bids stay below your maximum, you will be the leader. If you lose the bidding, don't worry. Another item like it or better will show up within a few days.

If you really want a hard-to-find computer part, collectible art object, or rare piece of jewelry, keep your impulses under control. Don't show your hand. Quietly push the bidding up by the smallest amount possible at each step. You may end up winning the auction for a lot less than you expected.

The Trust Factor

Most of us have bought something face-to-face from a stranger we thought we could trust. Then the merchandise turned out to be shoddy, counterfeit, or stolen—and we couldn't get our money back, because the seller was long gone.

The early years of online auctions were much like this. Between 1999 and 2002, online auction fraud was so rampant that federal and state agencies launched investigations and ran sting operations. Congress held hearings. Magazines and newspapers ran big headlines: "Online Auction Fraud Rises." In 2000, CBS News declared, "Internet auction fraud is the fastest growing crime in America."

FACT

The ongoing fight against online fraud sometimes forces auction sites to change their business model. In late 2002, for example, uBid.com "discontinued the ability for every day consumers to sell on uBid due to counterfeit, stolen and generally untrusted offerings." Company officials said, "Even though we agree with the basic premise that all humans are fundamentally good, a few can ruin it for everyone." Now uBid focuses on business-to-consumer auctions only.

Successful online auctions such as eBay try to make it as easy as possible for buyers and sellers to trust each other even if they are separated by thousands of miles. Still, you have to trust the seller's photographs and descriptions of the auction merchandise. You have to trust the accuracy of the feedback previous customers have posted. And you have to trust your own research and instincts. If necessary, learn how to protect yourself … from yourself, particularly if you are a compulsive shopper. Electronic access to a planet full of desirable goods can be dangerous to your bank account, as well as to your personal information.

Buyer Protection Programs

Buyer protections range from "none" to "some" at various online auction sites. For example, eBay's Standard Purchase Protection Program "reimburses buyers for eligible transactions when an item was purchased on eBay and either not received or was received but significantly not as described." Depending on how much you paid for the disputed item, reimbursement can range from $1 up to $175 (after the program's $25 processing fee is deducted).

Yahoo! Auctions' plan offers a similar reimbursement range:

- Only winning bidders are protected.
- Sellers are not covered if they have a negative rating at the time of the auction close.

- The program does not cover a payment if any part of it is sent by wire transfer or to a post office box or to any international location.
- The maximum protection is $200 per auction, minus a $25 processing fee.

Both eBay and PayPal generate excellent records of transactions and payments. But on any auction site, you should make copies of everything pertaining to your transactions. Yahoo! urges auction participants to "keep all email, notes, shipping documents, and payment information. Be sure to print a copy of the auction. This is your responsibility. Yahoo! does not provide user information or copies of old listings."

Amazon.com Auctions offer the "A-to-Z Guarantee" protection program for auction participants. It reimburses up to $2,500 and shipping charges for payments made through the Amazon Payments feature. A buyer is covered under this guarantee (1) when the buyer pays but the seller fails to deliver the item and (2) when the buyer receives the item but it is "materially different" than was depicted in the seller's description. These conditions qualify as "materially different":

- Wrong version or edition
- Item condition or details not as described
- Wrong item
- Missing parts or components
- Defective item
- Damaged item

In general, online auction protection programs for buyers cannot be invoked until certain other conditions and restrictions have been met, such as time periods and other attempts at dispute resolution.

Escrow Protection

An escrow service is a licensed, regulated company that collects, holds, and sends a buyer's money to a seller. The transaction must follow the instructions agreed on by both the buyer and seller.

In an escrow transaction, the buyer pays an escrow company the amount of money the seller requires for the merchandise and shipping. The escrow holds the money until the seller ships the merchandise and the buyer confirms she has received it. Then the escrow company pays the seller.

FACT

Yahoo! Auctions has termed using an escrow service as "probably the safest way to process a transaction between a buyer and a seller who do not know each other." That assumes, of course, that you are using a legitimate escrow service and not one of the phony services that cyber-criminals sometimes set up to steal information, merchandise, and money.

Both Yahoo! and eBay mention Escrow.com prominently in their recommendations for online auction buyers. Escrow.com is a licensed and accredited escrow company audited regularly for compliance by the California Department of Corporations.

Escrow services are generally employed as go-betweens in auctions involving high-priced items where there is greater danger of seller fraud and buyer fraud. For example, eBay defines "high-priced" as $500 or more. Escrow.com does not set any price minimums but states on its Web site: "Escrow is well-suited for items purchased on auction sites, automobiles, motorcycles, domain names, jewelry, specialized computer equipment and other high-ticket items." Some buyers, however, use escrow services for items costing less than $100, a tactic that often does not make sellers happy.

Escrow: Time Versus Money

Many sellers are not fond of escrow services because of the time it takes to receive their money after they ship the merchandise. The wait can often be a month or longer. Both the seller and the buyer must report to the escrow company that the transaction is completed before payment can be issued.

The buyer gets to inspect the merchandise and raise a dispute, if necessary, before the seller is paid. The seller has to cool his heels for a while but knows that the money is available and the payment will be good.

Escrow Steps

The escrow process generally requires five steps:

1. The buyer and seller agree on the terms of their transaction. This includes reaching consensus on the description of the merchandise, the sales price, the shipping details, and the number of days that the buyer can inspect the merchandise. They also must agree on whether the buyer or seller pays the escrow fees. Sometimes, buyer and seller split the escrow fee, so that each pays half.
2. The buyer pays the agreed-upon amount for the merchandise, shipping, and escrow service to the escrow company. Different escrow companies accept different forms of payment, but the choices typically include paying by check, money order, wire transfer, credit card, or debit card. The processing time for each payment method will figure into how long the seller must wait for his money and how long the buyer must wait for his merchandise.
3. The seller sends the merchandise after the escrow company authorizes the shipment. The seller also sends shipment-tracking information to the escrow company. The escrow company knows when the buyer is supposed to receive the merchandise and will contact the buyer to confirm its arrival.
4. The buyer's inspection period begins. During this time, the buyer can accept or reject the merchandise. If the buyer rejects the shipment, she must arrange to send the merchandise back to the seller at her expense. She may also be responsible for the escrow fees. The escrow company issues a refund only after the seller confirms the return of his merchandise.
5. If the buyer accepts the merchandise or the buyer's inspection period expires without protest, the escrow company pays the seller, and the process is completed.

Escrow Dispute Resolution

On its Web site, Escrow.com spells out what happens if a buyer and seller cannot resolve a dispute within sixty days. The matter goes to dispute resolution, "an arbitration process administered by the American Arbitration Association in accordance with the provisions of its Commercial Arbitration Rules."

The nonprofit American Arbitration Association (AAA) describes itself as "the world's leading provider of conflict management and dispute resolution" and states that it works to try to resolve "a wide range of disputes through mediation, arbitration, elections and other out-of-court settlement procedures." Disputes for arbitration or mediation can be filed through local or regional AAA offices or through the AAA's Web site (*www.adr.org*).

ALERT!

Beware of fake online escrow services. Cyber-thieves have created some sophisticated-looking temporary sites that do nothing except steal money and personal information from a few sellers and buyers, and then vanish from the Web. Use only the escrow services recommended by the auction site.

For example, eBay recommends using only Escrow.com for transactions in the United States and United Kingdom. For other areas of the world, eBay recommends the following:

- Australia: *www.escrowaustralia.com.au*
- France, Netherlands, and Belgium: *www.tripledeal.com*
- Germany: *http://ebay.iloxx.de*
- Italy and Spain: *www.escrow-europa.com*

If a seller refuses to use Escrow.com (or its overseas affiliates) and demands that you use another escrow site, consider this a bright red flag with spotlights. Online fraud may be just one more click away. Don't complete the transaction, no matter how much you want the item. Report the seller to eBay immediately.

Personality Clashes

The online world can be a strange place. People who can't see each other and who will likely never meet can get into heated arguments over all sorts of issues.

Online auctions can be giant electromagnets for good people who get along well and treat each other with respect. But inevitably, some troubled or angry souls will come into digital contact and quickly get into a fifteen-round world-heavyweight-championship online bout—the digital equivalent of Shakespeare's famous *Much Ado About Nothing*. Message boards are particularly prone to "flame wars."

If one of your online purchases goes awry—maybe you never received it and the seller kept no shipping receipts—conditions will be ripe for a confrontation. It may escalate quickly from exchanges of e-mails, increasingly angry in tone, to threats, negative feedback, and reports to the police. You could pass each other on the sidewalk and never know that you have been snarling at each other online over a $10 plastic birdhouse.

From the buyer's perspective, if the seller gets defensive, then threatening over the condition or the nonarrival of a shipment, sometimes it is better just to walk away from a small purchase and not waste any more time and psychic energy on a fight.

Fighting Fraud

The online world is rich with wondrous conveniences—and it is a giant conductor for any imaginable kind of fraud. In online auctions, buyers and sellers alike must always temper their enjoyment and activities with a steady vigilance against Internet-based scams and crimes. The newest software and hardware can provide certain types of protection. But fighting online fraud also demands knowledge—keeping up with the latest schemes and warnings and using common sense in questionable situations.

For example, in 2005, computer hackers figured out how to remotely lock up all document files on a computer's hard drive and prevent the computer's owner from accessing them. The hackers then demanded ransom payments for sending the electronic keys to release the files. Computer security companies and software manufacturers quickly developed protections against these so-called ransom-ware attacks. But the incidents once again demonstrated the vulnerability of computers linked to the Internet.

Phishing Expeditions

Phishing (pronounced "fishing") is one of the biggest scams on the Internet, and online auction participants are some of its top targets. You probably have received bogus e-mails seemingly from eBay, PayPal, major banks, or other sites where you may or may not have performed financial transactions.

FACT

The Federal Trade Commission (FTC) has warned users to be suspicious of any official-looking e-mail message that asks for updates of personal or financial information. The FTC urges recipients to avoid the links in the e-mail and go directly to the company's Web site for confirmation of a problem with your account. If you suspect you have been phished, forward the e-mail to *uce@ftc.gov* or call the FTC help line, 1-877-FTC-HELP.

Online auction participants can get these e-mail messages almost every day from fake auction sites, fake payment services, and fake banks. Many of the messages look as if they have come from the real organization, but there are usually telltale signs, such as misspelled words or tortured sentences that the actual companies would never send out. Generally, the messages want recipients to do one simple thing: click on a link so they can "update" their credit card information or "fix" a problem with their account. The link, of course, goes directly to a phony site that resembles an eBay or PayPal page, and its sole purpose is to gather sensitive information.

Dear valued EOA member,

We regret to inform you that your EOA account has been suspended due to concerns we have for the safety and integrity of the EOA community.

Per the User Agreement, Section 9, we may immediately issue a warning, temporarily suspend, indefinitely suspend or terminate your membership and refuse to provide our services to you if we believe that your actions may cause financial loss or legal liability for you, our users or us. We may also take these actions if we are unable to verify or authenticate any information you provide to us.

Due to the suspension of this account, please be advised you are prohibited from using EOA in any way. This includes the update of your actual account.

If you could please take 5-10 minutes out of your online experience and update your personal records you will not run into any future problems with the online service.

Please update your records by the 10th of June.

Once you have updated your account records your EOA session will not be interrupted and will continue as normal.

To update your EOA records click on the following link:
http://EOA.doubleclick.net/clk;13012399,10693575;h?
http://mail.falke.de/horde/files/EOADLLupdate/saw-cgi/EOAISAPIdllSignIn.php

Beware the Social Engineer

A "social engineer" is a con artist with a computer who also knows how to charm people. In computer security circles, "social engineering" describes a non-technical intrusion in which the cyber-crook tricks other people into bypassing or even breaking normal security procedures.

A social engineer might do some simple "shoulder surfing" and learn how to access one of your online auction accounts by standing behind you while you are using your wireless laptop in Starbucks or in a restaurant. All he has to see is your user name and memorize your keystrokes as you type your password or record the information with a hidden video camera. Then he can go into your account, make changes, and either post bogus merchandise for sale or buy items and have them shipped to another address.

QUESTION?

How can I defend my online activities against social engineers?
Computer security specialists usually list three key defensive strategies:
(1) Be aware of the value of information, even seemingly innocuous
details. (2) Learn how to better protect your personal information, especially in Internet-related transactions such as online auctions. Pay close
attention to the security tips and security alerts provided at online auction sites. (3) Be aware of how social engineers operate.

Where to Go for Help

If you believe you have given sensitive information to a fraudulent auction Web
site or if you think your auction site account has been compromised in some
other way, contact the real auction site immediately and report your dilemma.

On eBay, you can get help by starting with the Securing Your Account
and Reporting Account Theft page:

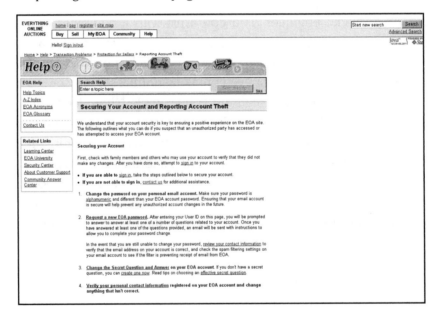

Also, eBay has a page devoted to E-mail and Web Sites Impersonating
eBay. To reach this page, go to:

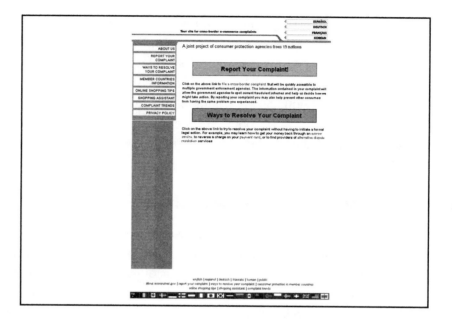

The page also contains a link to an online tutorial on how to spot spoof (fake) e-mails that claim to be from eBay.

On the Yahoo! Auction site, suspicious auctions can be reported at the Neighborhood Watch link:

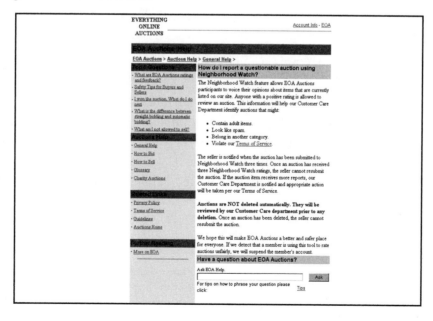

This link allows any participant with a positive rating to review other auctions. Negative review information can help the Yahoo! Customer Care Department identify auctions that look like spam, contain "adult" items, belong in another category, or violate the site's terms of service.

When an auction has been submitted to the Neighborhood Watch three times, the seller gets a notice and cannot resubmit the auction. If more than three negative reviews are received, the auction can be permanently deleted.

Dispute Resolution and Mediation

Buyers and sellers sometimes disagree over the condition or actual worth of an auction item that has been purchased and delivered. They are encouraged to try first to work out their differences among themselves. If they fail to reach a compromise, SquareTrade is eBay's preferred online dispute resolution service. Sellers on eBay who display the SquareTrade membership seal have had "their identity and/or contact information verified as a prerequisite to being approved for the Seal," according to the site's membership criteria descriptions. And: "[T]heir feedback has to remain strong" if they are to continue displaying the SquareTrade seal on their auction sites.

Econsumer

Econsumer.gov is a joint project of consumer protection agencies in nineteen countries, including the United States, Canada, Japan, South Korea, Australia, the United Kingdom, and others.

If your complaint involves an online auction seller or buyer in one of the member nations, you can file a complaint. "The information in your complaint will allow the government agencies to spot current fraudulent schemes and help us decide how we might take action," the site's main English page explains.

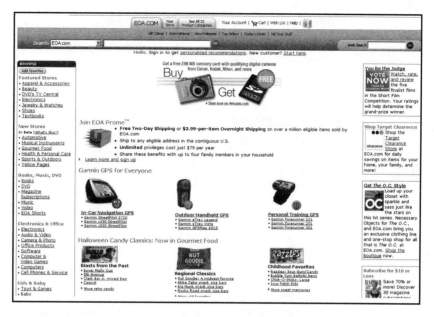

Feedback: The Ultimate Weapon

In the online auction world, feedback can be the peacemaker that keeps online auctions honest and fun. In the wrong hands, feedback can be a weapon of mass destruction. Unfortunately, feedback is far from foolproof.

If you are the first or second victim of an unscrupulous seller, buyer feedback won't help you. You can post negative feedback that will warn others to stay away. But you may be hit with some retaliatory feedback that will lower your ratings as a buyer.

Positive postings, on the other hand, can help buyers feel more secure about bidding on a particular seller's items. And sellers can feel more at ease about their winning bidders, when they can read feedback such as "Great customer … pays fast … no problems!"

Going Negative

Sellers and buyers alike fear negative feedback. Just one bad rating on a seller's record is enough to send many potential buyers scurrying to other listings. Several negatives can kill an auction business. Meanwhile, sellers often can block the bids of buyers with negative ratings.

Most online auction transactions are completed without a problem. Previously, eBay has estimated that only one transaction in 40,000 leads to a reported dispute between buyer and seller.

QUESTION?

Can negative feedback be erased?
Negative feedback usually cannot be erased after it is posted, even if you and the other party settle your dispute. Therefore, use it only when other means of resolution have failed.

The worst time to post negative feedback is when you are angry or disappointed in an item you have just received as the winning bidder. On some sites, you may be able to go back and add some comments stating that the matter has been settled in a positive manner. But as the FaithBid.com auction site cautions: "Once you've said something, you can't take it back." Angrily posting feedback that is malicious or untrue could leave you open to legal action by the seller.

Buyer protections are in place on most online auction sites. But it is up to you to learn the best ways to use them. In some surveys, roughly half of the auction participants admitted that they seldom look at the feedback other buyers post. Instead, they remain focused on the prize, the much-desired auction item, and little else. Don't run the risk of being the high bidder on a disaster. Know your buyer protections and use them.

Chapter 10
Getting Started Selling Online

Some people are naturals at selling and being in business. Most of us, however, probably never gave business a serious thought until we discovered the fun, the possibilities, and the stimulating challenges of being an online auction seller. Getting started as a seller is surprisingly easy, and the best way is simply to jump in and make your first online sale, using an auction site's basic selling tools as your guide.

Learning the Legalities

Yes, you're anxious to get started, but don't click on an auction site's Sell button just yet. First, be aware that many items cannot be sold online. Lists of banned or questionable items vary from one auction site to another. However, eBay's lists are an excellent and comprehensive starting place to review.

From eBay's main page, click on the small Site Map link just above the My eBay tab. The screen will display headings in the following categories:

- Buy
- Sell
- Search
- Help
- Services
- Community

Scroll down to the bottom of the page. In the lower-left corner, under the Help heading, click on the link: Is my item allowed on eBay? This will open the Is My Item Allowed? screen. On that page, several lists are displayed under the heading Prohibited, Questionable, and Infringing Items. Here is what these major categories mean:

- **Prohibited items:** These may not be sold, period.
- **Questionable items:** These require further investigation by the seller. Some may qualify to be listed for auction, but many will not.
- **Possibly infringing items:** These may violate copyrights, trademarks, or other protections if they are sold online.

Under each category, eBay has links to discussions of their meanings, plus expanded lists of the items rated as prohibited, questionable, or possibly infringing.

Seller, Be Aware

A seller is responsible for what she lists for sale on online auction sites. If something in one of the prohibited, questionable, or infringing categories is posted, auction site personnel may remove her listing as soon as they spot it. Some online auction sites ask their members to act as site monitors and report any questionable or improper listings. If you post a listing for a banned item, your selling privileges may be revoked. So, it is vital to know that there are items that may be trouble. You don't have to memorize the lists, but you will need to refer to them when choosing certain items to sell.

The best approach for your first auction is to steer clear of anything on the warning lists. Pick an item commonly auctioned. It can be something from your garage or closet or storage cabinet, such as a camera, a nice but unwanted vase, a floppy drive for a computer, or even an old lunch box. You may be surprised at what people need or collect.

If several items exactly like yours, or similar, are being sold on the online auction site and closed auctions can first be found, you can be sure there is a market for your item, and it will be a safe item to list and sell.

Choosing Your Site

By far, eBay is the world's biggest online auction site. So, new online auction sellers typically make their first sales there. With billions of successful transactions under its belt, eBay has automated and simplified much of the process of creating a listing. Beginners can follow an easy step-by-step flow, make changes as needed, and get help along the way.

Other online auction sites offer similar selling steps for beginners. By now, you may have explored several sites and found at least one, other than eBay, that you would prefer to try. The explanations in this chapter focus on eBay. However, many of the steps and procedures are similar on other sites, and online help is available on the sites when you have questions.

Registering as a Seller

Registering to sell on an online auction site usually is almost as simple as registering to buy. The process begins by clicking on the site's Sell or Sell Stuff or similar tab or button. If you don't already have a user's account on the site, your first task is to set up one. As discussed in Chapter 6, this is the account that allows you to bid and buy on the site. Your new account will likely be available immediately after you complete filling in a few online forms, and you will be able to continue registering as a seller.

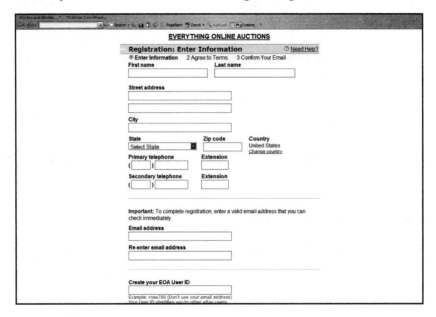

To become a registered seller on most sites, you will have to supply the following types of information:

- Name
- Address
- Telephone number
- E-mail address
- Credit card information
- Bank account information
- Shipping address (if different from address for bank account and credit card)

Some sites may require more information, including gender and age. As a rule, most sites require sellers to be at least eighteen years old.

QUESTION?

I'm seventeen and on my own. Why can't I sell?
When someone bids on an auction item, they enter into a legally binding contract with the seller. In most parts of the world, persons under eighteen years old are not allowed to enter into such contracts.

Getting Ready to Go

Now you've registered to sell, but to sell what? Sell it where on the site? This is the right time to log out of your new seller account and start organizing the details of your first auction sale. Follow these steps:

1. Pick out the first item you want to sell. It doesn't have to be something rare, vintage, expensive, or big. Common items from your closet or kitchen, such as a camera, a hand-me-down water pitcher, or an out-of-style suit, may attract a surprising number of bidders. (Remember to review the auction site's restricted or banned items, if necessary.)
2. Research the item. Use search engines such as Google.com and an auction site's search tools and advanced search tools to find the item and determine what makes it special and desirable to bidders.
3. Take notes on how similar items are described, pictured, and priced in current and closed auctions. Make special note of the categories under which the items have been listed, such as Cameras & Photo or Collectibles > Pinbacks, Nodders, Lunchboxes > Lunchboxes or Collectibles > Cultures, Ethnicities. Knowing these categories will help you place your auction listing in the right area.
4. Clean your item carefully and make notes on its condition, including any blemishes, chips, cracks, dents, scrape marks, tears, or other flaws. (Don't damage it during the examination and cleaning process!)
5. Measure the item's length, width, height, and diameter—any essential dimensions. Refer to current and previous auction sales to find out which dimensions of the item are considered important for buyers.

6. Photograph the item from several angles, using a digital camera, if possible. Get help from a family member or friend, if necessary. A film camera can be used, but have the film processing lab put the pictures on a CD-ROM disk so you can view them and edit them in your computer. Alternately, film prints can be scanned and converted to digital files. Again, refer to current and previous auctions to find examples of good pictures. Use similar poses or combinations of overall views and close-ups for your pictures. Get your pictures into your computer. Use photo-editing software to crop the pictures for best appearance.

7. Find an appropriate shipping box and protective packing materials to protect your item. If you don't have any of these handy, go to an office-supply store and get them.

8. Pack the item securely in the box, but leave the top open. Weigh the package on a good postal scale and record the weight. Allow an extra ounce or so for labels and final shipping tape. Also, measure and write down the package's length, width, and height.

9. Use the U.S. Postal Service Web site (*www.usps.com*) to determine how much it will cost to mail the packaged item to the most distant Zip Codes from your location. (To keep your first sale simple, just focus on selling to domestic buyers.) If you prefer to use another carrier, such as UPS, go to the carrier's Web site and enter the appropriate weight, measurements, and sample destinations. Record the shipping charges.

10. Open your word processing software and start writing the description of your item. Refer to your notes on how other sellers have described similar items. Save your text file. You can copy from it and paste the text into the description box once you are listing your item for auction.

You are ready to click on the Sell, Sell Stuff, or similar tab once again and start creating your first listing. Take your time. Read every prompt and explanation carefully. If you become unsure or confused at any point while following the steps, you can get help, refer to online tutorials, or cancel and try again after you gather your thoughts. Nothing will happen or be posted until you reach the final step in the process, review your new listing, and click on the final confirmation button to post it.

Creating Your First Listing

On the Sell page, review the short tutorial beneath the heading, How do you sell on eBay? Under the Prepare heading, you can click on the Research Similar Items link, but you already should have done this if you are ready to post your first listing.

The List heading contains a link to Easy Steps. Click here and read the explanations of the following six steps:

1. Choose a format.
2. Select a category.
3. Enter title and description.
4. Add pictures and details, and select pricing and auction duration.
5. Choose payment and shipping options, and enter shipping fees.
6. Review your listing details and submit.

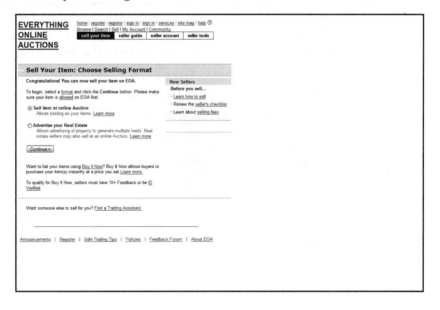

Choosing a format is easy. The Sell Your Item: Choose a Selling Format screen should have the Sell Item at Online Auction choice already set as the default. However, verify that it has been selected. For more information, click on the Learn More link. Otherwise, scroll down the page to the Continue box and click on it.

This will bring up the Sell Your Item: Select Category screen.

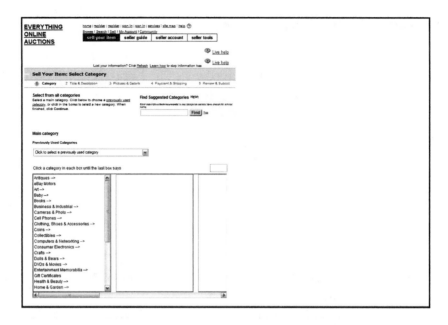

On the Select Category page, you will find the appropriate category for list-ing your item. Refer to your research notes and find the first entry, such as Col-lectibles, in the box under Main Category. Click on Continue. Scroll through the list of subcategories, if any. Choose the appropriate one, and then click on Continue. Next, you will see the Sell Your Item: Describe Your Item screen.

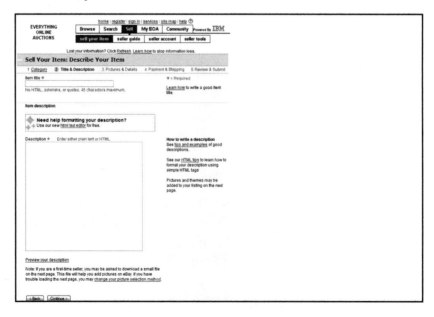

Your preselling preparations will continue to pay off when you reach the Sell Your Item: Describe Your Item screen. Here, you will click on the Title & Description option and start creating the description for your item.

Your first entry will be in the Item Title box. Once again, refer to your notes to see how others have titled an item similar to, or just like, the one you are selling. Create a new title using the other titles as a guide. Be sure your item is spelled correctly and includes identifiers such as brand name, type number, and style. Buyers will enter these terms when they are searching for an item such as yours, and using the right keywords will help them find it quickly.

Under the Item Descriptions heading on this page, you will enter your item's specific details. Open your word processor, find the description you previously wrote, copy the text, and paste it in the text box. Once the text is pasted, you can edit it, change fonts and type sizes, pick a type color, and do other formatting. However, you can also stick with the basic settings and continue to the next steps. Click on the Preview Description link to see how your item description will appear. When you are satisfied with your description, click on Continue. (You will have another opportunity later to change your description and other entries before posting the completed listing.)

The next screen that will appear is Sell Your Item: Enter Pictures & Item Details. Your first choice will be to select the Pricing & Duration of your auction. Choose a starting price for your auction. Many sellers start at $1, even for items that will sell for a lot more. Low starting prices often attract more bidders. And more bidders mean more competition, which can drive the final price higher than you expect. But you may be more comfortable setting the opening bid at the absolute lowest price you would accept for the item. Otherwise, if you begin at a dollar and only one bidder shows up, you will have to sell for a buck.

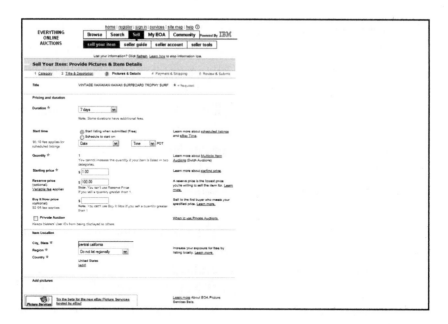

Seven days is the default duration for auctions on eBay, and experience shows that this duration works very well for most sellers. The default can be shorter or longer on other auction sites. For your first sales, however, stick with seven days. You can try longer or shorter durations later.

When you reach the Add Pictures prompt, you will again be glad you have done your advanced preparations. On eBay and some other sites, there is usually no charge for the first photograph. Then there will be a small charge for each additional photograph. A few items can be shown effectively with one photograph. But in most cases, two or three photographs are better. For expensive items, several more photographs may be needed to convince buyers that the merchandise really is of good quality.

The auction site will have online tools to help you upload your photographs and see how they will appear in the listing. Once you finish adding your pictures, click on the Continue button. You should be able to add photographs or delete photographs until you reach the point where you must make the final verification of your listing.

FACT

Clear photographs are often the most important part of an auction listing. Potential bidders typically examine pictures first, and then read descriptions and look at the photographs again. You want your item to look good in photographs, but you also want to reveal the flaws and blemishes that potential buyers must consider before bidding.

The next screen, Sell Your Item: Enter Payment & Shipping, will prompt you to choose which payment methods you will offer to buyers and which shipping methods will be available. You can also include flat shipping and handling fees or include an automatic shipping calculator that uses the buyer's mailing address to figure costs.

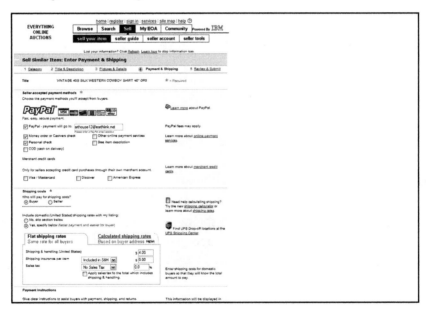

For most beginners, the easiest payment approach is to set up a PayPal account. With PayPal, which is owned by eBay, you can pay for items you buy, and you can accept credit card or debit card payments for items you sell. You also can create prepaid shipping labels with tracking information. You can print the labels with your computer and notify the postal service or UPS to stop by your house and pick up your package.

Generally, you will want buyers to pay shipping costs and to buy shipping insurance, if they want it. Be sure to include a delivery confirmation notice in the price of shipping. A few fraudulent buyers may try to dispute that you mailed an item, and then attempt to refuse to pay. Delivery confirmation will be proof that they received the item. Most buyers are trustworthy, but cover yourself at *all* times.

You should also post a very clear return policy with your shipping information. Some sellers post every item "as is" and refuse to accept any returns. Others are willing to refund the bid price if the item is returned in good shape, at the buyer's expense. Meanwhile, others will refund the bid price and the shipping price. Check the return policies of others that are selling similar items. If you find a policy that makes you comfortable, use a similar return policy in your own listing.

Making a Good Impression

The quality and appearance of your first auction listing will make an impression on prospective bidders. If you have an item they want and you have done a good job on your listing, you will soon start drawing bidders. Some of them may seek you out again to see what else you are selling.

For each item you post, keep copies of all documents, including your auction pages, e-mails, and shipping records. Send each winning bidder a receipt, and keep all paperwork accessible in a filing cabinet or three-ring binder.

Your job is not done, however, once your listing is posted. Some potential bidders may e-mail you with questions. You should answer them promptly, with attention to the details of their requests, and maintain a pleasant manner even if they question your honesty or make demands for more proof that something is vintage, valuable, or rare.

After your item is posted, if someone points out an error or omission in your description, you should make the corrections as soon a possible.

Errors in content and spelling can make many potential bidders suspicious of your item. If you don't trust your own spelling and grammar skills, get help from a friend or relative. Don't be embarrassed to get assistance. The most important thing is to get the description right so bidders will start showing up and making their offers.

The "making an impression" portion of your job will not be over even after you have sold your item, collected your money, and shipped the package to the winning bidder. Be sure to thank the winner, post appropriate feedback for them on the auction site, and get right back to work on your next listing. You want to start building momentum for your new business.

ALERT!

Once your first auction ends, you may expect to hear from the winning bidder right away. Don't be surprised if you don't get a response for nearly a week. On eBay, a seller cannot file an Unpaid Item complaint until at least seven days have passed and attempts to communicate with the winning bidder have failed.

No Bids? Don't Get Discouraged

What if you gave an auction and nobody came? It happens all the time on eBay and other sites. Some weeks you can post something and no one viewed it or bids on it. Other weeks, you may have ten people frantically bidding on it at the same time.

Remember, many bidders wait until the final minutes of an auction to place their bids. During the days before the end of an auction, they search for interesting listings. If they find yours and think they may want the item, they will keep checking the listing to see how the bidding is going. They may show up as one of the "watchers" of your item, or they may stay in stealth mode all week and suddenly appear with a bid at the last minute.

If your first item seems to be drawing little interest, don't worry about it. Start working on your next auction listing. If the first item doesn't sell, try again with the same item—now or later. Meanwhile, post your next item, too. You've already learned how, and you've mastered the basic process. It's now just a matter of a little more time until you make your first sale.

Picking Payment Options

In the movie *The Graduate*, Dustin Hoffman's character is given just one firm word of advice about his future: "Plastics." Many experienced auction veterans give one firm word of advice to new auction sellers: "PayPal."

PayPal lets buyers pay for winning bids with major credit cards or debit cards. Then PayPal transfers the money into the sellers' accounts (taking a small fee for its services). Many sellers on eBay and other auction sites now use PayPal exclusively and try to discourage other means of payment.

Of course, many auction buyers do not have credit cards or debit cards, and many other bidders are not comfortable with sending financial information over the Internet. To attract the most bidders for your first auctions, you may want to consider accepting money orders, cashier's checks, or personal checks. But you must take special care when handling these forms of payment.

If you agree to accept personal checks, for example, remember that you must not ship an item to a buyer until his check has cleared at the bank. Also, get verification of a money order or cashier's check before shipping an item. Some auction sellers have been victimized with counterfeit money orders and cashier's checks. Even banks sometimes have difficulty verifying that a cashier's check or money order is good. (See Chapters 8 and 17 for more information.)

No-Frills Selling

During the first weeks and months of your auction-selling career, the "no-frills" route can be your surest path to success. If you can gather some good items, describe them clearly and thoroughly, and show them with photographs, you will sell many of them without using anything other than the auction site's basic selling tools.

In this "learn as you go" approach, you can work gradually on improving your advertising skills and photography skills. Each time you have a new item to list, you can try one or two different features, if you wish, but never go overboard. Some inexperienced sellers think they must use every available tool, and the results often scare bidders rather than attract them. Also, online auction sites charge extra to use some of their fancier selling tools and features. If you stick to no-frills selling, you will keep your auction fees to a comfortable minimum. It is possible to spend hundreds of dollars on special selling features, yet end up selling your item for $20 or less—or not at all. No frills is the way to go for maximum profit when you sell and the lowest losses when an item doesn't sell.

Focus on posting the right information in the right category, with enough pictures to show potential bidders what's available. You won't need fancy borders, background colors, huge typefaces, or colorful fonts to grab your customers. To misquote the movie *Field of Dreams,* if you post it in the right category with the right title, the right description, and the right photographs, they will come.

Chapter 11
Organizing Your Business

You have set up buyer and seller accounts at an online auction site, posted a listing, made a sale, and shipped the treasure to the winning bidder. A surprising passion can be stirred by auctioning off an item for more money than you expected. You may decide, quite suddenly, to go into the online auction business full-time, perhaps with no clear idea of how and where to start. You can begin by learning how to organize and build the venture that has seized your imagination.

Developing a Business Mindset

Successfully selling something over the Internet has opened your eyes. Now you can really see and understand the vast possibilities created by instant access to the world. From the comfort of your home or from the comfort of an office with your name on the front door, you really can sell things without knocking on doors, mailing fliers, or making those dreaded cold calls. In the expanding universe of online auctions, you don't even have to spend big money on advertising. Millions of people are at their computers right now, restlessly seeking things. They will be seeking you and the items you offer, once your business is up and running on the Web.

All Things Considered

Those who bid in online auctions clearly want things: collectible things; practical things; impractical things; things they used to treasure as children; things they need to repair a house, a car, or a computer; things they can wear; art things—almost anything known to humankind. Again, to misquote *Field of Dreams,* if you list it, they will come, riding a search engine.

You can jump into the online auction business without any business training or experience in online commerce. This is the beauty of free enterprise. You can join millions of other people already prospering … or eking out a living … or losing their money in their online ventures.

The business world offers absolutely no guarantees of success, no matter how hard you try or how much you learn. There also are no shortcuts to success, only faster, more efficient ways to do necessary and hard tasks. Resolve now to skip the Get Rich Immediately! and Make Millions from Home! schemes you will encounter on the Internet. Stay focused on your dream to organize an online auction enterprise and prosper.

How deeply you go into business is up to you. Many newcomers keep their day jobs and dabble in online auction sales after they come home from work. Or, one spouse stays home and runs the auction business while the other spouse holds a "regular" job, with health insurance and other benefits. These are valid approaches. Not everyone stays enamored of selling online long enough to build up a business. Once the novelty wears off or the collectibles from late Aunt Edna's estate are gone, many would-be online auction tycoons take up other pursuits and let eBay, Yahoo! Auctions, Overstock, and the rest slide.

Others, of course, plunge headlong into setting up and incorporating a powerhouse auction firm that will ply the globe's electronic trade routes twenty-four/seven. They rent an office and some warehouse space. They set up their computers and shipping tables and start piling up merchandise to auction. They decorate their offices with motivational slogans and quotations from ancient warriors and generals.

It is perfectly okay to set your goals anywhere in this range. Maybe you want a family business where everyone under your roof can work and play together and earn a modest second income. Maybe you have lost several jobs to layoffs and are tired of worrying about when the next one will happen. You want to create your own job in your own business, so you can do satisfying labor with your hands and your mind any time you choose.

QUESTION?

How can I know I will like auction selling?
Easing into online auction selling may be the best and least expensive way to find out. Start with a few items, and gradually build up. Once you gain experience, you may discover a passion and expand your operations. Or, you may decide buying is more fun.

Many different types of sales or customer service pursuits could fill this need. But an online auction business may be exactly right for you.

What to Sell

You may have a specific notion of what you want to sell, and you may have reliable sources of the merchandise. Or, like numerous other successful online auction sellers, you may want to list many different items for bid. You might prefer to be an auction reseller, one who buys items online and tries to resell them at a profit on another site. Or, you may wish to be an online seller who accepts items on consignment and auctions them for others, in return for a percentage of the total selling price. Consignment selling can give you a larger auction inventory, without having to buy it or store it.

If one of these online auction methods is not enough, you can blend them in any combination. For example, you could specialize in buying and reselling specific types of merchandise, such as Depression-era dinnerware, but also accept many other items to auction on consignment. You can organize and build your business around your own preferences.

If you believe you have bought or been given stolen merchandise, do not auction it to get it off your hands. Report your suspicions to law enforcement and give them the goods, if necessary. Selling the items could drag you into a police investigation as a suspect.

Goods worthy of auction can be found almost everywhere. Many of the people who show up early for garage sales and yard sales are auction sellers looking for quick bargains that they can put online. You can join the competitive parade of cars rolling from one sale to the next. Estate sales, going-out-of-business sales, church fund-raiser sales, and end-of-semester moving sales are other good places to pick up auction items cheap.

Friends and neighbors will give you stuff just to get it out of their closets, cabinets, desks, or attics. Your own home may be a gold mine of stuff you can sell and never miss.

Work Structure

You won't have to tape your eyelids open and sit at your computer day and night, if you do go into the business. Many online auction sites have automated their key features for buyers and sellers and will keep you informed via e-mail alerts. These features mean you can structure your days like almost anyone else who holds a "regular" job: eight hours for work, eight hours for sleep, and eight hours for everything else.

However, the longer you are willing to work and the harder you are willing to try, the greater the potential rewards and satisfactions once your business is up and thriving. The first few months will be the toughest. You may have to put in many stretches of long hours while you build up your auction merchandise and learn how to price your items, display them in the right categories, and describe them for maximum sales impact.

FACT

Never underestimate what people will buy, and never underestimate their reasons for buying it. Common objects or pieces of clothing that seem trivial to you may hold special meanings for many people in the online auction universe. A teacup from your attic or a sweatshirt from your closet may draw several bidders into a fierce battle. You may never know why. Just thank the winner, ship the item, and move on to your next listings.

Determining Your Needs

At one level, the needs of an online auction business are very simple. You need merchandise to sell online. But what merchandise? Ask yourself these questions:

- Do you want to specialize in one area, such as antique furniture, collectible plates, rare books, or used parts for 1957 Chevrolets? Or would you rather be a generalist who puts a wide array of merchandise up for auction?
- Do you have the knowledge and experience necessary to be a specialist?
- Will you be willing to compete with the other auction specialists already battling for bidders in your area of interest?
- Where will you get your merchandise, how will you store it, and will any of it require special shipping and handling?
- Will you accept items on consignment to sell for others?

- If you want to specialize in a certain type of merchandise but feel you don't yet have enough knowledge, where can you get it quickly, before you launch your auction business?

You may be interested only in building up an online auction enterprise, but a key part of developing a business mindset will be learning as much as you can about business in general.

The Business of Business

You may be thinking, "What's to learn? I'll just list an item, wait for the high bid, collect the money, ship the purchase, and smile all the way to the bank. Sweet!" Actually, as your business grows, you will have plenty to learn and a lot to consider as you begin each new day. Things that happen half a world away or in your own neighborhood can have a direct bearing on how your enterprise fares on a day-to-day and long-term basis.

Your business needs may vary widely, depending on whether you take up online auction selling as a second income source or as a completely new career. A part-time business may require little more than a home computer, a digital camera, a few boxes, some packing materials and labels, a printer, plus a few items of auction-worthy merchandise. The authors are firm believers in simply starting a business from scratch and building up as you go.

Store your auction items out of the sight—and grasp—of relatives and friends. They may find something they like and expect you to let them have it for free or at cost. If you give in, you will cut into your potential profits and income.

To launch yourself into online auction selling full-time, however, you may need much more, such as:

- An office, either at home or in a building
- Warehouse space where you can store auction items and box them up for shipping after they sell

- A business telephone and high-speed Internet access
- One or more computers devoted to posting and monitoring your online auction listings
- Software to help you operate and manage your business, generate invoices and receipts, and track your sales and expenses
- One or more laser printers for labels, invoices, letters, catalogs, and other tasks

Buying into Knowledge

The smart online auction entrepreneur knows that knowledge really is power. It is also an indispensable link to stronger profits. Information should be one of your key needs, even if you plan to keep your auction operation no bigger than your kitchen table.

Start each business day by getting at least a brief overview of:

- What's happening in the world and how global commerce is reacting
- What's happening in national, state, and local news and how commerce close to home is reacting
- What's happening in the online auction industry
- What new changes or policies have been put into play on favorite auction sites

Admittedly, your first move may be to see how well your current auction listings have drawn bidders overnight. Once you have that perspective, give yourself some time to reconnect with the outside world and community around you before zeroing in on the process of posting your new listings.

Start reading general business publications such as the *Wall Street Journal, Fortune, Business Week,* and others, even if you are not yet in business. Stay on top of fast-breaking world and national events by checking online news sites and daily newspapers. Read the latest auction news at AuctionBytes.com and other online auction periodicals, and check for news releases on each of your favorite auction sites.

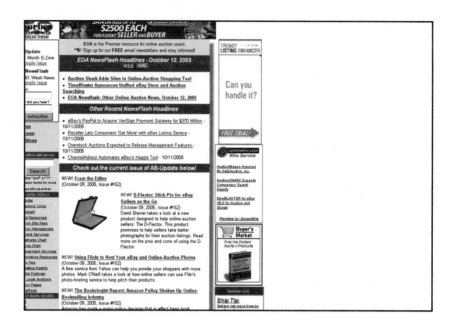

Watch for trends, tips, and interviews with people who have become successful in the online auction world. Determine if you can apply some of their experiences toward improving and building your new business.

Money and Time

If you take up auction selling full-time, one of your key needs, of course, will be income—more than enough to survive from check to check. You will be hoping to make enough profit to feed and clothe your family, pay for your house or apartment, make car payments, give your kids some allowance, pay for their education, fund a vacation, buy new furniture—the list of demands on your income can be never-ending.

Try, if you can, to fund your new endeavor with money you already have, even if you have to start very small and build up. You will not need banks and credit card companies waiting unhappily for their payments while you are trying to buy groceries and pay the mortgage from your first auction earnings.

The Family Factor

Many people quit corporate jobs and start businesses so they can spend more time with their families. Unfortunately, some of them can end up spending less time, not more, even when the business is launched from a spare bedroom or just a few steps away in the garage. Launching and nurturing a new business can consume every waking hour, if you let it. The process can strain relationships, anger your children and relatives, and even make old friendships rocky. You will need to take special care to balance your business life with your family life, whether you work from home or an office.

FACT

Even if your online auction business is "your" business alone, it will affect everyone else living under your roof. Kids may be pressed into service to help pack boxes or carry the packages into the post office. Your spouse may have to monitor your ending-soon listings while you race off to search for more merchandise at an estate sale or yard sale.

Home-based businesses can create some unique and sometimes unpleasant family issues. You may find yourself competing with your spouse, your small children, or your teenagers for use of home computers, printers, phone lines, and common spaces. You may be using the dining-room table to pack and ship an odd-shaped, fragile object, while your spouse is trying to serve dinner. Your once-neat-and-clean house now may be cluttered with boxes, bags of Styrofoam peanuts, rolls of bubble wrap, and piles of items you plan to sell. And all available surfaces may be covered with papers associated with your business.

Pace and Balance

Especially at the beginning, when your new business needs sustained attention, you must be very careful not to overwork. Focusing everything on your dream in too short a time will be unhealthy for you, your business, and those you love. Pushing yourself until you are very tired and irritated may cause you to make costly mistakes or use faulty judgment or hurt a loved one's feelings.

You will have more enthusiasm for your business goals if you turn away periodically from the online world and spend special time in the real world with your family and friends. We all need to recharge our personal battery packs. Rest and recreation—R and R—is vital to members of the military. It helps them cope with the intense stresses of combat or the intense boredom of being posted in isolated places. Your auction business will never be as stressful as battle, but you will still need to schedule regular times to get away from your computers, boxes, packing materials, and piles of waiting merchandise.

ALERT!

Your most creative ideas may pop up while you are doing activities unrelated to online auction selling. Something you see while playing softball, something your child says while eating ice cream, or something you overhear in a restaurant may trigger a new dimension for your business. Make time for serendipity.

Avoid Isolation

A solo entrepreneur faces a special challenge if he has no family to demand some of his time and attention. He may retreat into isolation and spend almost every waking hour online as he attempts to shape and build a business. A stay-at-home spouse who cares for small children while running an auction business can fall into a similar isolation and be desperate for adult conversation by the time the other spouse gets home. Meanwhile, the single parent who operates a home-based online auction business while caring for children faces an even higher risk of isolation.

Try to find time to get out for a while and be an active part of a group of people. Let a trusted friend, relative, or babysitter watch the kids for a couple of hours. Go to a luncheon sponsored by the local chamber of commerce or other business organization. You may become acquainted with other people who run online auction businesses and who want to swap war stories, tips, and experiences. You may also meet management specialists and sales experts who can offer some advice, as well as business beginners who will look to you for some insights.

Avoid getting addicted to e-mailing, checking bids, and watching competition online. Get up as often as possible and do something active around your office, your house, or neighborhood. The online auction world will not collapse if you don't pay attention for a little while.

Join some friends or relatives for lunch and talk about anything and everything except business. Take your kids to meet some other stay-at-home parents and their kids. Go as a group to an outdoor concert, a parade, a performance, or a movie suitable for kids. After the movie, while you are on your way home, watch for yard sales, garage sales, and salable goods that may have been left at the curb for the trash haulers.

Make Your Children Part of Your Business

You may have unrealistic expectations about how long you can work without paying attention to your children. Keep looking for ways to involve them in the business, rather than push them away. The more they know and understand what you do, the better they will be able to adjust to the idea that they must let you work sometimes.

As they grow up, your children can be given more and more responsibility within the business. They may even stick with the family business after they are grown and help perpetuate it. Or they may choose pursuits and careers totally unrelated to selling online. In either case, you will have played an important role in developing their work ethic, and you will have given them a solid head start in life and business.

If your children will not cooperate with the rules of behavior in your office, hire a trusted babysitter or a well-behaved older child from your neighborhood to watch and play with the kids for a couple of hours while you focus on the pressing needs of your business.

Friends Versus Work

Some of your friends may drop by your home or office unannounced, because they still think of you as someone who does not work. After all, you don't drive off to a "real" job, so you must have time for their visits. You may also have friends who want to drop by to talk while they paw through the merchandise you plan to sell. Unfortunately, something collectible may become worthless in one fumbled second.

Be candid even with your closest friends. Let them know you have gone into business and will be keeping regular business hours. Offer to meet them for lunch or after your workday or on weekends. If they want to see your latest merchandise, ask them to view it online and give you some feedback on how well you have displayed it and described it in your listing. They might be tempted to bid.

Setting Your Goals

Every business, no matter how small, needs a business and marketing plan. Online auction businesses are no exception. A business and marketing plan helps you establish your goals and markets and formalize the steps necessary to reach them. You can learn how to create this plan by reading some how-to books on setting up a small business or home-based enterprise.

For a kitchen-table business, the plan can be short and straightforward: "XYZ Auction Enterprises will sell almost any type of item, using eBay and PayPal only. No merchandise will be accepted on consignment, and no items will be purchased online for resale. All items to be auctioned will be gathered from personal belongings and local garage sales, yard sales, and estate sales. XYZ will gather, store, sell, and ship the items from its main location. XYZ will build and expand its reputation and customer base by (1) offering bidders a fair chance to obtain good items at low prices; (2) responding to bidders' questions in a timely manner; and (3) shipping items quickly in sturdy containers."

Spelling out what you want your business to be can help you set realistic, attainable milestones. Creating a strategy for marketing your business can help you better understand who might and might not be interested in the merchandise you intend to sell.

Another key reason for creating a business and marketing plan is to help you get a business loan or attract investors or business partners, if you need them. Depending on the types of products you intend to auction and the amounts of space you will need to store and ship them, you may require a big sum of cash to begin your business. You may also need to incorporate your business or create a partnership or limited liability company (LLC). These are matters to discuss with a tax attorney before you launch your enterprise.

Inventory and Expenses

To fuel your business and keep it alive, you will need to acquire items you can put up for auction. Indeed, you will need a steady stream of merchandise and sales to stay in business and keep prospering. Once you have some inventory, maintaining it and tracking it will be crucial to your success. So will recording and periodically analyzing your expenses, such as shipping, boxes, packing materials, and labels. If you discover that you are spending more on products, shipping, and auction costs than you are receiving, you won't be in business long. It will be time to scramble and learn how to have money left over—profit—after you have met all of the expenses for the sales.

Expenses can be tracked easily with simple software or old-fashioned bookkeeping logs. Be sure to keep all paper receipts after you enter their information into the accounting software. Also, keep a mileage log in your car, recording all trips to deliver or pick up packages or buy office and shipping supplies, plus other business-related errands.

Bookkeeping

The importance of accurate bookkeeping cannot be overemphasized in the online auction business. Learn how to keep very good books and maintain a solid paper trail of receipts, invoices, e-mails, payment notices, bank statements, and other items. If your business is successful and expands rapidly, you will have many transactions and many chances to make a mistake.

You will also encounter buyers who will erroneously or falsely claim that they did not receive something, or they will claim that they paid you when you know that they didn't. Your paper trail can silence them in a hurry and satisfy any investigators from the auction Web site. One very important part of bookkeeping is to do it daily or even several times a day, if needed. Don't let receipts pile up for a week or a month before recording them.

At the end of the year, you will thank yourself for being so diligent. Missing receipts can add up to a lot of wasted money. You may not be able to prove that you spent the amounts on business supplies, boxes, and shipping fees. Instead, you will have to report higher income and pay higher taxes as a result.

Your Partner the Tax Preparer

Ideally, you want an accountant, not an Internal Revenue Service agent, to prepare your taxes. An accountant or, at the very least, good accounting software, should be a key player in your online auction business. If you get at least some basic training in accounting, from a class or some books, you may be able to use accounting software to help keep track of receipts, invoices, shipments, and virtually all expenses of running an auction business, including the dreaded quarterly tax payments.

Even if you do your own books, however, you will likely need assistance from an independent accountant, the Internal Revenue Service, and possibly a tax attorney. They can help you cope with such matters as self-employment taxes, state business taxes, deductible versus nondeductible mileage, projected income and expenses, and the best ways to pay yourself from your business income.

If you track your sales income, expenses, and other details on the same software package your accountant uses, you can often save time and money when she reviews and corrects your books and clarifies your tax options. Keeping your own books will also keep you more aware of where your money goes.

Take it from those who have had painful experiences with casual— okay, sloppy—bookkeeping during their early years in the auction business. When your self-employment business has a good year, you can end up owing the IRS hundreds, even thousands, of dollars in income taxes and Social Security self-employment taxes. If you have failed to make adequate quarterly payments toward your estimated taxes for the year, you can spend the week before April 15 trying every desperate measure to raise cash. That can include, unfortunately, listing some of your own household belongings and treasures for auction. Take the time to keep good books, and this will not happen.

FACT

Developing a business mindset is not difficult, but the process does require a willingness to learn new things and techniques. It can involve staying in touch with the general economy and new trends in the online auction industry. It can also require closely tracking expenses, while cheerfully serving the needs of bidders.

The bidders at your auctions will want, and deserve, quality merchandise at attractive prices. They will want, and deserve, quick, well-protected shipping. And, they will want, and deserve, to know that a caring human is at the other end of the transaction. With the right drive and approach to the online auction business, you can develop a comfortable lifestyle for you and your family. But never lose sight of the needs of your bidders, as well. Treat them as you would like others to treat you.

Chapter 12
Preparing Your Sale

Every day is sale day in the online auction business. To get to the fun part of actually selling things and getting paid for them, however, you need to spend time gathering your goods and getting them ready to list. Fortunately, this will involve some of the most interesting and entertaining parts of online auction selling: Discovering what you really have and determining which sites and categories will be the best places to list your merchandise.

Having the Goods

The majority of online auction sellers start small, with items found inside their own homes or attics. In a consumer-driven society, we all tend to collect stuff—amazing quantities of it—over periods of a few years. The explosive growth of self-storage mini-warehouses in America is one testament to our long-term prosperity. Periodically, we end up with too many things in our houses or apartments, and either we have to find more space ("Put it in storage!") or we have to pare down ("We need to have a garage sale!"). Increasingly, people are realizing they can sell almost anything on eBay and other auction sites.

For a short time, at least, your own home or apartment can supply you with enough goods for a small-scale auction selling business. Family and friends may also want to get rid of things and may gladly donate them to you just to get the boxes, bags, and excess furniture out of their way.

Some good things from your household that can sell online include:

- Antiques (items at least 100 years old)
- Vintage items (The definitions of "vintage" can vary widely and often depend on the item. But at least twenty to thirty years old is a good starting point.)
- Old china, serving utensils, silverware, and cooking appliances
- Toys, games, posters, trading cards—almost anything that has been boxed up or stored for at least a decade or two
- Clothing that is new or barely worn (i.e., because it was too small when you bought it or received it as a gift years ago)

This is only a partial list. Do a simple test. Look around in your home and gather up five items that you could easily live without. Find each item's identifying information, such as model name, type number, and manufacturer. Use the search tools on eBay to see if similar items are listed. If a few have been auctioned or are for sale right now, there is a market for your item. Note the final selling prices. Repeat the test as desired and start setting aside any items that have a market. You may be surprised at how quickly your "sell" collection can start to grow. With just a handful of things to auction, you can launch your business and start learning—and earning—as you go.

Can online auction selling be a good family business?
Absolutely. Some family members can scout for goods to sell while other family members manage the listings, collect the payments, and ship the sold items. For variety, swap jobs.

Focusing Your Business

At some point, of course, you will run out of personal items to sell. Before you get there, start giving this question some serious thought: Do I want to keep doing this as a part-time, second-income business, or do I want to become a full-time online auction seller? You can keep a small selling operation supplied with inventory just by spending some weekend time going to garage sales, yard sales, flea markets, moving sales, estate sales, and other common events. Of course, you may find yourself bumping elbows with other people grabbing for the same goods to sell online.

Another common approach is to bid on certain items from other auction sellers, and then try to sell them again online for a profit. This can work if you are familiar with particular types of merchandise and with the trends in their prices. A variation on this theme is to look for listings with poor pictures that have no reserve price and are about to expire with no bids. You can often win the item for a dollar or less and have it shipped to you the cheapest way. Then you can take new photographs, create a new listing, set a reserve price that would give you a profit—and hope bidders will show up wanting to win it.

Yet, another approach is to buy merchandise online from so-called below-wholesale suppliers such as Specialty Merchandise Corp., or travel to going-out-of-business sales, fire-damage sales, storm-damage sales, and other sales where merchandise, office equipment, and related items may be priced artificially low.

FACT

Several online auction sites, including eBay and uBid, offer online merchant programs that can help you move from individual seller to small business owner and beyond. Consider these programs carefully and examine your own needs and goals before enrolling and paying. It may be prudent to take some basic business courses first, and then reassess your selling goals before focusing on entering an online merchant program.

If you choose to grow your online auction business and make a run toward full-time employment, be prepared for issues such as renting an office or some warehouse space to store inventory and getting a part-time worker to help you. In a business that relies heavily on inventory, you cannot spend all of your time managing auction listings and shipping packages. You will need someone else to pack and ship the sold items while you are rounding up more goods to list.

Selling on Consignment

Many online auction sellers like to work with consignment sellers, people who scout around and find things that others can sell. In a consignment arrangement, you don't have to gather and maintain an inventory. You agree to auction the consignor's items in return for a percentage of the selling price, typically 25 to 50 percent. The best advantage of this approach is that you are paid first when an item sells. You subtract your commission and give the balance to the consignor.

A key disadvantage is that you have to know and trust the source of the goods. You don't want to discover, as some have, that you have been selling stolen merchandise on consignment. Another drawback to consignment sales is that many auction sellers already have rushed to embrace the concept. Since 2003, thousands of franchise and independent auction drop-off stores have opened across the United States. People can simply bring items to these stores to be sold on eBay or other sites, and the stores take care of selling, shipping, and paying the consignor's proceeds if the item sells. The people who have the merchandise don't have to fool with auction sites or computers. Unfortunately for individual eBay sellers, the concept has caught on and grown.

People who used to give old items away or sell them to the first taker have realized that they can get more money by selling them online, even if they don't have a computer. So, they have been flocking to auction drop-off stores. More than 7,000 of the stores had opened nationwide by mid-2005, but some auction experts were questioning the long-term viability of the concept.

Another example of the spreading consignment trend is eBay's Trading Assistant program, which has been around since 2002. People who want to sell something on eBay but don't have the time can use an eBay directory to find a local Trading Assistant. These are independent businesspeople who run consignment-selling operations on eBay. Trading Assistants will often pick up an item from a seller's house, list it for auction, and then pay the seller after subtracting their fees from the proceeds. The individual Trading Assistants set their own fees with no involvement from eBay. To qualify as an eBay Trading Assistant, a seller must have a feedback score of at least 50 and a minimum feedback percentage of 97.

Drop-Ship Sales

Another approach to selling without inventory is to team up with a wholesale drop-shipper. MegaGoods.com and DropShip.com are two of the numerous examples. Typically, as the seller, you become a member of the wholesale drop-shipper and are give access to an online catalog of goods such as consumer electronics or household items. They supply photos and descriptions of an item so you can place it on an auction site. To make a profit, you must set a reserve price greater than what you will have to pay the wholesaler. Usually, there are membership fees and fees for the services you use. When a winning bidder pays you for the product, you pay the wholesaler the catalog price for the item, plus a drop-shipping fee, and pocket the difference. The wholesaler then drop-ships the product, with your return address on it, to the winning bidder.

ALERT!

If something grabs your interest, don't grab your credit card or check-book. First, spend some time doing careful background research on the program and its promoter. Never rely on a professional-looking Web site and e-mailed testimony from "satisfied customers." Before you pay, be sure you *know* what you will get for your money and how it might help you and your business.

You don't have to maintain an inventory when you use the drop-ship approach. You pick items from the wholesaler's catalogue and pay an auction site to list them for sale. If the item doesn't sell, you are out the listing fees, just as you would be if you posted one of your items and it didn't sell. You can try again with the same item or pick something else from the catalog to try to sell.

Knowing Your Stuff

Rule number one: You can't know everything. Still, you should try to learn the essential information about items that you list for sale. Some inexperienced sellers lose big money because they haven't bothered to find out if an item is rare. Other new sellers blindly accept someone's assurance that an item is valuable, and then try to sell it as a valuable collectible—until knowledgeable bidders let them know it's junk. Rule number two: Always take the time and effort to know what you have. Your long-term reputation as an online seller will depend on the work habits you develop starting now.

Auction site search tools and advanced search tools are excellent for discovering if there really is a market for the dusty yo-yo you've stored since childhood or for that ugly "heirloom" candy dish left to you by your aunt. As you move deeper into the auction business and start gathering goods from garage sales, thrift stores, store closings, and other sources, you will rely heavily on auction site search tools, as well as on Internet search engines such as Google.com.

You may be an expert in a particular category, such as antique furniture or sports trading cards, and will want to focus your auction business there.

Yet even with an extensive background in one category, you must be willing to spend time seeking out new items, verifying their authenticity, listing them for auction, and keeping up with the markets for your specialized goods.

Picking the Right Category

Online auction sites are typically divided into dozens of categories and hundreds of subcategories and sub-subcategories. Your challenge is to find the right place to list your item so the best bidders can find it. Some items can fit in more than one category, but you may have to pay extra to list it in a second grouping. Although you want casual browsers to be able to find your item, you especially want it to be found easily by motivated bidders who are looking for the very items you have.

Listing an item in the wrong category can cause it to not sell, and your reputation as a seller won't be helped by the mistake. Or, you may sell it for a lot less than it is worth, because only a few bidders can find it.

Selecting Your Reserve

Setting a reserve price—the lowest price at which you will let an item go—is a very controversial topic among online auction sellers. Some argue that bidders tend to shy away from auctions with reserve prices. Others counter that reserve prices ensure you will not sell your item too cheaply. Indeed, if you have purchased an item at a garage sale for $10 and need to resell it for at least $15 to realize a profit, setting a reserve price of $15 can ensure that you won't end up having it won by a low bidder.

Opponents of reserve prices argue that you could simply set the opening bid to $15 and not use a reserve price. Those who set reserves counter that more bidders are drawn to auctions when the opening price starts low, usually $1. If you can set a reserve price that protects your merchandise from being sold at a loss, you can start the bidding at a buck and not worry.

Sellers can use eBay's Buy It Now and similar features on other sites to let an impatient bidder pay a posted price for an item and end an auction immediately. However, setting a buy-it price will limit how high bidding can go. A bidder will have no reason to offer more than the Buy It Now price.

Using a reserve price can make good sense if you really don't want to sell a particular item below a certain price. Auction purists will argue that bidders should determine the auction outcome, not reserve prices. But the auction purists also won't be the ones who take the hit if your $10 item draws a $2 winning bid.

Placement Options

Online auction sites sometimes have fee-based options that can help you get more exposure for your listing. But the fees can be high and may exceed the value of the item you want to post.

Three examples offered by eBay include:

- Featured Plus! ($19.95)
- Gallery Featured ($19.95)
- Home Page Featured ($39.95 for one item, $79.95 for two or more items)

Using the Featured Plus! option puts your item in the Featured Items list that appears at the top of the category list and search results. It also will show up in the regular listings of items up for bid.

The Gallery Featured option adds a small version of your first picture to your listing in the Featured Items list.

The Home Page Featured option, according to eBay, gives your item "a chance to rotate into a special display on eBay's Home page."

There are restrictions on what kinds of listings can employ these features, and certain minimum seller feedback ratings are required.

A cheaper way to gain a little more exposure for your item is to list it in a second category and pay twice the regular listing fees. If you have an item that is a popular seller, you can also use a one-day auction listing. This will bring your listing much closer to the top, among those ending soon and may draw some fast bids. Don't try this technique with items that might not sell quickly. Otherwise, you will waste listing fees and photograph fees and will have to list the item again in a longer auction to sell it.

Auction Duration

In the online world, you can find auctions that plod along for a month and auctions that race from start to finish in three minutes. When auctions last for at least a day or longer, most buyers will wait until the last hour or even the final few minutes to get into the bidding. So why make any auction last longer than forty-eight hours or so? Exposure. Longer auctions give bidders seeking items like yours more time to find them.

Auction durations vary from one auction site to another. Amazon.com Auctions lets sellers choose almost any number of days between two and fourteen. Sellers on Yahoo! Auctions can choose any length between two and ten days. On eBay, the choices are one, three, five, seven, or ten days. There is a forty-cent charge for a ten-day listing. To use a one-day listing, you must have a feedback score of 10. It can be 5 if you have a PayPal account and accept PayPal as a payment method. A short duration can encourage bidders to jump in sooner than the last few minutes

Experience has shown that seven-day auctions are very popular with buyers and effective for sellers. A listing can be posted on a weekend and end on the following weekend, when bidders and sellers are home and have more time to be online. Some online auction experts pick Sunday evening as the best time to end a listing. Meanwhile, one of the worst times to end a listing is in the middle of a three-day holiday weekend. That's usually a Sunday, as well. Your best bet is to stick to weekend endings for most of your listings but occasionally experiment with other evenings. Some bidders actually like to turn off their computers on weekends and do other things with their lives.

A weekend ending is particularly prudent when you are selling on a site such as Amazon.com Auctions, which uses the Going, Going, Gone auction format. If a bid is received within ten minutes of a listing's closing time, the listing is automatically extended until ten minutes pass without another bid.

ALERT!

Set your listing's ending time to coincide with the time when the most bidders can be available, and don't forget the time zone differences. Some auction experts say the best times to end a listing are 9 P.M. to 11 P.M. Eastern Standard Time, which corresponds to 6 P.M. to 8 P.M. Pacific Standard Time.

It is easy to get hooked on selling things in online auctions. You may never cease to be amazed at what human beings will buy or sell, and you often may be amazed at some of the strange and delightful items you will get to list. Things will pop up in online auctions that will bring back warm memories of your childhood or memories of visits to a favorite relative's house. You suddenly may encounter surplus military gear like you once wore, and more memories—good and unpleasant—will flood back. You may find something you once owned, gave away and wished you had back, now being sold by someone living thousands of miles away. Your first sales may be small. You may not even turn a profit in the first weeks as you learn. But patience and persistence *will* pay off.

Chapter 13
Creating the Perfect Ad

People need and want information, yet their eyes often glaze over when confronted with too much of it. For each item you put up for auction, your challenge is to entice potential bidders with just enough facts presented in a clear, friendly, and honest manner that grabs their attention and makes them want what you are selling. Over time, with a little practice and study, you can become a master at creating clear, effective auction advertisements that will bring steady success to your online auction selling efforts.

Choosing Your Format

Online auction sites typically provide one or more standardized formats for posting auction listings. The standardized formats help beginners learn the selling process. Within each auction format, some sites also provide opportunities for creative advertising. However, you often have to pay extra to use background colors or borders, large, boldface type, or supersize photographs. In the end, using too many optional features and applying too much "creativity" to your ad could cost you more than your item is worth. So your challenge is to strive for a cost-effective balance between creating auction listings that do the job and those that stand out and draw higher bids for your merchandise.

Formats on eBay

On eBay, you can choose among three standardized selling formats:

- Sell item at online Auction
- Sell at a Fixed Price
- Advertise Your Real Estate

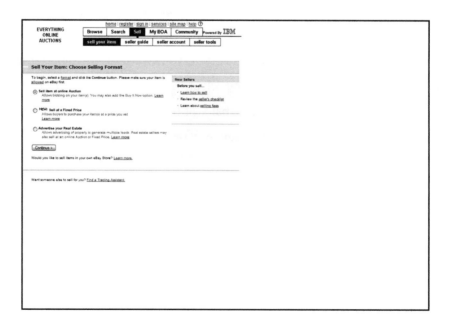

Some sellers who use eBay's online auctions are not satisfied with how their photos appear in their listings. So, they include a Web link in their item description to a page outside eBay. The Linking to Descriptions policy offered by eBay permits members to include one link "to a page that further describes the item being sold in that listing." The page outside eBay can have larger, clearer photos and provide more information about the item. The seller can be more creative with fonts and graphics. The outside page also can have a discreet link to—but no descriptions of—other items the seller has available outside eBay. But the link must conform to specific eBay policies.

If you choose to sell your item at a fixed price, a buyer can purchase it without bidding or waiting. Alternately, you can set a fixed price and add a Best Offer qualifier. Your asking price may be $500, for example, but the highest offer you get is $400 by the time your auction ends. The bidder with the best offer wins.

QUESTION?

Can a new seller use eBay's fixed-price formats?
Sellers cannot use eBay's fixed-price formats until their identifications are verified and they meet certain minimum levels for how much positive feedback they have received from buyers.

The Advertise Your Real Estate option is not an auction, but it does require creating an enticing description of the property or land you hope to sell. You pay eBay a flat fee to list your property for thirty or ninety days, and interested buyers can fill out a contact form if they want to get in touch with you. "The format aims to generate multiple leads rather than a single high bidder," eBay points out. The process of creating a real estate advertisement on eBay is similar to creating an online auction listing. You write and format the text, upload several photographs (for a fee), and pay extra fees if you want to add fancy borders or images or use specific photo layouts. Your property is displayed in the appropriate category and can be found by prospective buyers seeking land, houses, or other structures in a specific city or region. Below your listing, eBay posts a Ready to Contact Seller/Agent? form.

When a prospect fills out the form and submits it, you get her information and questions.

Formats for Yahoo! Auctions

Yahoo! Auctions' free listings provide fewer opportunities for getting creative than eBay does. Initially, you are offered only one format. You pick an auction category, upload your photographs, and then enter your listing details. Success hinges mostly on having good photographs and writing an enticing title and description for your item. Yahoo! allows up to three photographs with each auction listing, and the photos appear bigger and clearer than they probably would on eBay. Once your listing is posted, you can change the title, edit the description or add more details, and change the auction's category, if necessary.

Many auction sellers stick with this basic Yahoo! format. But once you have created and posted your first auction, you can add some personal flair and creative touches by setting up and customizing a Yahoo! Auctions Booth. To start the process, click on the Options link to the right of My Auctions. The Options screen will appear. Directly under the Buyer and Seller Options heading, click on the Customize My Auction Booth link. The options include:

- Name Your Booth
- Add an Image
- Add a Link
- Color Schemes
- Design Your Pages
- Promote Your Booth

If you assign a name to your booth—for example, "Rusty Nail Sales"—and add a graphics image, the name and image will pop up on a bidder's screen when he posts a bid for one of your items. The graphics image can have a link to your auction site, as well. Meanwhile, Yahoo! offers eight color schemes for the headings and subheadings displayed in your auction booth. Once you add an image to your site, you can do more formatting, using Yahoo! PageBuilder. Finally, the Promote Your Booth option gives you access to HTML text that you can copy and paste onto another Web site and provide a quick link to your Auction Booth.

Formats for Amazon.com Auctions

Many of Amazon.com's auction listings follow a standardized format that consists of entering:

- Title
- Minimum bid
- Short description
- Auction closing information
- Seller
- Detailed description
- One photograph or other image
- Item purchase information
- Customer service policy

The emphasis most often is on information rather than visuals. Even though one picture is free, many auction listings do not contain a picture. Therefore, much of the effort of creating a good ad on Amazon has to be focused on getting an auction into the right category, then writing a title that search engines can find, and creating clear, detailed descriptions of the item.

Be Specific

Few bidders will happen across your auction listings while simply browsing auction sites. Some of them may be category browsers: They'll spend an evening checking out the auctions that are ending soon in a few of their favorite categories, such as electronics and cameras or stamps and coins. More than likely, however, the bidders who find you will be looking for something very specific, and they are using the auction site's search tools to help them find it. This is when extra effort toward writing concise, complete titles will pay off.

Writing the Best Description

Professional writers know all too well that "writing is rewriting." Think of the text for your auction listings as drafts of a short manuscript. In the first draft, your job is to get the essential information into place and be sure it is correct. In your second draft, you should work on making the text flow more smoothly and fix any omissions or wordiness. In the third draft, give the text a final polish, run the spellchecker, and have someone else read the text to catch any errors you may have missed and point out wording they don't understand.

You don't have a lot of writing room when creating auction-item descriptions—a few hundred words at most. Therefore, many listings tend to be matter-of-fact and uninspiring reading. For example:

> This auction is for a new Cox .049 Black Widow model airplane engine that has never been mounted, fueled, or started. It is still in its original packaging and was purchased in 1982...

You never want to over-hype auction merchandise or gloss over its flaws. But if you know something of the aura or the history associated with an item, you can use it to help entice bidders. Here's an example:

> Remember that wonderful, high-pitched whine of a Cox .049 engine as it made your P-51 profile scale-model plane leap into the air and start dancing at the ends of 23-foot Dacron control lines? Here is a brand-new Cox .049 Black Widow engine that has never been mounted, fueled, or started. It has been stored in its original packaging since its purchase in 1982.

If you want to know what really makes people buy something, look at some marketing research books, such as Robert B. Cialdini's enduring business classic, *Influence: The Psychology of Persuasion*. According to Dr. Cialdini, there are thousands of different tactics that can cause people to say yes to buying something. Yet, all of the tactics boil down to a half-dozen basic categories. The explanations are too long to include here, but one of the categories, scarcity, is a key force in online auctions. "Collectors of everything from baseball cards to antiquities are keenly aware of the scarcity principle in determining the worth of an item," Dr. Cialdini notes, adding that "people seem to be more motivated by the thought of losing something than by the thought of gaining something of equal value."

Pictures Sell

On eBay and other online auctions, good pictures are worth a thousand words, and more, and possibly a thousand dollars, too. Experience shows there can be dramatic differences in the amounts bid for items shown with photographs and the same items described with words only. Indeed, some auction buyers specifically bid on items that have no photographs or only a solitary, fuzzy image. After they win the items at low prices, they take some good photographs and resell the items for a nice profit.

If you are not confident of your writing skills, try printing out the titles and descriptions from several completed auctions for items similar to yours. Borrow some of the best wording, and revise the sentences so they end up being written in your own words.

Taking the Best Photo

If you have a reasonably good digital or 35mm film camera, you are equipped for taking photographs of your auction items. What will matter more than the camera is how well you handle the focus, lighting, and background for each picture.

Focus

Many digital cameras are equipped with auto-focus. You aim, give the camera time to focus on the object, and shoot. If you use a 35mm film camera, a single-lens reflex (SLR) is best. This is the kind where you look directly through the lens rather than through a rangefinder that is offset slightly from the lens's perspective.

FACT

Rangefinder cameras are difficult to use in close-up photography, because what you see through the rangefinder is not what the lens sees. You can have your item centered in the viewfinder, but in the resulting picture, the top or bottom may be out of the frame. Also, some rangefinder cameras do not focus as closely as a 35mm SLR camera does.

Disposable cameras are better than no camera, but not by much. You cannot adjust the focus on a disposable camera. If you get closer than three or four feet from an object, the picture may not be in focus at all.

Scanners

Color photographs from film or digital cameras can be copied on a desktop scanner and saved as graphics files. The files can be pulled into image-editing software and then cropped and uploaded to an auction site. Amazon.com recommends setting the scanner to a resolution of seventy-two dots per inch (72 dpi). If higher resolution is used, the sizes of the graphics file will grow, too, and they will take longer to download. You may lose some potential bidders if they are impatient and get tired of waiting for a file to load.

Lighting

Lighting is the downfall of many online auction photographs. Some sellers simply plunk an object onto a table and pop it with a flash camera. The results are often garish, with deep, unappealing shadows and spots of harsh glare where the flash has bounced straight back into the camera.

For best results with a film camera, use diffused sunlight. If you can't get enough light near a window, take your pictures outdoors. Areas of shadow can be filled in with light reflected from a white cloth or piece of white poster board. You may need an assistant to help manage the reflected lighting. Do not take outdoor pictures before 10 A.M. or after 4 P.M. When the sun gets low in the sky, its light travels through more of the atmosphere. The light takes on a reddish tint that will appear more visible in your photographs than you will notice while shooting the pictures. Overcast days are often excellent for outdoor photography of auction items because the light is soft and diffuse and doesn't cast any strong shadows or glare.

ALERT!

Daylight color-film pictures take on a reddish-yellowish glow if taken under tungsten lights. They tend to turn green if taken under fluorescent lights. Filters are available to make daylight film work correctly with tungsten or fluorescent lighting. But you may have to go to a camera store to find the right filter and mounting adapter for your camera.

With a digital camera, try setting up two or three shaded lamps several feet away from the item you are photographing. Move the lamps around to minimize glare and shadows. Use a white reflecting board or white cloth to help cast extra light into troublesome dark areas.

Background

Use a neutral backdrop, such as a piece of off-white or light gray smooth cloth, to create an uncluttered background for your pictures. You may also want to cover the table If you are photographing an item that is off-white or light gray, pick another color that will provide some contrast but not detract from what you are photographing. The idea is to remove all background clutter and anything else that might distract the potential bidder from looking at your auction item. Try to keep the item at least a foot, and preferably more, in front of the backdrop.

More Tips for Good Pictures

The more pictures you can take, the better—but only to a point. Professional photographers often shoot several rolls of film just to get one or two special pictures. Similarly, some items can be shown with one picture, but for others, such as an antique juice pitcher, you may need to show the sides, the top, and the bottom, as well as some of the interior, if possible. If an auction item is very expensive, bidders may expect to see up to a dozen pictures or so. A standard eBay listing can accept up to twelve photographs (only the first one is free), or more if additional fees are paid.

The tips that follow can also help ensure that you will get the photographs you need.

- Keep the item in the center of the camera's viewfinder, but also leave a little bit of space around it to create a visual border. If the border is too wide or if background objects creep into part of the shot, use photo-editing software to crop the picture.

- Use straightforward camera angles. Merchandise photography is not art; it's a selling tool. Bidders want to see an object's condition, color, and any distinctive markings, such as brand name, serial number, or a symbol that verifies its description and vintage.

- With digital cameras, use the highest image resolution. Some digital cameras will default to 90 percent resolution, but you can often increase it to 100 percent just by pressing a button or choosing an option in the editing software. Just remember, the higher image resolution will increase the size of your picture file.

- Along with bad lighting and bad focus, many auction pictures suffer from camera shake. Brace your camera against a sturdy object, such as a table or chair, when taking merchandise pictures. Better yet, get a tripod. It is very difficult to hold a camera steady, especially when you are trying to shoot close-ups.

- Don't be afraid to show your item's damage or rust spots or areas of faded color. Buyers will need to know what they are getting. Also, shoot close-ups of logos, labels, model numbers, certificates of authenticity—anything that can prove your item is desirable to collectors.

- If you absolutely have no skills at photography and no patience to learn, try to get help from a friend or relative. High school or college photography students also can be hired to take the pictures you need.

You may be good at editing digital photographs, but avoid trying to edit out the flaws and blemishes in what you are selling. There should be truth in advertising, especially in online auctions where buyers must rely on pictures, descriptions, sellers' reputations, and little else when making bidding decisions. If you make an old vase look pristine, and the buyer gets a vase with several chips, she likely will complain and post negative feedback.

Choosing Photo Options

On eBay, you have several photo options. You can try to get by with just one photo (the free one) and hold your listing costs down. Or, you can pay extra to upload several photographs and hope that higher bids will help you recoup your investment. For a small extra charge, you can choose a picture layout.

On the Yahoo! Auctions site, your only choice is to upload one, two, or three photographs. Since they are free, try to use three pictures to illustrate your item.

Amazon.com makes the photo options simple on its auction site: You can download one image. It can come from your computer, or you can add a link in your listing to a photograph or other image out on the Internet.

Unlike Yahoo! and eBay, Amazon specifies that picture files or image files must be no larger than 100 kilobytes (KB). The recommended size is just 10 KB to 25 KB, with a resolution of 300 by 300 pixels. Files edited in image-editing software must be saved in JPEG (.jpg) or GIF (.gif) format. Amazon allows you to include a hypertext link in auction item descriptions. This link can display additional photographs and information stored on another Web site.

Excellent advertisements are not difficult to write and assemble for an online auction site. Still, many people feel challenged and even threatened by the amount of work that is sometimes required. You can learn from the examples of others. The ads you create may never be perfect, but, in the online auction world, they will often be better than good enough.

Chapter 14
Getting Paid

To be paid promptly, run your online auction sales operation like a business, even if your aim is simply to earn extra cash for the family grocery budget. Clearly stated policies for payments, shipping, and returns will help entice potential buyers to place more and bigger bids on your items and make faster payments. Clear policies will also minimize how much e-mail you must answer about the payment methods you accept, how you handle returns, which shippers you use, and how quickly you ship.

Setting Your Standards

Selling online is about earning a living, or at least generating a second income, while doing something you enjoy. Whether online auction selling is your livelihood or a hobby, you want to earn a return on the necessary investments, including the money you spend for auction merchandise, listing fees, photograph fees, and other sales features. The time you spend managing your auction sales is also worth money.

The quicker you can collect from winning bidders, the more valuable their payments will be to you, your family, and your business. The best way to ensure fast payments is to have:

- A clear list of payment preferences
- A definite deadline for when you expect payment to be made
- A list of the shipping services you offer
- A merchandise return policy (or a statement that you are selling "as is")

Payment Preferences

Many online auction sellers post just one payment preference: "I accept PayPal only." PayPal's instant-payment features means goods can be paid for and shipped almost immediately after an auction closes. PayPal is very popular with "weekend warrior" auction sellers who start seven-day auctions on a Saturday or Sunday. Once a listing closes and the winning bidder pays with PayPal, the goods can be boxed up, and a U.S. Postal Service or UPS shipping label can be printed with a computer and laser or inkjet printer. The shipping fees can be paid from the seller's PayPal account, and the balance—the profit—can be transferred to the seller's bank account. Meanwhile, Monday morning, the box can be dropped off at an appropriate shipping facility on the way to work.

To add PayPal to your payment preferences in eBay, click on My eBay. On the My Summary page, look for Preferences under the My Account heading. Click on Preferences and edit Payment from Buyers.

Payment methods can be different for each auction item you list. For example, if you have been accepting PayPal payments only and want to add personal checks, money orders, and cashier's checks, you can add these items in the Payment & Shipping section of a new listing. If you already have posted a listing but no one has placed a bid, you can open the listing and click on Revise Your Item. Scroll down to Edit Payment & Shipping and click on the link. Add or delete payment methods as desired. If a bid already has been placed, you can add more payment methods but not delete any of those currently in place.

Payment Deadline

In the online auction world, seven to ten days are common deadlines for receiving payment. A ten-day deadline should give adequate time to a buyer who prefers to mail a personal check, money order, or cashier's check rather than pay online with PayPal or a credit card.

If you require immediate payment (via PayPal or credit card, for example), you must specify the shipping costs and other related costs, as well as the price of the winning bid. The buyer must be told exactly how much to pay.

Shipping Services

The shipping services you offer can affect how quickly you are paid. Buyers needing a particular item in a hurry may bid in your auction or do a Buy It Now purchase because you offer faster shipping methods than a competitor does.

Return Policy

Your attitude toward merchandise returns can affect buyers' willingness to place bids on your items. Researchers at eBay have found that "difficulty in returning items" is one of potential bidders' key concerns, even though returns are rarely necessary. The eBay researchers also found that sellers with clear return policies typically sell a higher percentage of their listed items than do their competitors who don't have return policies. A clear return policy can give your buyers the confidence they need to bid on, and bid up, your merchandise.

A clear return policy states:

- What merchandise cannot be returned
- The conditions for return (such as "merchandise packaging unopened")
- How a refund will be issued
- The time limit for returning merchandise

Items sold "as is" generally cannot be returned to the seller by a winning bidder. Be sure to specify "as is" and "no return" in the descriptions for any "as is" items you list for auction.

Your return policy should be very clear on the conditions under which you will accept an item's return, such as "opened box with all original contents" or "unopened merchandise packaging." You should also specify: "Items will be inspected before refund is issued and must be the same items that were shipped." There is a practical reason for this warning. Idealistically, you may believe that all businesses, including yours, should offer a policy of "100% satisfaction guaranteed or your money back." This approach works well in a retail business where a customer walks into the store and physically returns a defective item. Store personnel can inspect it and issue a refund or swap the defective item for a new one on the spot. In the online world, however, you always have to be on guard against fraudulent buyers who will try to "return" a different or inferior version of the merchandise they bought from you.

Your return policy also should contain a clearly stated *refund* policy. For example: "Refund will be given as money back." Or, "Refund will be given as store credit." Or, if many items of the same type are in stock, "Merchandise will be replaced with similar item of equal value (subject to availability)."

Set a time limit for returns and stick to it. Otherwise, a buyer may try to send back an item and demand a refund several months after purchase. Online auction sellers typically set deadlines of seven days, ten days, fourteen days or thirty days for buyers to return merchandise.

Some successful eBay sellers do not post a return policy. Instead, they deal with problems, if they occur, on a case-by-case basis. When an item in question is not very expensive, a seller will often refund the buyer's bid price and possibly the shipping costs, too, and let the unhappy buyer keep the item. This avoids the hassle of trying to recover the merchandise, and it minimizes the chance of getting negative feedback from the transaction.

As Is

At times, you will want to sell certain items "as is." An "as is" item is auctioned off in its current state with no guarantees that it will meet its intended purpose. Likewise, it usually is sold with no opportunity for return. The buyer has to gamble that the item will work or can be repaired. "As is" items are often bought to cannibalize for parts that can be used to repair a similar item. Or, all useful parts are removed from the "as is" object and put up for auction by someone who knows, and can describe, how they are used and replaced.

To get the highest bids for an "as is" item, follow these steps:

1. Check current and closed listings for similar items.
2. Make notes on the categories used, how the item is described, and how it is shown with photographs in the most successful sales.
3. Create similar photographs for your item.
4. List your item in the best category and set the opening price low. Use a reserve price, if necessary, to avoid selling the item for less than the minimum you want to get for it.
5. Write a careful description of the item, listing any visible flaws and any mechanical or electrical problems that are known to you.
6. If you don't know the condition of the item, make this very clear to potential bidders. State that the item is being sold "as is" and that your return policies will not apply.
7. State that the buyer assumes all responsibility for the condition of the item and has bid with the understanding that the item may not meet its performance requirements or expectations.

Pick and Choose

Examples of good (and bad) selling standards are easy to find on eBay and other online auction sites. Make a buyer's tour of several auction listings posted by experienced sellers, those who have had at least 100 positive feedback postings from buyers. Read the information posted for shipping, payment, and return. Notice how the successful sellers handle special requirements such as shipping insurance. Take notes on any instructions or requirements that you can include in your own standards. For example, you might want to include statements similar to these in your sales policy:

- "I accept PayPal, money orders, cashier's checks, and personal checks."
- "Payment should be received within ten days after the end of the auction."
- "I ship in one to two days when payment is made with PayPal."
- "Shipment will be delayed until personal checks clear."
- "Shipping insurance is optional but recommended. It may be required on some items."
- "Negative feedback will be left for winning bidders who do not pay."

If you are not sure that your policies are clear enough, have a friend review them and point out any areas that raise questions.

Payment Preferences: Buyer's View

A cautious buyer may ponder several questions while examining your payment preferences, including:

- Are your preferred payment methods easy to use?
- How do you report that payment has been received?
- Do your preferred payment methods provide proof of purchase?
- Can payments to you be traced?
- How secure are the payment methods you offer?
- What liability coverage is available if something goes wrong with the transaction?

You can't please all of the buyers all of the time. Some may ask, or demand, that you accept a payment method you do not wish to use. Stick to your standards. Ask the potential bidder to use one of the payment methods you have specified. If they refuse and post a bid anyway, you may be able to cancel it and block them from bidding in your future auctions.

FACT

According to eBay, sellers and buyers should contact each other within three days after an auction closes. The Auction Police will not arrest you if you take four days or longer. However, a buyer may become restless, bombard you with e-mails, and consider negative feedback. Make it a policy to contact winning bidders as quickly as possible.

Terms of Sale

Be sure your terms of sale specify the following very clearly:

- How to pay
- What shipping methods are available
- How often you ship (daily, three times a week, once a week, and so forth)
- Whether shipping insurance is optional or required

After you establish your terms, stick to them. You may get several requests from potential bidders, asking you to offer another payment method or shipping method. Be polite, but explain that the methods you have chosen work best for you. Encourage them to use one of the payment methods you have chosen.

Many online auction experts recommend offering as many ways to pay as possible, including accepting personal checks and credit cards.

Other experienced auction sellers, however, have benefited from the explosive growth of PayPal. They have found that stating "I accept PayPal only" is not a deterrent to bidders. Indeed, PayPal's instant payment capabilities means the winning bidder can pay with a credit card or debit card, and the auction merchandise can be shipped the same day or within a day or so of the auction's conclusion.

Invoice E-Mail

Some auction sites, such as eBay, have features that enable you to generate and e-mail payment invoices to winning bidders. On some other auction sites, you have to create your own invoice and send it via e-mail.

On eBay, you can click on the Send Invoice button at any time after an auction ends but before the buyer completes the Checkout process. The Send Invoice button is accessible from the auction item page or from your My eBay page.

Experience shows that eBay's invoice program can confuse some buyers. The invoice picks one shipping method, such as Parcel Post, adds it to the item price, and displays the total. Other shipping options and their prices are listed in a separate column that is not totaled.

Free invoices can also be generated and e-mailed using PayPal's invoicing feature accessible from the Merchant Tools tab. PayPal offers a number of invoice templates as well; some can be stored for future reuse.

For more sophisticated invoicing needs, including customized invoices with graphics, a number of fee-based invoicing services are available, such as BillMyClients.com and SecondSite.biz. Sites such as these can be useful for large-scale auction sales businesses and online stores that include auction sales as part of their operations. Online invoicing services may also be useful if you accept consignment items for online auction sales. Research these services carefully and compare their fees and features. If possible, locate other online auction sellers who use the services and ask them for their opinions of the services.

Checks

The traditional personal check keeps losing ground to debit cards, check cards, and credit cards, which many merchants now prefer. Yet, an estimated 200 million Americans still have personal checking accounts, and many of them do not like to give out their credit card information online. They are leery of identity theft. They prefer to pay with old-fashioned paper, even when they know it will delay shipment of their auction winnings.

Accepting checks is one way to increase the market and the competition for your auction items. But you must state clearly in your selling policies that goods will be shipped only after the buyer's check has cleared.

QUESTION?

What if I clearly state "PayPal only," but a winning bidder pays with a check?
If the buyer has a good feedback rating, she probably won't jeopardize it by sending you a bad check. If the amount is reasonably small, under $50, you may be safe in shipping the item right away, just as you would with a PayPal payment. If the buyer is new or if a larger amount of money is at stake, tell her that since PayPal was not used, you will have to delay shipment until the check clears. Be kind. Don't risk negative feedback.

Some auction sellers take a chance and ship as soon as they receive a personal check, especially for small amounts from buyers with good feedback scores. Most of the time, the checks *are* good, and trust is rewarded. Many other sellers, however, state in their sales policies that goods will not be shipped until the check clears, and they stick firmly to that rule. Be aware that it is *very* difficult to collect on bad checks, especially out-of-state checks for small amounts.

Credit Cards

In any business, you can make more sales if you are able to accept credit cards. At the consumer level, credit cards are the number-one tool of e-commerce. Credit cards provide buyers with certain levels of protection when making purchases from online merchants or auction sites. Credit card users are more likely to make impulse bids or impulse purchases while roaming around online auction sites, and bidders in other countries can overcome currency differences by using a credit card.

PayPal provides the easiest way for an auction seller to accept payments from credit card holders. Winning bidders can pay for their purchases with MasterCard, Visa, American Express, or Discover or use the eCheck option to pay with an electronic check. Many online merchants and auction sellers who accept credit cards directly also accept payments through PayPal, because of the service's growing popularity.

If you expand your business into an online store with an inventory and access from the Web, you will likely want to accept credit cards directly. To do this, you need to establish a merchant account and choose a gateway, which connects you to the transaction clearinghouse and verifies that the credit card is good. Three types of gateways typically are available for merchants: (1) credit card swipe machines, such as you see at restaurants, doctor's offices, grocery stores, and retail stores; (2) desktop software; and (3) real-time Web gateways.

The traditional advice for setting up a merchant account in a small business is to go, hat in hand, to your bank, and then look for other possibilities if they say no. A number of online companies—such as Charge.com, MonsterMerchantAccount.com, or Merchant Accounts Express—now offer merchant accounts, and you can apply in a matter of minutes. Fees, services, and restrictions vary. You should carefully research several merchant account providers before choosing one.

PayPal for Sellers

Increasing numbers of auction sellers explicitly state in their seller's policies that they only accept PayPal. The reason is simple. The eBay-owned payment service enables an auction seller who doesn't have a merchant account to accept payments from winning bidders who pay with credit cards, bank transfers, debit cards, or checks.

PayPal's advantages include:

- Almost immediate payment when the winning bidder uses a credit card or debit card
- The ability to print postal service or UPS shipping labels from your computer and pay shipping charges online
- The ability to track your postal or UPS shipments while in your PayPal account
- Protections against buyer chargebacks and fraud
- Payments can be made in U.S. dollars, Canadian dollars, Australian dollars, euros, pounds sterling, and yen, with currency conversions immediately available online.

Some of PayPal's features and services are free for buyers and sellers. When a buyer makes an auction payment to a seller, PayPal deducts a transaction fee from the seller's receipts. In 2005, the transaction fee was thirty cents, plus 2.2 percent or more of the sales price (depending on the amount received), and bidders in nearly sixty countries could use PayPal. To ensure transaction safety, PayPal uses encryption technology and the Secure Sockets Layer protocol to keep computer hackers at bay.

Escrow—Yes or No?

Buyers and sellers frequently use online escrow services in transactions where the selling price exceeds $500. Escrow services help minimize fraud during transactions for high-dollar items. However, some buyers consider $100 a lot of money, so they may insist on using escrow for items well under $500. The buyer generally pays the fees for using an escrow service, unless the seller and buyer agree in advance to split the charges.

ALERT!

Western Union cautions: "Be wary of third party 'collection' or 'holding' services unless they are a reputable, licensed escrow service." Cyberthieves sometimes set up phony online escrow services and use them to steal merchandise, money, and credit card information.

Using an escrow service will slow down how quickly you are paid. The wait can be up to thirty days or more. If the buyer refuses the merchandise after inspecting it, you likely will have to pay the shipping charges to retrieve it. But the buyer will not be able to get his money back from the escrow service until your goods are returned. For auction items under $100, try to discourage the use of an online escrow service. But if the buyer insists, be sure he pays the escrow fees.

An amazing array of online tools and services can help you receive payment quickly after you complete a successful auction. These tools and services will get even better and more sophisticated over time as the popularity of online auction sales continues to surge.

Chapter 15
Shipping Made Easy

Shipping should never be an afterthought in a business built around online auctions. To misquote the poet Robert Frost: "Good shipping makes good customers." When you deliver auction purchases in a timely manner, in well-protected packaging, you project an image that says you care about the bidders who buy from you and care about the quality of the goods you sell. At the same time, you offer an unspoken but clear invitation to come back to your listings to buy again.

Be Ready to Go

Veteran online auction sellers know that buyers often give better feedback when their merchandise arrives well packed in a clean, sturdy shipping container. Want proof? Read some of the feedback that buyers post on eBay and other auction sites. "Items arrived nicely packed…. Prompt shipping with good packing…. Packaged well, shipped quickly…. Excellently packed!"

Shipping is not rocket science. But it definitely should weigh on your mind—literally. As a new auction seller, you must learn how to ship items efficiently and with the least expense in a wide array of weights and sizes, using several different delivery sources. These may include the U.S. Postal Service, United Parcel Service (UPS), Federal Express, DHL, freight trucks, independent couriers, and even intercity buses.

Do not list your first auction item on eBay or elsewhere until you have determined the quickest and most affordable ways to ship it from your location, and you have set up the appropriate accounts necessary to get the best service and rates. Learn how to ship before you sell, not afterward.

Shipping options will vary from city to city and hamlet to hamlet. If you plan to run an online auction business from an isolated farmhouse at the end of a gravel road that fades into a pig trail, you may have mosey down to your mailbox each day and wait for the rural mail carrier to pick up your shipments. Otherwise, you will have to hop into your truck or onto your tractor and haul your items to the nearest town for shipping. The good news is you can really do this. All corners of the planet are firmly linked by the Internet and a vast, crisscrossing web of shipping routes that include highways, air paths, railroad tracks, and well-traveled sea lanes. You can farm a little Iowa corn, then go into your home office, get online, and sell a collectible baseball card to an eager software programmer who works for Microsoft in Redmond, Washington. Or, you can sell an antique, vacuum-tube radio to an aircraft mechanic who works at a small hangar somewhere in Florida.

The millions of bidders who now hang out and buy at online auctions often will not bid unless they are offered several shipping choices. Experience has taught that they are more likely to bid when they at least have the option to select a quick or standard delivery method. They may choose quick shipping and willingly pay more, simply because they need or want the item *now*. Or, they may be bargain shopping and want to hold down shipping costs. They can wait a week or ten days or longer to get the item, if slower shipping will save them a few bucks.

Shipping Checklist

As an online auction seller, your main shipping concerns will include:

- ✓ Package weight
- ✓ Package dimensions
- ✓ Shipping methods
- ✓ Shipping price
- ✓ Container
- ✓ Protective packing
- ✓ Insurance
- ✓ Proof of delivery

Scaling Your Profits

Much of your profit from auction listings will depend on how well you can monitor and control shipping costs each time you send an item to a winning bidder. Potential bidders are very sensitive to shipping costs. If the price of shipping seems too high, they won't bid. Meanwhile, many new sellers lose money on some of their first auction sales, because they fail to pay attention to shipping costs and forget to specify that the buyer will pay to have the item delivered. A seller may have to spend a hundred dollars on shipping an item that sold for only five dollars.

One of the first purchases for your online auction business should be a well-calibrated and accurate scale. The bathroom scale you have been eyeing will never do! Look for postal scales, shipping scales, freight scales, or even food-weighing scales. You can work with almost any scales that are accurate and can handle the lightest or heaviest package you expect to send.

FACT

Scales suitable for online auctions generally come in two flavors: mechanical and digital. You can find them at office supply stores, in office supply catalogs, and at online sales sites such as OfficeDepot. com and Staples.com. Scales are also hot items on eBay, Yahoo! and other auction sites.

Typical prices for new weighing devices can range from under $20 for a mechanical scale with a two-pound capacity to around $150 and more for freight scales capable of weighing shipping containers up to 400 pounds. Mechanical scales are often specified by maximum weight and measurement accuracy, such as "100 lb. + 1 lb.," meaning accurate to one pound. Several brands of digital scales are also on the market. Some digital scales can weigh packages with an accuracy of less than a half-ounce, and some can connect to the Internet and download the latest postage rates and shipping rates from several leading carriers.

Measure for Measure

Your second purchase should be a tape measure. This can be the metal kind used by carpenters and construction workers or a cloth tape measure used by tailors and seamstresses. Ideally, you may need both types. The tape measure will be used to measure the length, width, and height of shipping boxes.

To ship online using UPS, for example, you will need to know the girth and length of a package. The girth is determined by measuring completely around your package "at its widest point, perpendicular to the height." For this, you will definitely need a very flexible tape measure. To measure the package's length, place your tape measure against the longest side and note the distance from edge to edge. Add the girth and length together, and you will have the total package size.

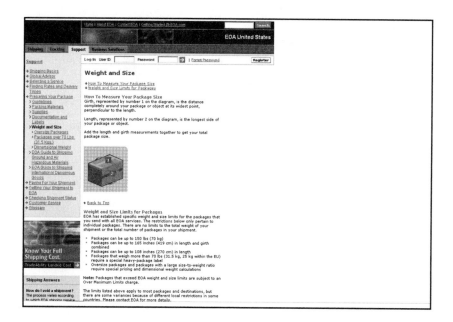

ALERT!

Never guess at shipping costs. Take the time to figure out how you will package the merchandise and how much the buyer, or you, will spend to get it to its destination. Experienced auction sellers often pack their items into boxes, ready to seal, before they post their listings.

Once you have the weight and dimensions of your package, you can use convenient online calculators to figure out how to price the postage or delivery charges. These calculators are found on mailing and shipping sites such as the United States Postal Service, *www.usps.com*; United Parcel Service, *www.ups.com*; and Federal Express, *www.fedex.com*.

The calculators will require such information as destination Zip Code, package weight, type of package, package dimensions, and declared value. Some of the sites, such as FedEx, will have convenient links to pictures and dimensions of their standard shipping containers.

> You may need at least two scales: one to weigh letters and packages up to five pounds and one to weigh heavier boxes. Pick accuracy over price when shopping for a scale. Missing a weight boundary by as little as an ounce can cost you extra shipping dollars each time.

Is it Really Worth It?

Even if you plan to haul all of your packages to the post office or UPS Store and let others take the measurements and do the weighing, experience has taught many that owning a scale and a tape measure can save significant money and time. Knowing the shipping weight and package dimensions is vital when creating a new auction listing. Knowing exactly how much you should pay for shipping can save you from shelling out extra when a clerk makes a mistake.

Will I need a postage meter?

A postage meter can save time and money in almost any active small business. Pitney Bowes estimates its meters save users an average of 20 percent a year in costs, because exact amounts of postage can be applied to mailings.

Shipping as a Profit Center?

To some online auction sellers, shipping costs are a built-in way to squeeze a few more dollars out of buyers. They charge shipping fees that are more—sometimes a lot more—than the actual cost to send the merchandise. Many other auction sellers, however, strongly oppose and reject this practice. Buyers hate it, too, once they catch on to it.

To survive and thrive, an auction business requires repeat customers as well as a steady flow of new ones who might become "regulars." You can consign your auction business to a slow death if you keep scaring off potential repeat bidders by overcharging for shipping. Any short-term profits from the jacked-up prices will be lost once the negative feedback begins popping up and buyers start shunning you.

The better procedure, from our experience, is to give buyers a straight deal on the shipping costs and try to get a little more profit from the auction item itself to cover some of the shipping expenses. When you are pricing it and setting a reserve, factor in a little extra to cover the cost of the box, packing materials, tape, and labels. The expenses associated with shipping can be tax deductions in an auction business.

Pack your first auction item and shipping material into a box but don't seal it to weigh it. If the weight is very close to a boundary where the cost will go up, try reducing the packing materials slightly to allow a little more weight margin for the final tape. If a few ounces are still available, more packing can be added for extra safety.

Choosing the Shipping Procedure

Online auction sellers usually want buyers to pay the shipping costs. But you have to let bidders know up-front what they can expect to pay for shipping if they win the auction.

Choosing the shipping procedures for your auction business may be fairly simple. You may simply camp out in the eBay Shipping Center and let buyers choose to have their items shipped by the post office, UPS, or a freight company as needed. Or, you may face some tougher choices. For example:

- Your shipping choices may be limited to just one or two services because of your geographical location.
- You may have had a bad experience with one shipping service and absolutely refuse to do any more business with them.
- You may have to limit buyers to just one or two shipping choices and require them to buy insurance because your auction specializes in easily broken collectible dishes or delicate electronic instruments.
- Many of your auction items may have to travel by freight truck or in the cargo hold of a bus because they are too bulky or too heavy for conventional delivery services.

Through a Buyer's Eyes

You can learn a great deal about effective shipping by paying closer attention to how goods are packaged for transport. Even a lowly cardboard box can project a positive image for your auction business, especially if the container is clean, sturdy, neatly sealed with shipping tape, and with professional-looking labels applied to its outside. Most auction sellers have been buyers first and still spend a lot of time looking for treasures and bargains that they can resell or add to their personal collections. Learn the online auction world from the buyer's side before becoming a seller. You will have more empathy for auction customers who need an item shipped a special way or who insist on more packaging materials and insurance "just in case."

FACT

Your experiences as a buyer can teach you plenty about shipping and sellers' attitudes. Bid on a few items you want or will need in your business and see how well, or poorly, they are packed when they arrive. Make notes on the good ways and bad ways they have been boxed. Save any boxes, bubble wrap, padding, or Styrofoam peanuts that can be reused once you start selling.

When you are ready to start selling items on eBay and other auctions, take careful stock of your packing and shipping preparations. Ask yourself:

- How much do I really know about the shipping methods and delivery services that I plan to use?
- Do I have the right scales and a good tape measure?
- Have I found, bookmarked, and tested useful online tools such as locator maps, delivery service Web sites, and the U.S. Postal Service Web site?
- Have I carefully read the how-to information and tips presented on each shipping site?
- Have I set up the appropriate accounts with the services that I plan to use?
- Do I have shipping supplies, including boxes, tape, scissors, box knives, foam pads, Styrofoam peanuts, bubble wrap, and other quality cushioning materials?

Save your old rolls of duct tape and masking tape for repair jobs and painting tasks around the house. These tapes should never be used on the outsides of shipping boxes. They won't hold up to the stress of shipping. They may also gum up important sorting machinery. In addition, a buyer receiving a box festooned with these tapes will be appalled at your shoddy handiwork. Use only real shipping tape.

FACT

UPS recommends sealing boxes with (1) pressure-sensitive or nylon-reinforced tape that is at least two inches wide or (2) three-inch-wide, water-activated, reinforced tape. Use three strips of tape on the bottom and top of each box. One strip should seal the middle seam. The other two should seal the edge seams.

Always treat shipping as an essential function of your business not as a necessary evil. Devote part of each day to replenishing shipping supplies, researching new or cheaper ways to ship, and gathering how-to packaging tips from shipping Web sites and other online auction sellers.

Clarifying Shipping Rules

Be very specific about shipping options when you create the description for each new auction listing. Invite potential bidders to contact you with questions. Many inexperienced auction sellers focus too closely on selling their items and then get into wrangles over shipping after the bidding concludes.

Generally, in the online auction world, the buyer is expected to pay for shipping and for insurance, if she wants it. The seller pays for the box, the packaging material, the tape, and the labels necessary to send the merchandise. These can be tax-deductible expenses for an auction seller.

Many online auctions leave all shipping arrangements to the seller and buyer. Some provide little support beyond a few links and online advertisements for shipping services. Unfortunately, these free-market approaches can leave many buyers confused and many sellers irritated with the volume of e-mail and other contacts that have to be swapped before the shipping methods, prices, insurance, and arrival schedules can be worked out.

The Godzilla of online auctions, eBay, maintains a Shipping Center that eats all other auction sites' shipping efforts for breakfast—in one gulp. The Shipping Center has online tools for calculating shipping charges and printing shipping labels. You can click on the online shipping services of the U.S. Postal Service and UPS, which have integrated many of their services with the eBay and PayPal sites.

In the Shipping Center, you can do virtually everything necessary to get your packages moving toward their destinations. You can pay online for postage or shipping, print labels, buy shipping insurance (covering up to $200), and arrange for pickup of your packages. You and your buyer can click into the Shipping Center and track the progress of your shipment as it moves through the postal system or UPS network.

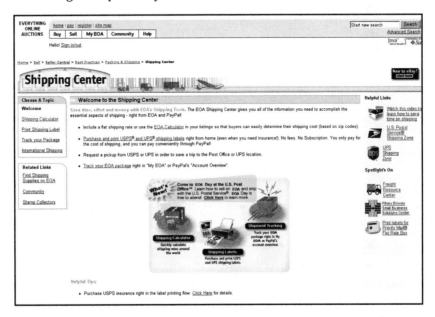

When you aren't shipping or tracking, you can go to the Shipping Center and order free boxes in various sizes from the post office. The Priority Mail boxes are co-branded with U.S. Postal Service and eBay logos. You also can watch a Pitney Bowes video that shows how to save time on shipping. You can jump over to the UPS Shipping Zone page and take a very detailed Packaging Tips mini-course that covers almost everything you need to know about preparing and shipping packages of many different sizes and weights. UPS's Global Advisor site introduces the intricacies of international shipping. Likewise, you can download the UPS International Shipping How-to Guide from eBay's Shipping Center site.

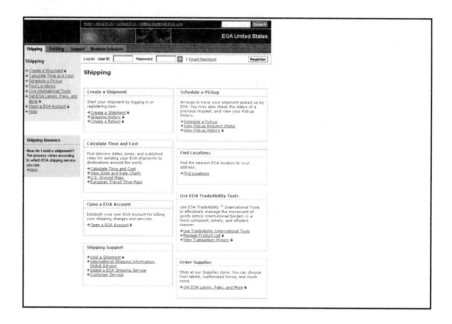

Check out the UPS FAQs (frequently asked questions) for information on how to open a Daily Pickup Account or Occasional Account. If you are a frequent seller on eBay and other online auctions, you can have UPS stop by your house or other location every day, Monday through Friday, to pick up your latest shipments. Daily Pickup accounts are billed weekly. If your auction shipments are more sporadic, an Occasional Account can let you schedule less-frequent pickups but still be billed weekly. Other shipping arrangements and rates are also available from UPS.

To stay profitable, almost all businesses need a steady flow of new customers, as well as a dependable base of repeat customers. Effective shipping is one of the most important ways to win the hearts, minds, and loyalty of online auction bidders. Keep them happy, and you can keep them coming back for more of your auction listings.

Specialized Shipping Services

If your auction items are too bulky or heavy for conventional delivery services, consider shipping them by freight truck. Many freight haulers are set up to handle LTL (less than truckload) shipments. Some of them cater to the needs of online auction sellers who suddenly have to send something huge, such as a pinball machine or an antique cupboard, to a buyer hundreds of miles away. Goods can be moved by truck to virtually anywhere in the Continental United States in five days or so. You will have to search and negotiate for the best shipment prices to the desired destination. You will also have to learn how to fill out a bill of lading. According to Yellow Freight, "the bill of lading is the most important document in the shipping process." This document "is required for each shipment, and acts as a receipt and contract." Once a bill of lading is accepted, the carrier is obligated to deliver the shipment to the consignee, in good condition. The bill of lading acts as a shipping guide all along the route of transport. It gives freight personnel a variety of details, including where the container is going, how it is billed, and how it must be handled on the docks and in the truck trailers. At some LTL carriers' Web sites, bills of lading can be completed online.

Prices can be reasonable for LTL shipping, under $10 per hundred pounds in some cases. But so-called absolute minimum charges may apply, for example, for goods hauled less than 1,000 miles or across the Canadian or Mexican border. Also, there will be different prices for standard or expedited delivery. For an extra charge, some LTL carriers offer time-definite delivery guarantees as well.

FACT

Online sellers who specialize in large, heavy, or delicate items typically learn how to do their own packing and crating. They do this not only to save costs but also to ensure that their auction items get better-than-adequate protection.

The two main types of freight delivery are terminal-to-terminal and door-to-door. In terminal-to-terminal delivery, you take your crated or boxed merchandise to the shipping center for loading and transport. After it reaches the destination terminal, the buyer must go there and pick it up.

Shipping from your door to your customer's door will be more expensive, but the convenience and savings in time may far outweigh the extra cost. In typical door-to-door shipping, a truck is dispatched from the nearest shipping center to your office or home. The merchandise is picked up, already crated or packaged, and delivered to the truck terminal. From there, it is loaded into a truck trailer and transported to the truck terminal nearest its destination. After the container is unloaded from the trailer, it is put aboard another truck and carried to the recipient's door.

Objects that need crates usually cost more to ship than objects that can be "blanket wrapped"—protected with a number of cushioning blankets. Sometimes, special protective crates can cost much more than the transportation itself.

Here are some starting points for your LTL shipping research:

ABF Freight Systems (✐*www.abfs.com*), based in Fort Smith, Arkansas, and Yellow Transportation (✐*www.myyellow.com*), based in Overland Park, Kansas, are two LTL carriers with convenient Web sites that include online tools for setting up accounts, calculating rates, creating bills of lading, checking transit times, scheduling pickups, and tracking shipments. ABF also has a special site (✐*www.shipabf.com*) for first-time and infrequent freight shippers.

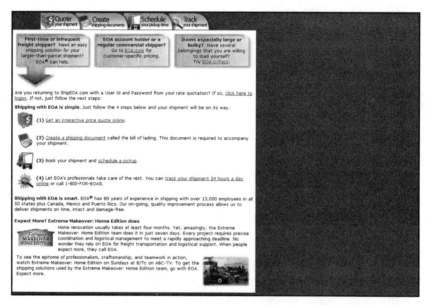

Craters & Freighters, headquartered in Denver, is a specialty freight-handling company that picks up and ships items "too big, fragile, valuable or uniquely shaped for traditional shippers." The company (✐*www.cratersandfreighters.com*) now operates crating and shipping franchise centers in many metropolitan areas. Full insurance is available.

FreightQuote.com, based in Overland Park, Kansas, helps its registered members get shipping estimates from more than fifty freight haulers, including big names such as Roadway, Emery, and Overnite, as well as several ocean-transport companies. A member can go online and compare prices and transit times, pick the best deal and make the shipping arrangements, print freight documents, and keep track of shipments.

Don't rely on a bid from just one freight site. Get bids from several at the same time, and get recommendations from other sellers who auction heavy items such as car parts or arcade games and ship them by truck.

Austin, Texas–based uShip.com takes a very eBay-like approach to shipping. Members can "list shipments once and receive bids from the largest community of feedback-rated movers, carriers, transporters and independent drivers on the planet," the uShip Web site proclaims. When bids are posted, the potential shipper can read each bidder's feedback from previous customers. And some drivers may bid bargain prices so they can pick up some extra cash and fill spaces in truck trailers that otherwise would be empty on a return trip. Shipment is available for special-care items such as antiques and works of art, as well as your late uncle Joe's highly prized jukebox.

Boxes, Boxes, Boxes

Many online auction sellers know a tidy little secret: The world is awash in free boxes. Astute auction sellers scoop them up like loose diamonds. Yes, you can and often should buy sturdy new shipping boxes at office supply stores and from office supply catalogs. But many boxes can be recycled and used for at least one more shipment, saving trees, energy, and money.

Almost any time you get a package in the mail or have a computer or household product delivered, you end up with a box and packaging that can be reused. When people move into or out of a neighborhood, some of their boxes end up piled at the curb or in the alley, awaiting the next trash pickup.

Cardboard boxes and padding materials often spill out of overstuffed Dumpsters behind businesses and grocery stores and are fair game for auction sellers.

ALERT!

Do not pull boxes and packing from inside Dumpsters, unless you have permission. Business owners often earn extra money by recycling cardboard and other shipping materials stored in Dumpsters. "Dumpster diving" is illegal in parts of the United States. You could be arrested and charged with theft or trespassing.

Saving Through Recycling

There are many ways to get free boxes and other shipping materials. Your friends and relatives get merchandise in the mail or have new household items delivered in sturdy boxes. They have to get rid of the containers and packing materials some way. Encourage them to donate the leftover boxes, cushioning material, and peanuts to you, so you can recycle them through your business and help hold down your shipping costs.

Garage sales and yard sales can be surprisingly good sources of useful shipping items. Foam mattress pads, for example, can often be purchased cheaply. The pads can be cut into pieces of many different sizes and used to help cushion paintings, breakable artwork, and other fragile items.

UPS, eBay, and others recommend using corrugated cardboard boxes to ship auction merchandise. According to the Corrugated Packaging Council (CPC), based in Rolling Meadows, Illinois, corrugated cardboard gets its strength and lightness from its easily recognized structure. It employs a layer of arched paper known as "fluting" that is tightly sandwiched between two flat layers known as "liners."

Fragile items can be double-boxed for added protection. Double boxing is also known as overboxing. The most effective way to double-box is to cushion the auction item carefully inside one box, then place that box inside a larger box that will be filled on all sides with cushioning materials such as bubble wrap, Styrofoam peanuts, or foam padding. Do not use shredded or crumpled paper.

Your Tax Dollars at Work

The U.S. Postal Service offers a number of free mailing containers and envelopes to patrons who use Priority Mail or Express Mail. Post office lobbies often have a few boxes displayed as flat pieces of cardboard that you can take home and bend and work into shape for your next Priority Mail shipment. The giveaway boxes are labeled "property of the U.S. Postal Service" and are covered with Priority Mail logos. Don't try to use them to ship something via UPS or FedEx. And don't get clever and try to turn the box inside out, so the Postal Service logos are all inside. The Feds have conveniently printed *Priority Mail* on the bare cardboard, too.

Always send your merchandise in clean, undamaged boxes. You or the buyer may have a difficult time proving a shipping-damage claim if you have used a torn, dented, or warped container. Cardboard cut from damaged boxes can be used to help cushion and strengthen the insides of good boxes.

Insurance: Yes or No?

Many auction sellers let their buyers decide whether they want shipping insurance. But some sellers require their winning bidders to purchase insurance, particularly if the shipment involves delicate electronic, computer, or camera items or fragile art objects. Insurance adds as little as a dollar to the cost of many auction shipments.

Whether you offer or require shipping insurance in your auctions be sure to spell this out very clearly in your listing descriptions. Insurance is inexpensive, especially for items worth less than $200. Many buyers, however, are just looking for the best overall price. Often, they will skip buying insurance and take their chances with the Postal Service or their favorite delivery company.

The Secret of Greyhound Bus

In car-crazy America, most drivers pay scant attention to passenger buses, unless they are stuck behind one in traffic, breathing its exhaust fumes. However, venerable Greyhound buses do more than haul people from place to place. The baggage and cargo holds also carry large packages. Greyhound buses can conveniently get large or heavy auction items from one city to another in one day, at rates far below those charged by UPS, FedEx, DHL, or the Postal Service.

According to Greyhound, packages accepted for bus transportation must be no more than 30 inches by 47 inches by 82 inches in size. Single packages must weigh less than 100 pounds, although packages weighing up to 150 pounds can be accepted for shipment to certain geographical areas specified on the ShipGreyhound.com site.

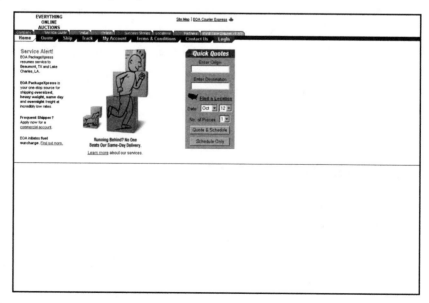

Packing for the Bus

Greyhound posts the following packing restrictions on its online shipping site:

"Fragile items must be packed so as to be separated by corrugated partition, individually wrapped in air-bubble plastic, Styrofoam™ sheets or pellets, or molded plastic. The interior must be completely filled with any of the above materials to prevent the items contained in the shipment from touching each other or the exterior shell of the container."

Greyhound specifically warns that it will not assume responsibility for fragile items that are packed with clothing, linens, or crumpled paper. These "do NOT constitute packaging materials, and will not adequately cushion or protect fragile items," the transportation company emphasizes.

Shipping Out

Every carton you send to a buyer can be a stealth sales pitch that helps bring him or her back to your auction listings. Each time you seal up a box for shipment, slip a thank-you note inside and invite the buyer to view your other auction items. Something this simple can help you build a loyal base of repeat customers eager to bid repeatedly.

The items you sell at online auctions will help determine the success or failure of your business. But how you send merchandise to buyers can make a much bigger difference between barely surviving and steaming ahead toward long-term growth and prosperity. The rules, costs, and methods of shipping will change almost every month. Stay on top of the changing trends. Selling and being paid will be your number-one priority. But shipping the goods to buyers in a safe, timely fashion definitely should be number two.

Chapter 16
Seller Etiquette

You've heard it said, and maybe you've said it yourself: "No more Mister Nice Guy." This attitude can produce effective results in some parts of the business world. However, it is the wrong approach for the quiet, calm flow of online auctions. The spirit and tone of your auctions can leave a lasting impression on buyers. If you put extra emphasis on trouble-free selling, efficient shipping, and quick responses to questions, many buyers will continue to return to your listings.

Remember, Your Business Is a Business

How you treat bidders is crucial to building up and maintaining a loyal customer base for your online auction business. The best approach is to be nice to bidders and competitors alike, even when some of them are not being nice to you. Avoid anger, even if it seems richly deserved. Stay focused on listing items that buyers will find irresistible and on shipping quickly when the winning bidders pay. Experience shows that a genial, laid-back approach can work very well in online auction sales, even for dedicated Power Sellers who are determined to keep expanding their operations.

Profit and Pleasure

In any self-employment business, you can work as long as you want to, as hard as you need to, or as little as you desire, and no boss will nag you, except yourself. *You* define the scope of your workdays. Unfortunately, some people can't handle this much freedom and let their businesses flounder, while they have fun.

Business and pleasure can mix very well in online auction selling. But fun must be balanced with dedication to the daily tasks and details necessary to keep a sales enterprise running. In other words, don't get sloppy with your bookkeeping, don't be slow to answer questions from potential bidders, and definitely don't be slow to ship a winning bidder's purchase.

Try, each day, to give at least passing thought to these necessary questions:

- What will I sell next?
- When will I list it?
- How long should I list it?
- Have I researched similar listings and made notes on descriptions, photographs, and selling prices?
- Do I have the right shipping boxes and packing materials?
- Can I add a payment method or shipping method that will attract more bidders?
- What other types of items can I offer that may help expand my sales base?

You can simplify your work efforts and workdays by auction site automation features, as well as payment services such as PayPal. You can schedule your auction listings so that most of your labor—listing, invoicing, and shipping—involves just two or three days per week. The rest of the time can be spent on enjoying life—and finding more items to sell. Each time you post a group of items to sell, start working immediately toward your *next* auctions.

Your Sales Policy

Having a sales policy can help bidders know exactly what to expect if they bid on one of your items and win. A sales policy typically consists of several statements, including:

- How soon payment is expected from winning bidders
- The payment methods you accept
- The shipping methods you offer
- How merchandise can be returned and what type of credit will be given
- A reminder for potential bidders to contact you if they have questions about the item, payment, or shipping

A basic sales policy might be structured something like this:

> Thank you for bidding. Payment must be made within ten days of close of auction. I accept PayPal, money orders, and cashier's checks. Unfortunately, I am unable to accept escrow payments or personal checks. I offer shipping within the United States only, using Parcel Post, Priority Mail, or UPS. If the item received is materially different than advertised, it can be returned within seven days for a refund of the bidding price. Items returned are subject to inspection before a refund is issued. If you have questions, please contact me via e-mail before bidding.

In the online auction world, there are two schools of thought regarding sales policies: (1) you definitely need one and (2) you probably *don't* need one. Confused? Don't worry. As you build your auction business, you will keep hearing arguments for and against posting strict sales terms with your listings. However, some buyers want to know exactly how long you will give them to send their payment, and other buyers may take their sweet time if no payment deadline is posted.

Having no sales policy at all can leave many things open to assumption or interpretation. For example, a buyer may assume that you will let him use an escrow service or a personal check or use a shipping service that is not available in your area.

Be careful how you present your policies, however. Many potential bidders may go away if you have posted sternly worded requirements, such as: "Escrow payments and personal checks are ABSOLUTELY FORBIDDEN!!!" Instead, use your seller etiquette to create a kinder, gentler statement. For example: "Unfortunately, I cannot accept escrow payments and personal checks. However, I welcome PayPal payments, money orders, and cashier's checks and can ship quickly when you use one of these methods."

Some sellers take a minimalist approach to sales policies. They state only what they will not do, such as use an escrow service or ship overseas. Otherwise, they stay flexible. They use the auction site's tools to list their preferred payment and shipping methods, and they remain open to inquiries from potential buyers who might want to pay with a personal check or use a specific freight carrier.

The good transactions at online auction sites will far outweigh the bad ones, and the risk of a bad transaction can be reduced if you have a clear sales policy. Keep clarity and politeness at the forefront of your sales etiquette.

Internet Courtesy

The Internet is like a big city—a very big city. It has many nice neighborhoods with many good people, and it has a few bad neighborhoods with bad people.

As an eBay seller, you should try to be nice to everyone you encounter online, even if they are not nice to you. It may be difficult to avoid getting angry with a winning bidder who insists on using a payment method or a shipping method that you don't support (and have stated such in your sales policy). If the buyer has good feedback, you may be able to work out a compromise. For example, you could agree to accept his check, if he will agree to let you use one of your preferred shipping methods. Of course, the buyer's check will have to clear before the merchandise can be shipped.

No matter how hard you try, you won't make all of the people happy all of the time. You *will* encounter difficult situations. Fortunately, these will be rare.

When you encounter an angry buyer, do whatever is necessary to avoid negative feedback. Ask her what would fix the situation. Maybe she will settle for a partial refund and the merchandise. If she demands a full refund, including shipping, have her return the merchandise. Send the refund promptly. The one-time loss of $20 or $30 is a small price to pay for avoiding negative feedback that could hurt your sales for a long time.

Personal Contacts

Some sellers try to have as little contact as possible with buyers, before, during, and after an auction. In their view, their listing, photographs, and posted sales policy should be sufficient to answer almost any questions. The better sellers, however, welcome and respond to e-mail inquiries about their merchandise. Some of them also welcome telephone calls when there are questions about listings, shipping methods, payment methods, or returns.

Things can get a bit more complicated if you start meeting a few buyers in person. Some of them may start pumping you for information on your next auctions. They may ask to see your stockpiled merchandise and try to buy some of your items on the spot. If you become friends with some of your buyers, you may be tempted to make them some "special deals" that will end up costing you money and leave other bidders out in the cold.

ALERT!

If you don't want buyers coming to your house or storage and shipping site, don't list auction items that are too big to ship. If you sell items that must be picked up, have at least one friend, relative, or employee present with you, for safety, at the site.

Keep relatives away from your treasures, too. Otherwise, they may ask you to give them certain items, or they may want to buy the items at "cost." You don't want to risk stirring up a big family feud over a Brazilian butterfly tray. One possible compromise: If they see something in your listings that they really want, encourage them to bid on it, and if they win, you can save them the shipping costs by delivering it personally.

Spammer? Spammee?

Just a few years ago, online business owners were encouraged to develop e-mail lists of customers and potential customers. The idea was to send them frequent messages bearing the details of a forthcoming sale or a new product in a catalog. Unfortunately, most people's e-mail boxes soon became overloaded with unwanted sales messages, scam messages, and links to computer viruses. Many computer users started adding e-mail filters and "spam blockers" to stop unwanted messages from reaching their screens. E-mail rapidly lost its sheen as a cheap and easy selling tool.

You still might be tempted to put together an e-mail list to alert buyers who previously have won some of your auctions. But the woman who bought a vintage vase from you last week likely will not care that you have just listed a power screwdriver. In fact, she may get angry at your "junk e-mail," block your future messages, and take you off her Favorite Sellers list. Unless you specialize in a specific type of merchandise, such as 35mm cameras, and deal with a base of regular customers, you may find e-mail lists to be a waste of time and goodwill.

CAN-SPAM

You definitely don't want to put yourself into violation of federal CAN-SPAM statutes. The Controlling the Assault of Non-Solicited Pornography and Marketing (CAN-SPAM) Act became law in 2004 after huge numbers of computer users complained to Congress about the junk e-mail that was pouring into their inboxes. Several leading "spammers" ignored the law and kept sending out unwanted and deceptive e-mail solicitations. So, the Feds cracked down. In 2005, several spammers received prison sentences and large fines, and many computer users noticed a significant drop in the volume of junk e-mail they receive.

Here are the main provisions of CAN-SPAM:

- It bans misleading or false header information in e-mail messages. The From, To, and routing information, including the originating domain name, must be accurate and show who originated the message.
- It prohibits deceptive subject lines. For example, if you sent an e-mail message proclaiming Huge Sale on Computer Hardware, but the text reveals you are only auctioning some "vintage" Y2K mouse pads, you could be in violation of the law.
- It requires that your e-mail advertising message must give recipients a way to opt out of receiving further messages from you. If they tell you they don't want to get any more of these messages from you, you must honor their request. A menu of choices can be used. For example, a recipient may not want to receive advertising messages but continue to receive a monthly newsletter.
- It requires commercial e-mail to be identified as an advertisement, and the message must include the sender's valid physical postal address. This is why you now see—and can easily filter out—messages with ADV: or ***SPAM*** at the front of the subject heading.

Spam has not been eliminated, of course, and unwanted messages still arrive from prolific spamming sites in foreign countries, where the U.S. laws have no jurisdiction. But in America, at least, the anti-spam legislation has slowed the practice of sending out e-mail to millions of recipients at one time.

For your online auction business, the best advice is to forget unfocused, mass-market e-mail campaigns. At any given moment, most people on the planet will not need what you are selling and will resent you for adding more clutter to their inboxes. Focus, instead, on creating carefully worded listing titles, ones that can make a good showing in an auction site's search window. Do such a good job of selling and shipping that buyers will add you to their Favorite list and keep coming back, looking for more things to bid on.

Sales Follow-Ups

The CAN-SPAM law does not prohibit you from staying in touch with e-mail recipients with whom you have a business relationship. If someone buys from you or e-mails with a listing question, a business relationship is established.

Some auction sellers like to e-mail their buyers, thanking them for bidding and letting them know that their package has been shipped. Some sellers also send messages to buyers thanking them for the positive feedback they have received. Some sellers like to follow up with buyers a few weeks later and find out if they are still satisfied with their recent purchase. In messages such as these, it can be appropriate to include a short sales pitch, such as: "By the way, I have just posted another vintage flower vase similar to the one you purchased last month. I invite you to check it out or let a friend know. Thanks!"

Auction buyers tend to search by item name or category, and sometimes they just browse until something catches their attention. The more efficient buyers, however, add certain sellers to their Favorite Seller list and check their auctions regularly for new items. Your goal should be to become a Favorite Seller with as many buyers as possible. Do not, however, send out e-mail that asks or begs them to add you to their list. Earn their respect by listing good items with low starting prices, cost-effective shipping, and quick delivery. Have a clearly stated sales policy. Finally, always maintain a positive attitude, even when you are under verbal assault from a buyer who obviously didn't read the item description and list of flaws before placing the winning bid. Soon, once you have made a few sales, you will begin seeing familiar screen names popping up and leading the lists of bidders.

Chapter 17
Protecting Yourself as a Seller

The online auction world is mostly populated by honest citizens eager for bargains, collectibles, hobby items, and repair parts. Unfortunately, technology-savvy criminals also see online auctions as an opportunity to steal money or merchandise or both. Sellers must stay on guard against schemes while giving good service to legitimate bidders. You cannot rely on "gut instincts" or "an honest face" on the Internet. To keep your business safe, you must practice common sense and make use of the available seller-protection features.

Potential Problems

By some estimates, rip-offs occur in less than one percent of all online auction transactions. This sounds very low, and yet if you auction several hundred items per year, you can almost always count on encountering at least one or two troublesome buyers and maybe a cyber-thief or two during that time.

Using realistic-looking Web sites, cyber-thieves have concocted everything from fake banks to fake escrow companies and fake drop-ship companies, all set up to victimize online auction sellers. This point cannot be stressed enough: *Always verify the physical existence of any bank, escrow company, or drop-ship company before doing business with them online.*

This means finding their phone book listing, calling them, and getting a business-location address—a real location, not a post office box—and verifying that address. You may also need to call a Better Business Bureau office in the same city to see if they have a listing for the company and if any complaints have been lodged against it. Depending on the amount of business you expect to do with an escrow company, drop-shipper, or bank, you may also need to get credit references.

ALERT!

Never rely on Web site postings alone to verify a business. What seems to be a fully functioning online bank in Detroit actually may be a digital front for crooks overseas who are using the site to steal money, credit card information, and auction goods.

Yes, the process can be time-consuming. It may also cost you few dollars in phone calls. But your losses can be severe if you deal with a fraudulent buyer who pays you with counterfeit money orders or counterfeit cashier's checks, and then gets away with your merchandise and gets you in trouble with law enforcement and your creditors.

Payment Protection

These days, sellers are more vulnerable than buyers to losing money in online transactions that go wrong. Indeed, most protections offered by online auction sites are focused on buyers. Some of the programs include PayPal Buyer Protection and the Yahoo! Buyer Protection Program. The focus on buyers is a carryover from the early days of online auction selling when bidders were often the victims of sellers who unloaded shoddy merchandise as "new" or failed to ship what they sold.

As a seller, you must take advantage of any protections offered by an online auction site and know the risks associated with each payment method you accept.

PayPal's Protection for Sellers

PayPal says it takes a three-prong approach to protecting sellers.

1. It screens transactions for fraudulent buyers.
2. It employs a team of chargeback specialists and a resolution center for disputed transactions.
3. It provides a Seller Protection Policy (SPP) that covers eligible sellers for up to $5,000 a year against unauthorized credit card use or fraudulent claims of non-delivery.

The policy only covers sales of "tangible goods" and does not cover claims of merchandise being "not as described" by the seller.

To qualify for coverage, a seller must:

- Have a qualified Verified Business or Premier account with PayPal
- Ship merchandise to the confirmed address on a Transaction Details page
- Use online delivery tracking and keep proof of shipping and delivery
- Require the buyer to sign for receipt of items costing $250 or more

Also, a transaction must be marked as "SPP eligible."

Meanwhile, sellers who qualify for PayPal's Buyer Protection program can display its special logo in their listings. The program's goals are to help new buyers feel more secure and more willing to do business with sellers recognized by PayPal. If there is a dispute between a buyer and a recognized seller, PayPal will encourage the parties to settle the matter themselves. If they cannot, PayPal will decide the outcome, either in favor of the buyer or the seller. To become eligible to display the PayPal Buyer Protection logo, a seller must:

- Have a PayPal Premier or Business account in good standing (in the United States, United Kingdom, Canada, or Germany)
- Have an eBay feedback score of 50 or more and a feedback rating of 98 percent or better
- List items on eBay
- Use PayPal as a payment method during the eBay listing process (only items paid for with PayPal are covered by the program)

Chargebacks

A buyer and a seller sometimes get into a dispute over an item, and the buyer initiates a "chargeback." A chargeback occurs when the buyer asks his credit card company to remove a charge from his account statement. It is the buyer's way of refusing to pay because of a problem with the merchandise or service. The buyer's credit card company will ask him for details on why he is disputing the charge. If they agree with him, the charge is removed, and the seller becomes responsible for several different fees. Also, his merchandise is gone.

Fortunately, chargebacks are not very common in online auction transaction. Credit card companies have tightened some of their chargeback policies, making the process a little harder for buyers. When chargebacks do occur, they often involve honest differences that can be settled through better communication between buyer and seller, or through arbitration. For example, the buyer claims the item was damaged before it was shipped, or she strongly disagrees with the seller's description of the item.

Some chargebacks, however, are fraudulent. For example, the buyer claims he didn't make the purchase and didn't receive the merchandise (even though he did) and asks for the charge against his account to be canceled.

The best ways to protect against chargeback losses include:

- Avoid misunderstandings in your auction listings. Provide clear, concise descriptions, measurements, and photographs. Describe and show the item's flaws as well as features.
- Ship to a verified address and use online delivery tracking and proof of delivery. If the item is expensive, require a delivery signature.
- If your auction item is fragile, consider videotaping the packing process. Show the undamaged item being placed into its shipping box and surrounded with protective packing materials. Some sellers shoot a continuous tape of themselves packing a box, sealing it, and printing the shipping label, and then driving the box to the post office or shipping center and dropping it off.
- Be sure to post a clear return policy in all of your auction listings. You may wish to restate the policy in each invoice and e-mail you send to buyers.
- Keep copies of auction listings, online tracking information, and e-mail from buyers.
- Save every bit of information related to a buyer refund. Some fraudulent buyers may try to file a chargeback after you have refunded their money.

PayPal's Resolution Center tries to help sellers and buyers reach an agreeable settlement in a dispute. If a buyer has paid you via PayPal with a credit card and then filed a chargeback, PayPal says it will "ask you for information regarding the transaction and use it as evidence when disputing the chargeback with the credit card company."

FACT

A buyer who leaves positive feedback for you can still file a chargeback several weeks or months after an auction. Also, a chargeback can be filed even if you state clearly in your listing that all sales are final and returns are not allowed.

While a chargeback is being investigated, an amount of money equal to the disputed total is placed on temporary hold in the seller's account. Investigation of a chargeback can take up to seventy-five days or longer, and PayPal warns, "the decision is ultimately made by the credit card company and PayPal cannot control the outcome."

Bottom line: The better you cover yourself *before* a chargeback occurs, the better chance you will have of proving your case if one is filed.

Shipping Protection

Rule number one: Never send merchandise to a buyer without using delivery tracking. Even if the buyer is just across town or in the next county or parish, spend a little money on proof of shipping and delivery verification. A buyer who claims she didn't receive her purchase will not have much of a case if you have the tracking and delivery information showing that she did.

The postal service and major delivery services (such as UPS, FedEx, and DHL) offer online shipment tracking.

For expensive items, an online escrow service such as Escrow.com can protect sellers against claims of non-delivery. The seller is not paid until the buyer receives and approves the merchandise.

For transactions exceeding $1,000, PayPal recommends getting and keeping "an online receipt in the form of a signature from the recipient as proof of shipment."

Deadbeat Bidders

In the early days of online auctions, sellers were plagued by seemingly eager bidders who would push up the price of a listed item and then never show up to pay for what they had won. On eBay and other sites, feedback can be posted for buyers as well as sellers, and bidders with bad ratings can be blocked or have their bids canceled. As a result, the numbers of deadbeat bidders have dwindled. But they haven't totally disappeared. You will still encounter bidders who win an auction and refuse to pay. You can block them from bidding again on your listings under their current screen name.

You will probably lose your listing fees for the unpaid item, but you may be able to recover at least some of the sales fee that the online auction site collects for each completed sale. On eBay, you can file for a Final Value Fee credit. This is the fee the seller must pay after a bidder wins an auction.

Also with eBay, if a high buyer doesn't pay, the seller may have the option to make a free Second Chance Offer to runner-up bidders.

Individual and Organized Buyer Fraud

Sellers get the most focus in online auction fraud discussions. Most fraud complaints involve (1) sellers who don't send the goods that buyers have paid for, and (2) sellers who send items that don't live up to the descriptions in auction listings. However, fraudulent buyers are also on the prowl, constantly looking for opportunities to steal money and merchandise from honest and naive sellers.

Sometimes, you may deal with individual opportunists who are trying to trick you. Other times, you may be going head-to-head with organized crime. However, if you stay alert and know the warning signs of buyer fraud, you can protect your auction sales operations, your valuable feedback ratings, and yourself against identity theft.

Individual Fraud

Unfortunately, not all winning bidders are model citizens. Some of them will:

- Demand that you accept a payment method you don't want to use
- Claim that you didn't ship the merchandise and demand a refund
- Claim that you deliberately shipped damaged merchandise and demand a refund
- Return an item similar to the one you shipped (but not the same one) and demand a refund

If you have stated clearly in your sales policy that only certain payment methods are accepted and the buyer refuses to use any of them, you can notify the online auction site and not complete the transaction. For example, you can click on eBay's Dispute Console link to report an unpaid item dispute and also file for a refund of eBay's Final Value Fee that it charges a seller after a bidder wins his auction.

To handle claims that you didn't ship the merchandise or that you sent something that was broken, you may have to deal with the U.S. Postal Service, credit card companies, and online auction site personnel.

If small amounts of money are involved and you have no proof that the buyer is trying to commit a fraud, it may be easier to surrender the refund and avoid a long-running dispute. You can block the user from bidding again in your listings, and you can try to do a better job of screening bidders before they become winning bidders.

To set Buyer Requirements for future listings, go to the Buyer Requirements page. On this page, you can:

- Block buyers who registered in countries to which you don't wish to ship
- Block buyers who have a feedback score of –1, –2, –3 or lower
- Block buyers who received strikes for two Unpaid Items within the past month

There is also an option to block a bidder who is winning or has won a certain number of items in the past ten days. This option can be applied to all bidders or only to those with feedback scores of 5 or less. Yet another option on the Buyer Requirements page enables you to block bids from any buyer who does not have a PayPal account. This feature is very popular with sellers who accept PayPal only.

If a winning bidder makes a fraudulent payment, contact a local law enforcement agency and the police department in the buyer's location. Notify the online auction site as well.

Sellers of expensive items often encounter a buyer tactic that is forbidden on many auction sites, yet still occurs with predictable regularity. Soon after posting a new listing, a seller may get an e-mail message from a potential buyer offering to buy the item for a certain price if the seller will end the auction right after she bids. Sometimes, the price is attractive. But experience shows the under-the-table bid frequently is less than half the price that ultimately wins the bidding. The potential buyer knows the item's real value and is trying to scoop it up cheaply so *she* can sell it for the higher price.

Organized Fraud

Organized crime groups in Eastern Europe, Africa, and other areas have become enthusiastic users of the Internet to perpetrate frauds in other countries. Online auction buyers and sellers have often been their prime targets. Some of their scams involve:

- Fake auction support sites
- "Accidental" overpayment
- Fake escrow companies
- Fake drop-ship companies
- Fake online banks

If you sell and ship items to overseas customers, watch out for the following warning signs of buyer fraud, as identified by participants in eBay's international shipping forum:

- A buyer asks you to end the auction early and offers to pay more than the current high bid.
- The winning bidder is in Indonesia, Nigeria, or Romania and wants to pay with a Western Union money order. Unfortunately, counterfeiters in these countries have created thousands of fake money orders.
- The winning bidder asks you repeatedly to send the item before you have received the payment.

- The winning bidder wants you to ship overseas FedEx overnight (so they'll have the merchandise before your bank discovers their payment is bogus).
- A potential buyer contacts you via e-mail and asks you to sell the item to them off the auction site.
- The winning bidder wants to pay with a credit card but wants to use your merchant account, rather than pay through the auction site.

ALERT!

Be wary of brand-new buyers with very slow feedback scores, such as zero. All buyers and sellers start at zero and work their way up. However, if someone opens a buyer's account one day and starts bidding on very expensive items the next day, proceed with caution. When creating listings on eBay, Yahoo! and some other auction sites, you can screen out bidders who don't meet minimum feedback levels.

Specific Types of Buyer Fraud

As a seller, in order to protect yourself against buyer fraud, you need to be able to recognize and watch out for different types and perpetrators of fraud. Some of these include fake support sites, "accidental" overpayment, fake companies, and fake banks.

Fake Auction Support Sites

It isn't hard for computer criminals to create a fake Web site that mimics a real company's Internet operation. Users of eBay and PayPal get frequent e-mail from cyber-thieves trying to get them to click on a Web link so they can "fix" an urgent problem with their account. If you do click on the link, you are taken to a site that looks very much like a page within the real eBay or PayPal. Online auction veterans know these sites are set up specifically to steal credit card numbers, passwords, and other personal information. Yet, online auction newcomers often are fooled and become victims of identity theft and credit card theft.

"Accidental" Overpayment

If you accept money orders from winning bidders, be very careful of the "accidental" overpayment ploy. A number of auction sellers have been hit hard by this scam. For example, suppose you have listed an item and gotten a winning bid of $18. The buyer sends you a money order—oops, for $180. He says he can't get a replacement and pleads that he needs the merchandise soon. Just cash the money order and mail him a refund when you send the merchandise, he suggests. The money order looks good. The bank accepts it and credits the money to your account. So, you buy a $162 money order and send it to the "hapless" buyer. Unfortunately, a few weeks later, you get a message from your bank. The money order the buyer sent you was counterfeit. You now owe the bank $180 and fees. Meanwhile, the crook has happily spent the $162 you sent him, and he's enjoying or reselling the free merchandise he got from his scheme.

ALER

Under Federal Reserve Regulation CC, a bank must make the funds from a bank draft or cashier's check available to you within forty-eight hours. But the average bank draft or cashier's check can take two weeks or longer to clear. It may take several more weeks to discover that the instrument is counterfeit. Don't spend the money from a bank draft or cashier's check until you're sure it's good.

Never accept overpayments from buyers. They know the winning bid price, and they should know the shipping costs from your listing or e-mail contact. If they can't do the math and get within a few dollars of the correct total, or if they claim poor English language skills and misunderstood your listing, a red flag should go up.

Fake Escrow Companies

Criminals sometimes set up phony online escrow companies and victimize sellers who are new or too busy to do a verification check. The scam works like this: Your high bidder says he wants to use an online escrow company and gives you a link to one that he says has done a good job for him in the past. So you go to the link, fill out the transaction forms and receive confirmation that the buyer indeed has put the agreed price into escrow. Trustingly, you ship the merchandise to the "buyer." After the inspection period is over, you go back to the online auction site—and it's gone. So is your high-dollar merchandise. Unknowingly, you shipped it to the address of a motel, and the "buyer" checked out soon after he got your package.

Online auction sites generally recommend only one online escrow company: Escrow.com. If a buyer refuses to use that link and says she wants to deal through another site instead, be certain that it is a real, bonded escrow company. Notify the online auction site if you suspect that you are dealing with a fraudulent buyer.

Fake Drop-Ship Companies

Many online auction sellers use drop-ship companies as a source of salable merchandise. The seller picks an item from the drop-shipper's catalog and lists it for auction on eBay or Yahoo! or another site. The drop-shipper usually supplies a photograph and a description of the item. When the winning bidder pays, the seller keeps the profit but sends the rest of the money to the drop-ship company to pay for the catalog item. The drop-ship company then sends the item to the buyer, with the seller's return address on the box. Numerous legitimate drop-ship companies are online, offering auction sellers everything from cameras to purses.

Unfortunately, cyber-crooks also can set up phony drop-ship companies, and these sometimes victimize auction sellers who don't do any verification checking. The crime usually happens like this: An auction seller decides to try using drop-shipping to increase his sales. So, he goes online and starts looking at drop-shipper Web sites. One site catches his eye. The prices in the catalog seem very good. He believes he can auction the items for a decent profit. So, he opens an account on the spot, gives them a credit card number and other personal information, and picks an item from the catalog to list for auction.

The winning bidder, however, never receives the merchandise after paying for it and files a chargeback.

The online world is also alive with distribution schemes involving inter-mediaries and advisers who, for a fee, will try to act as your go-between when dealing with drop-ship companies. It may be best to avoid them all. Work directly with reputable drop-shippers or find other sources of merchandise to sell.

Fake Banks

Astute criminals with computers can create seemingly real online banks with little effort. Fake banks have been used in schemes involving counterfeit cashier's checks. The seller gets a handsome winning bid and receives an official-looking cashier's check apparently issued by a bank. The seller goes online to the financial institution's Web site to verify that the check is good. Naturally, it is. The crooks have set it up that way. The unsuspecting seller ships the merchandise, deposits the check, and lives happily ever after, until his bank contacts him a few weeks later with the double-whammy—the check was phony and he is now part of a criminal investigation.

QUESTION?

Who can I contact if I become a victim of online fraud?
Contact the nearest law enforcement agency and the Internet Fraud Complaint Center (IFCC) via its online site. The IFCC is a partnership between the Federal Bureau of Investigation and the National White Collar Crime Center.

Most of the time, online auction transactions will proceed without any problem whatsoever. Still, you must stay on guard. The best way to protect yourself as a seller is to keep common sense well ahead of profit motives. Never forget that the online world is alive with illusions and traps, as well as real wonders and conveniences. What you see may be a lot less than you will get, no matter how good and convincing the Web site appears. Be persistent and thorough when you check out the background (and the *actuality!*) of online escrow sites, drop-shippers, and banks. Read the feedback of winning bidders, too. Even feedback can be faked. Never take anything for granted on the Internet.

Chapter 18
Feedback and Ratings

In the online auction world, buyers and sellers use a system known as feedback to publicly describe and rate their transactions with each other. Feedback is sometimes given other names, such as buyer ratings and seller ratings. Feedback scores are posted for all site users to see, and they provide a reasonably reliable means for keeping buyer-seller interactions fair and honest. Good feedback scores should be carefully nurtured and protected. They are the main measures of your reputation and your trustworthiness as an online auction seller and buyer.

What Is Auction Site Feedback?

Most online auction sites have a public forum where buyers and sellers can rate each other on how well they have upheld their ends of a transaction. Pierre Omidyar, eBay's founder, generally is credited with creating the first rating system in 1995. He called it Feedback Forum. An evolved form of the system is still in use today.

Soon after feedback systems began appearing on auction sites, however, unscrupulous sellers and buyers figured out ways to manipulate their scores. They created inflated positive ratings for themselves by bidding on and winning their own auctions under different user names. Some of them used their self-generated positive feedback scores to lure buyers into auction fraud schemes. For example, in one auction-related crime, laptop computers were listed for bid and had very attractive Buy It Now prices. Buyers quickly snapped up the "bargain" computers and rushed their payments to the seller. A couple of weeks later, when their computers still had not been delivered, the buyers started making inquiries and discovered that the seller had disappeared, taking their money with him. They had completely believed his posted feedback and had made no other efforts to verify his status.

A decade later, safeguards are in place to help make auction feedback systems more honest and secure. But feedback systems still are not foolproof, and feedback postings should be viewed as just one part of the buyer-seller trust equation. Online auction sites frequently urge potential bidders to do the following:

- Read all of the feedback comments posted for a seller—good, bad, or neutral—before placing a bid.
- Contact some of the members who have left positive, negative, or neutral feedback. Ask for updates on how they feel about doing business with a particular seller.
- E-mail the seller a question or two about the item that interests you. An honest seller likely will give you quick, detailed responses.
- Be sure you understand the seller's preferred payment methods, return policy, and shipping policy. Again, send questions to the seller if you need clarification.

Some of the investigative processes may be too time-consuming for small items costing less than $50. Frankly, most buyers just glance at a seller's positive feedback count and feedback percentage. If a negative rating has been posted within the past twelve months, they will often go straight to it and make their bid/don't bid decision based on what the disgruntled buyer reported and what the seller posted in response.

ALERT!

Before bidding on any item listed as "rare," "vintage," or "collectible," research its market value carefully. Scrutinize the seller's auction-site record and contact the seller with questions. A simple search of current and closed auction listings may turn up dozens of similar "rare" items that have drawn little or no bidder interest.

Take the time and effort necessary to protect yourself, particularly when expensive merchandise is involved. Use the steps presented earlier to do a thorough check of the seller's reputation, record, and sales and return policies. Also, know *what* you are trying to win.

How Does Feedback Work?

Online auction sites try to simplify the process of leaving feedback for a seller or buyer. Typically, there is a Leave Feedback link somewhere on the page confirming the successful end of an auction.

Sellers often click on their Leave Feedback link as soon as they receive payment from the buyer, and the payment clears at the bank. If the buyer pays with PayPal, his feedback from an inexperienced seller may be posted within a matter of minutes. However, a seller should *never* give feedback as soon as payment is received, even when using PayPal.

A transaction is *not* over until the buyer has received the item, inspected it, and left positive feedback for the seller. That is when the seller should leave feedback for the buyer.

Feedback is a seller's only real leverage when problems arise. *Never* give it up early. Otherwise, you may leave positive feedback for a buyer whose shipment then is lost or broken, and they respond by posting negative feedback for you. Hold your feedback until the buyer receives a shipment, so you can have the opportunity to correct a problem, if one arises, before it escalates into hard feelings.

On eBay, the Feedback Forum's rating system works like this:

- Your feedback score is increased by one point each time a positive comment and rating is posted for you by a different individual member.
- For each negative comment and rating posted for you by a different individual member, one point is subtracted from your score.
- Nothing is added to your feedback total if someone posts a neutral comment and rating after dealing with you.

For example, "si8ai9 (25)" means that the eBay member using the screen name *si8ai9* has received positive feedback postings from twenty-five other eBay members. Below that rating total, another line will express the feedback score as a percentage. If twenty-five positives and one negative were posted, the positives would be divided by the total number of feedback postings (26) to produce a positive feedback score of 96.2 percent.

ALERT!

If a seller has received as few as two negative ratings over the past twelve months, many potential buyers will not bid on his items. Likewise, if a buyer has negative feedback—for not paying, for example—a seller can cancel the buyer's bid and block her from bidding again on his auctions.

Why Is Feedback So Important?

In the traditional brick-and-mortar world, a customer walks into your store, selects an item from a shelf, and brings it to the checkout counter. He may ask you a question about the item, and to help close the sale, you may tell him that if the item doesn't fix his problem, he can bring it back for a refund, as long as it hasn't been damaged. During the transaction, you and he may also have a brief conversation about the weather or a recent news event or discover that you both attended the same high school.

Levels of trust can be created quickly when buyer and seller are face-to-face in a well-kept store. Afterward, the buyer may tell a friend: "They had exactly what I needed at the XYZ Store. It was on sale for ten percent off, and they were very helpful. I'm going back next Saturday to look at their power tools." Your store has just gotten some positive feedback, but the only way you may find out is if the customer does return to shop again or if his friend drops in and says: "I hear you're having a ten-percent-off sale."

Positive Feedback in the Online World

Transactions generally are much more anonymous in the online world. You go to a Web site, click on an item to read its description, click on another link to buy it, then key in your credit card information and shipping address, and finally click on a sales confirmation link.

You may be buying from someone on the other side of the planet or on the next block in your neighborhood. In any case, the digital store you are visiting is simply a collection of images, text, and data-entry boxes, all floating in cyberspace. You can't walk through the front door and touch the merchandise. You can't watch the merchant's face and body language and how she handles other customers and get any sense of whether she is trustworthy or not. You simply must trust that the store is "there." Unfortunately, cyber-thieves sometimes have set up virtual stores that do nothing but steal money and credit card information.

At online auction sites, positive feedback postings help buyers trust that they can get an honest deal from a particular seller. They can send e-mail to the seller and try to get a better feel for how he runs his business and treats his bidders. But the clearest measure of an online auction seller's reputation is what his previous customers have said about him.

Meanwhile, astute sellers know that having a good feedback score can often help them get higher prices for their auction merchandise. Buyers feel more confident about bidding when the seller has a strong positive percentage and many dozens of winning bidders have left glowing reviews.

Buyer feedback ratings are also important to sellers. Good, positive scores give them confidence that their winning bidders will be honest customers who meet the sales terms, pay on time, and don't make outrageous demands or false claims.

The Power of Positive Feedback

Your reputation as an auction seller or buyer absolutely will depend on how others rate their dealings with you. Two negatives *never* make a positive in the online auction world. Each negative simply lowers your posted score as a seller or buyer. Each negative also makes others wary of doing any transactions with you. Experienced buyers typically do not place a bid until they have checked a seller's feedback score and carefully read the comments previous customers have posted.

Cautious sellers, meanwhile, are equally mindful of bidders' feedback scores. On some sites, such as Yahoo! Auctions, a seller can set up an auction to reject bids automatically from any buyer whose feedback score is below a predetermined level.

Just a few negative feedback postings can render a seller's screen name or buyer's screen name virtually useless on an online auction site. However, an affected seller or buyer can often open a new account and quickly start over with a new screen identification and a clean feedback slate.

For a buyer, building or rebuilding a high feedback percentage is quick and easy. Just make a few winning bids on small items where the listings have drawn almost no interest and are about to expire. The grateful sellers will give you good feedback. Have the items shipped the cheapest way possible to hold down costs. Of course, it is best to do this with merchandise you actually want or can put to use, but you could put the items up for auction. You could try to turn a profit from them by creating better photos or more interesting descriptions than the previous seller used.

The Perils of Retaliation

One of the key flaws of feedback systems is that they are usually wide open to retaliation. Suppose you post negative comments and a negative rating for a seller who has taken two months to ship your purchase and who sent it in a box with inadequate padding. In return, the seller may post negative feedback for you, claiming that you didn't provide correct shipping information and didn't answer e-mail or were rude and refused to use his preferred payment method. When other sellers and buyers become aware of this exchange, they may not be able to judge who is right and who is wrong. So, they try to avoid both of you.

Once negative feedback is posted, it usually cannot be edited or removed, for legal reasons. However, eBay does have a mutual feedback withdrawal procedure, for situations in which both the buyer and the seller agree that the negative feedback is no longer appropriate. The withdrawn feedback remains in both members' profiles, but it not included when calculating feedback scores.

Sometimes, for a buyer, it is safer to walk away from a bad encounter and post no feedback at all, particularly if the troubled transaction was small. For a seller, meanwhile, it is often better to head off negative feedback by reaching some kind of agreement with the buyer. Will a partial refund satisfy her? Or does she want a full refund? Offer to buy back the item and pay for the return postage as well, particularly if small amounts of money are involved.

Understanding Feedback

Often you have to read between the lines to understand what a buyer's or seller's feedback comments really mean. A seller or buyer may have a perfect rating (100%), yet there may be notes of caution or even red flags written into some of the "positive" feedback. Also, a buyer may post negative feedback prematurely when a shipment or a payment is delayed. Later, when the errant shipment or payment suddenly shows up, there is no way to reverse the outburst. The seller or buyer who received the negative feedback may be able to post a response. Or, the buyer and seller may be able to "withdraw" the feedback by mutual agreement. The "withdrawn" feedback will remain visible to others, but a notice will be included that it has been withdrawn by mutual agreement, and it will no longer count in the recipient's feedback scores.

Help-screen discussions of feedback on eBay include the following caution: "Feedback cannot be edited or removed once it has been left. It becomes a permanent part of a member's eBay record and is viewable by the entire eBay community. Members could be held legally responsible for damages to a member's reputation if a court were to find that the remarks constitute libel or defamation."

If remarks fall within the realm of "feedback abuse" described on the Feedback Abuse, Withdrawal and Removal page, eBay can remove the feedback. A few of the reasons that can trigger that removal include:

- A court has ruled that the feedback is "slanderous, libelous, defamatory or otherwise illegal."
- The feedback includes personal identifying information about an eBay member, such as real name and address.
- The feedback mentions investigations by eBay, PayPal, or a law enforcement agency.
- A bidder whose sole intent was to leave negative feedback left the remarks.

If an eBay member posts more than one negative rating for another member, the multiple reports count as only one negative. The same is true if a member leaves more than one positive rating. A feedback score reflects the *number* of individual members who have had dealings with that particular seller or buyer and left comments summing up their opinions of the experience.

Feedback Wars

A buyer who works hard at maintaining a good reputation with sellers will often receive exuberant feedback such as: "Paid instantly with PayPal! Very Highly Recommended! A++++++++++." Meanwhile, a conscientious seller always likes to get buyer feedback such as this: "Great communications and shipping! Nice product! Will buy again!" Sometimes, however, something causes a buyer and seller to be at odds with each other, and their disagreement escalates into exchanges of negative feedback.

To avoid such a battle, an unhappy buyer may use positive feedback to express irritation with a seller while cautioning others about dealing with him. For example: "Good merchandise but dirty. Shipping was very slow." If you read some of the seller's other feedback and see similar comments about tardy shipping or dusty merchandise, you will know what to expect if you bid and win one of his auctions. A seller who is unhappy with a buyer may also post her complaint in an otherwise "positive" feedback message: "Money orders are inconvenient & cost me a fee. But thanks for bidding!" Negative feedback immediately affects a seller's or buyer's ratings and reputation. It also invites retaliatory feedback. It is much harder to retaliate against positive feedback, even when it contains a "negative" message. However, the feedback recipient is usually allowed to respond to comments in positive, negative, or neutral feedback.

ALERT!

The negative feedback posted on a particular seller or buyer may be just the tip of the digital iceberg. Some buyers and sellers walk away from bad experiences and post no feedback at all. They don't want to invite retaliatory feedback from the other party—or from some of his friends.

Using Feedback to Buy and Sell

Some sellers loudly—and too proudly—trumpet their positive feedback ratings in big letters in their auction text. Buyers can't do this and often are turned off by such overt ratings boastings. They'd usually rather judge for themselves, by studying the photographs and descriptions the seller has posted for his goods and by reading feedback from other buyers.

If you are a newcomer to an online auction site and want to start selling things, you very likely will need to be a buyer first. Bid on and win a few inexpensive items, so you can build up some positive feedback on the site. This feedback will encourage others to bid once you post your first listings. If you really don't need the items you buy to establish your feedback foothold, you can auction them later.

For sellers, the general rule is: Do whatever it takes to avoid negative feedback from an unhappy buyer. Try to communicate with them and find out exactly why they are unhappy. Ask what will satisfy them and try to meet that desire or request. If necessary, offer a partial refund or offer to buy the merchandise back at the winning bid price. Pay for the return shipping, too, even if that is not your normal sales policy. Never get into a feedback war and negative feedback for an item that brought you $20. It will cost you a lot more than that to rebuild your good reputation.

Influencing Feedback

You can influence what kind of feedback you will receive, but you should always use indirect methods. For example, the best way for a seller to influence a buyer's feedback is to strive to be honest and prompt in all transactions. Answer questions quickly and completely. Ship goods in clean, well-cushioned packaging, and never try to score a few extra bucks by over-charging for postage or delivery.

Meanwhile, the easiest way for a buyer to influence seller feedback is to make contact with the seller soon after the auction ends and pay immediately using one of the seller's preferred payment methods. Also, if the seller says he only uses the U.S. Postal Service for his deliveries, don't insist on DHL or FedEx. The Postal Service may be the seller's only convenient means for shipping. The same applies to payment methods. It may be difficult or inconvenient for the seller to cash a money order, and he may have to pay a fee when he does.

To get the best feedback as a buyer, pay close attention to the seller's preferences and try to stick to them. If you need to use another payment or shipping method, contact the seller *before* bidding, briefly explain your situation, and ask if he can accept your best payment or shipping method. Often a seller will say yes, and you will get good feedback for your courtesy and consideration.

QUESTION?

What is feedback manipulation?
When a seller or buyer tries to directly influence the feedback rating she will receive, that is called "feedback manipulation." Online auction sites generally forbid the practice, but it still happens.

To get the best feedback as a seller, treat the buyer as you would want others to treat you. Only sell merchandise that you have checked thoroughly. Don't skimp on the box and packing materials, even if it costs you a little more than you listed in the shipping charges. Get the goods out the door and into the shipping channels as soon as possible, and let the buyers know their packages are on the way.

Feedback Manipulation to Avoid

Sellers and buyers want and need the best feedback possible. Unfortunately, some of them try coercion to guarantee that they will get a good rating. For example, after you win an auction and pay a seller, he may e-mail you: "I will leave positive feedback for you after you leave positive feedback for me." Or, the message may be less direct: "Thank you for bidding. I'm very proud of my 100% seller rating." The hint, of course, is that you should do nothing to cause any threats to that record.

Other common forms of feedback manipulation include:

- Directly or indirectly creating positive feedback for yourself
- Posting negative feedback for others by using secondary accounts or willing associates
- Leaving unwarranted negative feedback for a buyer or seller whom you dislike or view as a rival

Yahoo's auction site includes a warning against trying to manipulate feedback by "leaving negative feedback if a user fails to do something that is unrelated to the auction." The warning does not explain what that "something" is. But a buyer, miffed at losing a desired object at the last second to a bid sniper, might decide to take her anger out on you by winning another of your items, and then posting negative feedback about the auction she lost.

When used properly, feedback helps minimize fraud, and it shines a clear spotlight that helps separate the good buyers and sellers from the questionable and the bad. Your goal should be to get and give the best feedback possible, while protecting the reputation of your business. The law of averages says you will never please all of the people all of the time, especially in online auctions. Problems will arise, and negative feedback situations will happen. But these can be overcome with knowledge, effort, time, and a positive attitude.

Chapter 19
Additional Online Opportunities

After a few months or years of online auctions, you may yearn for something "bigger," such as a Web-based store where you have more control over how you display and sell your merchandise and over how and where you can advertise. Once you reach this point, resist all urges to jump at the first appealing offer. First, determine which areas of business suit you best. Get trained to run a bigger enterprise and find the help you need to make the store happen. Your do-it-all-yourself days are now behind you.

Create Your Own Web Business

Virtually anytime you sign on to your e-mail account, you can be bombarded with "opportunities" to start a Web-based business or buy a Web-based franchise. Some of the offers clearly are scams. A few may sound appealing and actually may be legitimate offers. However, don't buy anything yet. Don't sign contracts, don't pay money, don't commit, and don't agree to anything. Back away from the keyboard and start taking the time to figure things out. Ask yourself these four important questions:

- What kind of business do I really want to be in?
- What materials, equipment, permits, and facilities will I need to get into that business?
- Do I have the necessary skills, or do I need more training?
- Do I know how to find and hire the help I will need to set up and maintain a Web-based store?

You can create and launch a Web-based store very quickly if you are willing to pay to get help from consultants and service companies. But if you are not ready to run that store, keep it stocked, advertise it, handle the needs and complaints of customers, *and* manage long-range planning, you may be rushing headlong into a costly disaster. Take your time; take more-than-enough time to figure out your goals, qualifications, and needs. The world will not run out of things to sell or customers willing to buy them while you are trying to get your store organized and online.

How to Advertise on the Web

Online auction sites generally do not let you add links to a Web site in your auction listings. So, your auction experiences may have given you little or no experience in how advertising is purchased and placed on the Web. The paramount rules are to (1) help search engines such as Google and Yahoo! find your business as easily as possible and to (2) position its information as near the top as possible in displayed listings. For example, if your online store sells or auctions specialized home-and-garden items, the name and URL of your business might show up at the 19,000th position in a list of 1,136,000 Web sites with "home and garden" somewhere in their descriptive text. Of course, even the most dedicated people using Google or Yahoo! to find a home-and-garden supplier probably will not scroll down below the first 100 or so businesses in the list. Therefore, your enterprise will remain out of sight and out of mind for them unless they accidentally find it while browsing the Web.

Building Your Link Popularity

Owners of small businesses often adopt a simple and free but time-consuming technique to improve their visibility on search engines. They arrange *link exchanges* with other online businesses. Web sites typically have link pages or link lists where the names and URLs of other businesses can be displayed. In a link exchange, the owners of two different Web sites (not in competition with each other!) agree to add each other's site name and site address to their link list. The most apparent goal is for a visitor to one site to find the link to the other site and click on it. Each Web site thus helps the other generate Web traffic and business.

However, search engines also use *link popularity* as one of their guidelines for determining where to position a listing. Therefore, the positioning of your Web site can vary from search to search. But the more links you can establish, the more often the search engines will see the name and URL of your business, and they will give it a higher "page ranking" when responding to someone's search request.

Exchanging Links

There are at least three general ways to exchange Web site links:

- Contact other Web site owners and ask for an exchange.
- Use a link exchange directory.
- Hire a link exchange service.

Most link exchanges are set up via e-mail. You simply send a message to another business briefly describing your business and giving its URL. You ask the recipient for permission to post his business's URL on your links page, and you ask if he would be willing to post a link to your business on his links page. The drawback to this approach, of course, is time. It can take many hours just to find some appropriate sites, send the e-mail, and do the work necessary to add the approved links to your Web site.

Internet search engines often use processes called "spiders" to go to Web sites and follow the outward links posted on their links pages. These outward links are added to the total results that help determine where a particular Web address will be displayed in a search list.

Adding your business name and URL to *link directories* will not eliminate all the work of creating link exchanges. But the link directories can help spread the visibility of your Web site and indicate greater link popularity to search engines.

Some sites, such as Iconcave.com and Link2Me.com, operate free link exchange directories where you can post the URL for your Web-based business. Often, but not always, you are expected to add the link exchange directory's URL to your links page in return.

Hiring a *link exchange service* may be a more efficient and cost-effective way to add good links and increase your site's link popularity, but be careful. Many of these services are available on the Web. Research them carefully before committing any money. Typically, they will charge fees in return for providing links to certain numbers of sites that are relevant to your business. The more you pay, the more links you will get. Often, you will not be required to create any return links on your site, but you may wish to, so the spiders from the search engines will keep finding them each week and including them in your link popularity total.

Some link exchange services can provide you with links to companies that consistently have very high page rankings in the major search engines. You likely will have to pay, however, to keep the link active, and it won't be cheap. Monthly fees ranging from $50 to $5,000 per link are not uncommon.

FACT

When setting up link exchanges or using link directories, focus on getting your business listed among other sites that have related content. Search engines look for these connections when calculating where in a search results list to display your URL. Beware of so-called link farms, however. Link farms offer hundreds or thousands of immediate links that may have nothing to do with your business. These links can hurt, not help, your search engine rankings.

Ways to Advertise on the Web

For several years, the hot trend in Web advertising was to send text advertisements using e-mail addresses purchased in bulk. Sometimes, the lists contained hundreds of thousands or even millions of contacts. But it was blind scatter-shooting, and most of the sales pitches reached uninterested or unqualified addressees or inactive accounts. Still, companies persisted, because it was cheap and easy to keep pumping out the messages. Finally, weary spam recipients starting resisting by blocking the messages, responding with phony information, or sending back hundreds of replies to overload the senders' systems. Anti-spam software was quickly improved and became readily available. Meanwhile, complaints to Congress led to legislation severely restricting the use of bulk e-mail messages.

Along with link exchanges, other methods are now popular for advertising products and services on the Web. Some of these methods include:

- Banner advertisements
- Banner exchanges
- Pop-up and pop-under advertisements
- Advertising in online directories
- Pay-per-click advertising

Unfortunately, Web-based advertising can get very expensive very quickly, especially if you attempt several different methods at one time to get the word out about your business. Do not commit to any method of online advertising until you have studied it carefully and determined how it might actually bring in enough sales to pay for itself and generate a profit.

Banner Advertising

Banner ads are big, colorful notices that stretch across most of the top or bottom of a Web page. For example, on a Web site devoted to screenwriters, a banner ad for a bookstore may appear in a box across the very top, while another banner ad for a writing seminar may be positioned at the bottom of the page. Some of the advertisements may be static displays of text and images. Others may use flashing words, changing pictures, or other techniques to grab the viewer's attention.

Unless you have a background in advertising, you will probably need help to design and post an effective banner advertisement for your business on other Web sites. If you can't find a skilled friend or college student willing to do the work for the experience or a future reference, you may have to hire a Web content creator who specializes in advertising. You will find no shortage of people willing to sell you their services. (For example, a Yahoo! search of the term *banner ad design* turns up more than 10 million hits.) The usual rules apply: Ask to see samples, ask for—and follow up—on referrals to satisfied customers, and ask for pricing.

Some online services promise they can create effective banner advertisements in a matter of hours. At least one site, BuyerZone.com, lets you post information about the type of banner ad, the assistance you need, and how quickly you need it. You will then receive bids from companies wanting to do the work.

Pop-Ups and Unders

For many years, online advertisers have been blitzing Web users' screens with ads that automatically pop up on top of a Web page display or hide beneath it until the page is closed. Many computer users have learned to hate these ads as much as they hate spam e-mail messages. Software to block pop-up and pop-under ads is now popular, and Microsoft added similar ad-blocking features to its XP operating system in 2004. Campaigns to eradicate pop-ups and pop-unders are expected to continue, so relying on these ads to promote your business may not be a good or cost-effective strategy.

Advertising in Online Directories

If part of your business strategy includes offering products or services in your own city or region, you may want to consider advertising in an online directory, such as local online Yellow Pages, or Yahoo! Local Listings, or in smaller directories operated by local companies. Likewise, you may be able to list your business free in certain online directories sponsored by county, city, or private agencies.

You can buy listings in online directories that have a business-to-business focus. For example, Business.com offers inclusion in an annual online directory for a flat fee ($199 in 2005). The directory "contains more than 400,000 listings within 65,000 industry, product and service categories" and is accessible only to other members of Business.com who are using its business-focused search engine, the company states.

Pay-Per-Click Advertising

When you advertise in online directories or on many other Web sites (including Google and Yahoo!), you often have the option to sign up for pay-per-click (PPC) advertising. With PPC, you generally can set your own advertising budget and decide how much each "click" is worth to you. Then, each time someone finds your link and clicks on it, the cost of the click is deducted from your account. If your PPC budget runs out, your listing disappears or your link no longer works until you pay more money.

At some sites, you may be able to sign up for as little as $5 per month and have as little as a penny deducted each time a prospective customer clicks on your link. Google recommends setting a PPC budget of at least $30 per day on its site.

Search Engines

Search engines have likely become a very important part of your daily routine. You probably use Google, MSN, AOL, or Yahoo! search tools several times a day, along with the search features on your favorite online auction sites.

Some other popular search engines include:

- Altavista: *www.altavista.com*
- Gigablast: *http://gigablast.com*
- Lycos: *http://search.lycos.com*
- Teoma: *http://s.teoma.com*

Sometimes, you may not give search engines a second thought. Other times, you may wonder how we ever got along without these marvelous tools that can plough through millions, maybe billions, of Web pages in seconds.

When you enter your search term, the search engine's job is to gather, sort, and report the information that seems most relevant to what you are seeking. There are three general types of search engines:

- Spider-based (sometimes called "crawler-based") search engines
- Search engines that use combinations of online directories and spiders to present their findings
- Online directories built and maintained by people (with help from online search engines, of course)

One example of the third type is the DMOZ Open Directory Project (dmoz.org), which is maintained by a worldwide network of volunteers.

Google and You

One of the constant battles for Net-based businesses is to maintain a good "position" on Google.com. Here's why. The name Google has become a verb in American culture. For example: "I Googled that new company last night and found them, but they haven't posted any pricing information yet."

Yahoo! often claims to have a bigger search engine and access to more content than Google. But what really matters is being sure your Web-based business can get good visibility on as many search engines as possible.

Search Engine Placement

There are two basic ways you can improve your placement or "page ranking" on search engines such as Google. First, you can "optimize" the information about your business before you submit it to be listed on the search engine. Second, you can buy advertising space at the search engine's main site.

Google is not the only search engine that sells advertising space. Yahoo! has several advertising programs, including Sponsored Search, which can list your business in the search results of five major search engines:

- Altavista
- CNN.com
- InfoSpace
- MSN
- Yahoo!

Optimizing Your Information

You should optimize your Web site's information *before* you submit it to a search engine for listing. However, you can make improvements to a site that is already registered, and let the spiders pick up the changes during some of their regular crawls.

Your Web page's title is your site's most important contact point with search engines. A short, specific title such as "Vintage Postcards—Buy, Sell, Trade" will have a much better chance of being found and seen by Web searchers than "Hello! Welcome to my Web site! Let me introduce you to the fascinating hobby of collecting vintage postcards!" Title lengths no longer than five to ten words are usually recommended.

Your site's main page, also known as an index page, should have "keywords" on it, as well. Keywords are terms that Web users might employ while doing an online search, such as "how to collect old postcards." Put yourself in their situation. If you were curious about how to become a screenwriter, for example, you might go to Google's search window and enter "how to become a screenwriter." Search engines often display links only to pages that have the same keywords as your query. So, you might not get links to sites that don't have "how to become a screenwriter" somewhere on their index pages. Similarly, Web sites that rely mostly on pictures do not score well with search engines, which require text. Even if your index page is little more than a title and an eye-catching picture, be sure to put some descriptive text with important keywords and key phrases somewhere on the page.

If you have difficulty coming up with the right keywords and key phrases to put on your Web site, consider hiring a keyword consultant. That's right—more proof that you can find almost anything you need or want via the Internet. If you don't have trouble coming up with keywords and key phrases and think *you* should be the consultant, you can launch that business online or quickly find companies willing to offer you franchise opportunities and digital storefronts for a few hundred dollars a year.

Good Google, Bad Google

When you buy basic advertising space on Google, you aren't buying a guaranteed appearance in the search results. You are buying advertising space in the AdWords display area next to search results. You may not need a consultant to help you create an AdWords posting. Google has established a basic format with limited line lengths for each AdWords text advertisement and related limitations for image-based ads. On the other hand, if you have little patience for restrictions, you may need assistance.

FACT

Google has set up strict editorial guidelines for the text-based ads and image-based ads. Review the guidelines at *https://adwords.google.com/ select/guidelines.html* and print them out, if necessary, for easier reference.

Some of the style and grammar restrictions in Google's *Text Ad Editorial Guidelines* include:

- No exclamation marks in ad titles.
- Ad text may contain no more than one exclamation mark.
- No excessive capitalization, such as "FREE REPORT."

- No gimmicky repetition, such as "HOT, HOT, HOT."
- Proper grammar must be used (no "then" for "than," for example).
- Ad titles must be twenty-five characters or less, and the two lines of description and URL line are limited to thirty-five characters each.
- No deceptive keywords or text. They must relate to your site and your products or services.

Google also monitors and restricts the content of AdWords advertisements. Its guidelines specify that:

- Ads must not violate Google's content policy. (The policy can be accessed from a link in the Editorial Guidelines.)
- Double-serving is generally not permitted. To "double-serve" is to try to have more than one AdWords account promoting the same business or keywords.
- Trademarks must be used correctly. (The trademarks policy can be accessed from a link in the Editorial Guidelines.)
- Claims of being "better" than competitors must be proven with a supporting display on the landing page of your Web site.
- Claims that your business is "the best," "the lowest-priced" or "#1" in a category such as service must have verification from a third party on your Web site's landing page.

Google has several other restrictions associated with text advertisements, including a ban on pop-ups when someone jumps to your Web site from your ad on Google or leaves your site.

The *Image Ad Editorial Guidelines*, meanwhile, generally follow the same guidelines for text that is displayed in an image. Some other requirements include:

- Graphics images must be properly sized for the type of ad that is being created.
- Images must be clear and recognizable.
- Images must be family-safe and must not violate Google's Terms and Conditions, which can be reviewed from a link in the Image Ad Editorial Guidelines.

- Unconventional layouts, such as upside-down pictures, cannot be used.
- Images displayed must relate to your products, services, or Web site.
- Ads may not imply an affiliation with Google.

If these restrictions and limitations leave you stymied or unsure, you can consider hiring a content specialist who has created AdWords advertisements for other businesses. Be sure to get references and check them out, along with a few ads that the specialist has produced. Google also will design an AdWorks for you through its "Jumpstart" program, for $399. Google personnel will collect information from you, review your Web site, and then create an Adwords ad. If you approve it, it will be posted.

An online business with a small budget may not be ready to pay consultants and sites for advertising. For a while at least, you may be limited to do-it-yourself choices such as link exchanges, listings in free directories, and optimizing your Web pages for the search engines. Try a few targeted e-mail messages, but be careful of the anti-spam laws. Likewise, you may be able to find cheap advertising space in a few online newsletters devoted to your area of business.

There is one other free method of advertising, and it works somewhat like a cold virus: viral marketing.

Viral Marketing

Viral marketing is a technique for spreading product or service information the same way a nasty flu virus is spread. One person spreads it to another, the second person spreads it to three others, and so on.

E-mail is the main tool that makes viral marketing work. Someone happens across your Web site or sees an item you are auctioning online and forwards your Web address to a friend. That friend has several other friends who might be interested in what you are selling. So, she forwards your URL to them. One of the friends has a cousin overseas who has been looking for an item just like what you are selling. He contacts the cousin; the cousin isn't interested, but his mother is, and she e-mails three of her friends with the news. Suddenly, you start getting inquiries and bids from all over the place.

The ubiquitous E-mail to a Friend link on eBay's auction pages is a prime example of viral marketing. Imagine Joe in Buffalo checking eBay with his wireless laptop computer while enjoying an after-work cappuccino. He comes across an auction item that amuses him or brings up a specific memory. He quickly dashes out a message to a friend: "Hey, remember that really ugly bike you had when we were kids? This may be it—or one just like it." As he sips his drink, another memory pops up. Someone at work told him recently that the in-dash radio had died in her lovingly restored 1957 Chevrolet and finding another one was going to be a pain. Joe decides to do a Web search—and finds the one you have just put up for sale. *Zip, zip,* the news goes out, and another potential buyer shows up, thanks to viral marketing.

Unfortunately, viral marketing only succeeds on a larger scale if the pass-along rate stays high for a while. If only one person needs the in-dash radio for a '57 Chevy, the "virus" quickly dies. However, if you are selling something outrageous that has just been in the news, such as the ball that hit a batter and sparked a two-hour riot at Fenway Park, word may spread quickly and widely. Hundreds, even thousands of sports fans may e-mail each other with the news, and then start clicking on your Web store to see the infamous baseball.

Only one of them can buy it, of course. But chances are good that at least a few of them will click on some of the other items in your inventory and buy something. Either way, you win.

Chapter 20
Where to Go from Here

Some economists predict that by the year 2008, American consumers will spend at least one out of ten retail dollars online. Many computer users, however, have already surpassed this ratio. Unless they need to buy something immediately, they often order it online or find it at an online auction site. The future promises more and better opportunities for online shopping. Understanding the possibilities and working them into your planning can help ensure that your online auction business will adapt and grow with the rapidly changing times.

20

Online Auction and Web Communities

On an eBay page, one simple word serves as the gateway to a much wider world. When you click on Community in the eBay toolbar, you move beyond your immediate concerns for what you are selling, who's buying, who's paying, and who still owes you money. The Community page gives you the option to connect with:

- Discussion boards where you can discuss any eBay-related topic
- Public and private groups where you can share common interests
- An answer center where eBay members can help other members with questions or problems
- Chat rooms where members can talk with other members in informal sessions

While focusing on selling, buying, and building your business, you may be tempted to skip these facilities. Yet, they can be excellent sources of information, helpful tips, ideas, and contacts. If you invest a few minutes periodically in exploring these sites, you can learn about features you haven't yet tried or hear details of new scams that may victimize sellers or buyers. You may meet someone who has worked his or her way through a business problem similar to one you are experiencing now. This advice may be the catalyst that gets you going in a new and more promising direction.

Discussion Boards

The eBay discussion boards are divided into three major categories:

- Community help boards
- General discussion boards
- Category-specific discussion boards

The *community help* discussion boards focus on topics ranging from escrow services and shipping insurance to PayPal and various policy and technical issues. The *general* discussion boards provide gathering places for eBay members who want to talk about almost any topic under the sun.

The *category-specific* discussion boards, meanwhile, zero in on problems and questions involving different auction categories or aspects of eBay. For example, someone seeking help with improving the lighting of their eBay photographs can get tips and advice from participants in the photography discussion board.

Groups

The Groups link takes you to a Groups Center where you can search for discussion groups that share your interests. You can search by Zip Code or keyword. The page also provides links to:

- Collectors clubs, for items ranging from antiques to trading cards
- Mentoring groups, for help with buying and selling
- Regional groups, organized by state or regions, such as eBayers who live in east Texas
- Seller groups, for sellers, Power Sellers, Trading Assistants, and others
- Special interest groups, for computers, crafts, fan clubs, stay-at-home parents, and other categories

Answer Center

The Answer Center is a collection of member-to-member forums where you can get help with issues related to using eBay, such as international shipping, packaging, policies, and user's agreements.

Reaching Out on Amazon.com

The Amazon.com site offers a link to its Seller Connection message board, where sellers can post questions or comments and get answers or responses from other sellers. To find it, look under the More to Explore heading in a box on the left side of Amazon.com Auctions page. The choices at Seller Connection include:

- Listing Management & Reports Discussion Board
- Shipping, Feedback & Returns Discussion Board
- Seller Soapbox Discussion Board

- Help for New Sellers Discussion Board
- Third-Party Software & Services Discussion Board

Amazon.com's sellers can post questions, share experiences, and get responses from other Amazon sellers. Most of the postings relate to how-to questions and technical points regarding Amazon's features or services. But in the Seller Soapbox area, sellers can vent their anger or concern over issues of the day, warn others of possible scams, voice complaints, or argue with each other, as people might when they meet face-to-face.

Yahoo! Community Page

The Yahoo! Auctions site offers a Community page, which includes links to Yahoo! Groups, where members can interact in a variety of settings. The Community link is found within the Getting Started box in the upper-right corner of the Auctions page in the Yahoo! Shopping area.

Another link on the Community page leads to the Yahoo! Auctions Sellers Group, a discussion board that offers help to all independent sellers using the Yahoo! Auctions site.

Networking and Online Relationships

It doesn't take long online to build a network of contacts and even become friends with contacts you have never met—and may never meet—in person. It usually is preferable to deal face-to-face with people, but the future promises more online interactions and electronic relationships. Businesses, government agencies, and other organizations are using Web links to lower costs by reducing the telephone contact and personal contact between customers or citizens and service representatives. No longer do you simply pick up a phone, call someone, explain your predicament, and have him or her transfer you to someone who may be able to help you. More often, a recorded announcement tells you to go to a Web site, click on a link that leads to another link, and another and another. There, after you have slogged through a pre-posted list of Commonly Asked Questions and their answers, you may find an e-mail link—not to a person but to a virtual department, such as helpdesk@thisveryimpersonalcorp.com. At last, you get to pose your question or explain your predicament.

Expect more of this when dealing with large organizations. Building and expanding a network of business, government, and personal *e-mail* contacts has become a necessity and will be even more of a necessity in the near future. Your only other recourse may be to deal with smaller organizations and independent businesspeople whenever possible. For instance, you may grow weary of wading through multilevel online menus to order a laser printer toner cartridge from a major source of office supplies. Instead, you may go *down* the supply chain to an online auction seller who (1) has a small stock of the cartridge you need and (2) answers questions from buyers personally, because just he and his wife run the business and they need every sale they can get.

Making the Most of Your Good Reputation

In the online auction business, your reputation as a seller is determined mostly by the feedback buyers post after trading with you. Thus, protecting the good name of your business should be one of your highest priorities at all times.

According to a report from the Pan West e-Business Initiative: "Bad feedback can cost you money. Many eBay buyers will only purchase items from sellers who have a positive feedback rating of 98+%. The lower your rating, the less active bidding you should expect on your item. Further, a strong seller rating may have a 5% or more increase on price."

To make the most of your good reputation:

- Focus consistently on delivering high-quality customer service and fast shipping, even when an auction sale item brings in only a few dollars' profit or represents a net loss.
- Remember that the customer is always right, even when she is wrong. However, try to provide information, in a very polite way, which may help the customer realize and understand her mistake. If possible, also offer at least a partial refund to reduce the likelihood of negative feedback.
- Promptly post good feedback for buyers.

- Follow up by e-mail to be sure they have received their shipment and are satisfied with their purchase.
- Minimize encounters with troubled buyers who could hurt your feedback reputation. To do this, use the online auction site's buyer requirements feature. It can be set to block bids from buyers with negative feedback scores or strikes for unpaid items.
- Avoid posting negative or neutral feedback unless necessary. Try dealing with an angry buyer directly to defuse and resolve a situation.

Buyers sometimes develop false expectations of an auction item as they look at its photographs and read its description. They mentally fill in some blanks and fail to ask enough questions. Then, when their expectations of an item don't match its real condition, they are angry with the seller for sending them "shoddy" or "damaged" merchandise. To minimize these incidents, concentrate on writing clear, accurate descriptions. Be sure your item photographs reveal the flaws as well as the positive features.

A constant focus on honesty and consistency will go a long way toward helping you make the best of your online reputation.

The Future of Online Auctions

Can't imagine what the next decade will bring? Try doing some Google and Yahoo! searches of "the future of online auctions." They will turn up a range of wild guesses, plus some serious predictions from five or six years ago that are largely obsolete. The truth is, no one really knows what the future holds, nor what the online auction world will look like five or ten years from now. Most likely, however, the pace of technology advances will be fast, and keeping in step with the times will be a constant challenge. Still, you should try to stay aware of new technology and new features that will affect online auctions. You should also try to take advantage of advances and improvements that can improve your sales, boost your profits, and simplify your work.

Universal Auction Registration

Imagine the possibilities and the convenience. What if you could sign up at one central online clearinghouse, then go to any auction site, and bid without having to repeatedly register and give out credit card information? What if your feedback scores traveled with you, so you didn't have to keep juggling several screen identities and building up good reputations on each auction site you frequent?

These conveniences haven't been created yet. But their development and adoption in the future could turbocharge the use and growth of online auction sales.

Niche-Within-Niche Auctions

Many buyers don't care that eBay currently offers hundreds of categories and sub-categories of auction items. They prefer to specialize in one narrowly focused corner of one auction grouping, such as early twentieth-century Appalachian art, 1950s electric guitars, World War II movie posters, or Soviet-era Russian navy uniforms. For sub-categories that have enough buying and selling of valuable items, it might become possible to create effective niche-within-niche auction sites that specialize in just one thing, such as baseball trading cards, first-edition books signed by their authors, or vintage balsa model airplane kits. However, such sites will likely not appear until more growth surges into the Internet and brings new buyers and sellers into the sphere of online auctions.

Big Sites Getting Bigger

Hundreds of auction sites are online, with more showing up almost every day. They can't all succeed. Failures already have happened, and other sites, new or old, will collapse in the near future. Consolidation is inevitable. It is not likely that Amazon, Yahoo! or uBid will displace eBay as the runaway market leader in online auctions. But some of the smaller sites may be consumed or may give up the auction business if they can't steal away more of eBay's market share. The smart auction seller will not focus on one site. Instead, she will try to use the best features of at least two or three auction sites and heed the ancient warning against putting all of your virtual eggs in one digital basket.

The Future of Web Commerce

Experts tend to agree on at least two predictions. The Internet will continue to get bigger and more pervasive in American and world society, and much of the action will happen out on the "edge" of the Net as computer users increasingly employ smaller, more mobile, more powerful devices.

A bigger, more pervasive Internet will mean greater availability of Web commerce at all levels of buying and selling. It will also mean that online auction sites will have more buyers and sellers competing with each other.

Greater mobility, however, will ensure that you will be able to combine travel and pleasure more easily with running online auction sales. As you find new items to sell, you will simply pull out your wireless multifunction digital device, take the necessary photographs, create the descriptive text, post the listing, watch for bids, handle other transactions, send and receive e-mail, and make voice phone calls. As long as you don't misplace or lose your Miracle Multi-communicator device, you will be fine. The panic you feel now when losing a cell phone certainly would be multiplied because of the number of other functions supported by the future device. Imagine yourself running your auction business while hiking in the Grand Canyon. It could happen soon. Now picture yourself suddenly and completely cut off from your auction business because you have just dropped your Miracle Multi-communicator into the Colorado River. That could happen, too. Adopt new technology as it fits your needs, but always have a backup means for keeping your business going.

QUESTION?

What is Internet2?
Internet2 is a consortium of more than 200 universities working with industry and government. They are trying to develop new network services and applications and ensure their rapid transfer to Internet users.

Several groups and organizations, including Internet2, are looking ahead to the so-called next-generation Internet, which may start appearing within a few years. For example, the National Science Foundation has proposed basically starting over, viewing the current Internet as a "clean slate" in its Global Environment for Networking Investigations (GENI) initiative. GENI is expected to focus on improving Internet security, as well as making the Internet easier to access and more useful for monitoring sensors and controlling devices within a building or home.

Internet changes may be years away from having any impact on your online auction business. Or, they could start arriving much faster than you think. Always keep one eye on the outside world while you stay focused on building your auction business and providing top-notch customer service.

Expanding Your Empire

You may hope to create a full-time, online auction business that keeps expanding and bringing in more money. Or, you may desire to keep your enterprise small and maintain it as a part-time source of secondary income. In either case, you will face challenges and constantly changing markets along the way.

Expanding your auction empire may entail:

- Finding, listing, selling, and shipping more items at a much faster pace
- Offering more payment and shipment choices
- Holding auctions in more categories
- Using more auction sites
- Using more of the seller's convenience features on each auction site
- Improving the quality of your auction items' photographs
- Posting photographs offline at other Web sites so they can be given bigger, clearer, and cheaper display than the auction sites offer
- Opening a Web store independently or using the Web store services available at major auction sites
- Moving your business from your house to a warehouse
- Getting serious about business insurance
- Installing a security system to protect your stored merchandise
- Hiring and training employees

- Hiring outside contractors such as an accountant to handle your books and a janitor to keep the packing and shipping area and your company's offices clean

If you desire to keep your business small and secondary to your career, focus on selling in just a few auction areas. Even then, you will still have to try new auction categories periodically, and you should keep track of new features offered by the auction site.

For example, you may have a few hard-to-categorize or semi-shabby items taking up space in your merchandise storage closet. You haven't been enthusiastic about trying to sell them, so they keep getting pushed back and buried under better items. Yet, you can't throw them away, because you know they might have value to someone and bring a fair price.

You may be able to find buyers for some of them if you use one of eBay's newer features, Want It Now. The link to Want It Now, a reverse auction, is found on the eBay home page. The Want It Now page lets buyers post free want ads for items they are seeking. The ads are posted in the same major categories that sellers and buyers use to post or search auction listings, and the notices can stay visible for sixty days. For example, a buyer would use the Art category to post his desire to buy a certain lithograph by a particular artist. If you happen to have a copy of the lithograph in your closet, you could create a Sell listing for it and then use the Respond button to send the item's listing link to the buyer. The buyer could check it out and decide whether to bid. If you already have the lithograph listed, you can use the Respond button to send the buyer the link.

ALERT!

Do not make direct sales offers to buyers when using eBay's Want It Now feature. Only send them links to listed auction items that *specifically* meet their posted needs. Attempts to sell them something else by sending e-mail addresses, Web links, phone numbers, or live chat links can lead to account suspension and other sanctions.

Many outside forces and events will help shape the near-term and long-term future of online auctions. But so will you and so will those who buy from you or sell to you. Any choices you make to expand your business or keep it small will also have an influence. As will any decisions you make to move away from major online retailers and start buying more of your goods and business supplies from online auction sellers.

In the online auction world, *you* are the market. *You* have the power. *You* make things happen. Go for it.

Appendix A
Additional Resources

Anti-Phishing Working Group
www.antiphishing.org

AuctionBytes
www.auctionbytes.com

eBay Security Center
http://pages.ebay.com/securitycenter

Federal Reserve Board, "Consumer Handbook to Credit Protection Laws"
www.federalreserve.gov/pubs/consumerhdbk/cost.htm

Federal Trade Commission ID theft information page
www.consumer.gov/idtheft

Identity Theft Resource Center
www.idtheftcenter.org

Internet Fraud Complaint Center
www.ifccfbi.gov

National Consumer League's Internet Fraud Watch
www.fraud.org

PayPal Security Center
www.paypal.com/security

Stopping Overshopping
www.stoppingovershopping.com

Appendix B

Glossary of Auction Terms

Absolute Auction

Better known as a "straight auction," an absolute auction has just one item up for sale. The seller sets an opening price and does not use a reserve price. The high bid wins the item, even if only one bid is received, and it is no higher than the opening price. Many online auction sellers use this format.

Antique

In some categories of goods, an item at least fifty years old is considered "antique." Under U.S. Customs regulations, an item must be at least 100 years old to qualify as "antique."

Appraisal

An expert's opinion of an item's value. An appraisal may be given informally ("Old chairs like this one have been selling for around $200 lately."), or it may be stated in writing.

As Is

Property "as is" is sold without any warranties or guarantees regarding its condition or suitability for a particular use. When you buy something "as is" in an online auction, it is up to you to examine and judge whether the property will meet your needs or desires. This may mean trusting the seller's descriptions, posted photographs, and reputation on the auction site. Other terms with similar meaning: "As is, where is" and "In its present condition."

Auction Value

An auction item's current bid. The value changes as the bidding goes higher.

Auction with Reserve

See Reserve Auction.

Bid Cancellation

The process of removing a potential buyer's bid from an item. A seller may cancel a bid only under special circumstances.

Bid History

A list showing the user IDs of bidders, how much they have bid, and when they placed their bid in a current auction.

Bid Retraction

The act of removing a bid from an item in an online auction. A bidder may retract a bid only under special circumstances.

Dutch Auction

An auction in which the seller has listed multiple quantities of an identical item. Several buyers can bid and win, or one bidder can try to buy up many or all of the quantities. This practice is known as "buying up lots." In a Dutch auction, all winning bidders pay the same price: the lowest successful bid. This is the opposite of what happens in a Yankee auction. There, each winning bidder pays his exact high bid.

Federal Reserve System

The Fed is the central bank of the United States. It incorporates twelve Federal Reserve branch banks, all national banks and state-chartered commercial banks, and some trust companies. In general, the Fed tries to keep the U.S. economy on an even keel by raising and lowering short-term interest rates and the money supply.

Federal Trade Commission

The Federal Trade Commission tries to ensure that America's markets are "vigorous, efficient and free of restrictions." The FTC also enforces consumer protection laws and guards against Internet scams, among its other duties.

Insertion Fee

This is eBay's term for an auction listing fee. Other online auction sites often use "listing fee" when charging an item to be listed.

Live Auction

An auction that takes place in real time, either in an auction venue with an auctioneer and buyers or online.

Lot

A single item or a group of items being auctioned.

MIB

This label on an auction item means "Mint in Box" condition. That means its original package has never been opened.

MOC

This label on an auction item means "Mint on Card" condition. This often refers to a toy or other item that is still packaged on its original card and usually inside protective plastic

NR (No Reserve)

This description means that an auction item does not have a reserve price that has to be met before it can be won with a bid.

Provenance

This term refers to an item's line of ownership. For example, an unusual or interesting provenance can add to an item's value, if ownership by a celebrity, a notorious person, or an important historical figure can be demonstrated.

Proxy Bidding

At an online auction site, this is the process of entering the maximum price you are willing to pay, and then letting a computer bid on your behalf. The proxy bidding agent will raise your bid just enough to keep you ahead, unless the price rises above your preset maximum.

Registration

The process of opening a buyer or seller account on an online auction site. Typically, you have to provide personal information including name, address, telephone number, and e-mail address, as well as credit card information. Some online auction sites may require other information, as well.

Relisting

This is to put an item up for bid again, after its first auction didn't attract any bids, or its reserve price was not met.

Reserve Auction

In a reserve auction, the seller posts an opening price but also sets a reserve price, which is the lowest he will accept. The reserve price is not revealed to bidders. If bidding exceeds the reserve price, the online auction site will post a message stating that the reserve price has been met. The seller is then obligated to sell the item to the highest bidder.

Reserve Bidder

The bidder who places the second-highest bid. If the high bidder backs out or is disqualified, the item can go to the reserve bidder, if she still wants to buy it.

Reserve Price

The price established by an owner for a lot to be sold at auction. The owner may legally refuse to sell the item for a price below this amount. The reserve price does not have to be disclosed before the attempted auction of the item.

Retaliatory Feedback

When a buyer posts negative feedback for a seller, because of shoddy merchandise or some other dispute, the seller sometimes may retaliate by posting negative feedback for the buyer.

S&H

This is auction site shorthand for "shipping and handling."

Shilling (or Shill Bidding)

This is a fraudulent practice in which the seller, using another auction account, bids on his merchandise to push up its price or has a willing associate do the bidding.

Sniping

The process of placing bids in the very last minutes or seconds of an auction, when there is almost no time for another bidder to respond. Bid sniping software sometimes is used to place a bid at the very last moment.

Terms of Service

Online auction sites usually have these sets of rules and guidelines that buyers and sellers must observe. Otherwise, they may lose their ability to buy or sell on the site.

Valuation

An expert's written or spoken opinion of an item's worth.

Value

In online auctions, an item's "value" is measured by how much money the highest bidder is willing to pay for it. Before auctioning it, a seller may have a good sense of its value but will not know exactly how much until the auction ends.

Vintage

This term, popular in auctions, applies to something that is old, relatively speaking, within its group or category. It may not necessarily be very old in terms of years. For example, a "vintage" record might be fifty years old, while a "vintage" Beanie Baby might be ten years old.

Viral Marketing

A marketing technique that encourages people to pass information such as a Web address to their friends and others, via e-mail. If the recipients also pass the information to their contacts, it can keep spreading from person to person, like a virus.

Index

The EVERYTHING Series!

BUSINESS & PERSONAL FINANCE

Everything® Budgeting Book
Everything® Business Planning Book
Everything® Coaching and Mentoring Book
Everything® Fundraising Book
Everything® Get Out of Debt Book
Everything® Grant Writing Book
Everything® Home-Based Business Book, 2nd Ed.
Everything® Homebuying Book, 2nd Ed.
Everything® Homeselling Book, 2nd Ed.
Everything® Investing Book, 2nd Ed.
Everything® Landlording Book
Everything® Leadership Book
Everything® Managing People Book
Everything® Negotiating Book
Everything® Online Business Book
Everything® Personal Finance Book
Everything® Personal Finance in Your 20s and 30s Book
Everything® Project Management Book
Everything® Real Estate Investing Book
Everything® Robert's Rules Book, $7.95
Everything® Selling Book
Everything® Start Your Own Business Book
Everything® Wills & Estate Planning Book

COMPUTERS

Everything® Online Auctions Book
Everything® Blogging Book

COOKING

Everything® Barbecue Cookbook
Everything® Bartender's Book, $9.95
Everything® Chinese Cookbook
Everything® Cocktail Parties and Drinks Book
Everything® College Cookbook
Everything® Cookbook
Everything® Cooking for Two Cookbook
Everything® Diabetes Cookbook
Everything® Easy Gourmet Cookbook
Everything® Fondue Cookbook
Everything® Gluten-Free Cookbook
Everything® Glycemic Index Cookbook
Everything® Grilling Cookbook

Everything® Healthy Meals in Minutes Cookbook
Everything® Holiday Cookbook
Everything® Indian Cookbook
Everything® Italian Cookbook
Everything® Low-Carb Cookbook
Everything® Low-Fat High-Flavor Cookbook
Everything® Low-Salt Cookbook
Everything® Meals for a Month Cookbook
Everything® Mediterranean Cookbook
Everything® Mexican Cookbook
Everything® One-Pot Cookbook
Everything® Pasta Cookbook
Everything® Quick Meals Cookbook
Everything® Slow Cooker Cookbook
Everything® Slow Cooking for a Crowd Cookbook
Everything® Soup Cookbook
Everything® Tex-Mex Cookbook
Everything® Thai Cookbook
Everything® Vegetarian Cookbook
Everything® Wild Game Cookbook
Everything® Wine Book, 2nd Ed.

CRAFT SERIES

Everything® Crafts—Baby Scrapbooking
Everything® Crafts—Bead Your Own Jewelry
Everything® Crafts—Create Your Own Greeting Cards
Everything® Crafts—Easy Projects
Everything® Crafts—Polymer Clay for Beginners
Everything® Crafts—Rubber Stamping Made Easy
Everything® Crafts—Wedding Decorations and Keepsakes

HEALTH

Everything® Alzheimer's Book
Everything® Diabetes Book
Everything® Health Guide to Adult Bipolar Disorder
Everything® Health Guide to Controlling Anxiety
Everything® Health Guide to Fibromyalgia
Everything® Hypnosis Book

Everything® Low Cholesterol Book
Everything® Massage Book
Everything® Menopause Book
Everything® Nutrition Book
Everything® Reflexology Book
Everything® Stress Management Book

HISTORY

Everything® American Government Book
Everything® American History Book
Everything® Civil War Book
Everything® Irish History & Heritage Book
Everything® Middle East Book

GAMES

Everything® 15-Minute Sudoku Book, $9.95
Everything® 30-Minute Sudoku Book, $9.95
Everything® Blackjack Strategy Book
Everything® Brain Strain Book, $9.95
Everything® Bridge Book
Everything® Card Games Book
Everything® Card Tricks Book, $9.95
Everything® Casino Gambling Book, 2nd Ed.
Everything® Chess Basics Book
Everything® Craps Strategy Book
Everything® Crossword and Puzzle Book
Everything® Crossword Challenge Book
Everything® Cryptograms Book, $9.95
Everything® Easy Crosswords Book
Everything® Easy Kakuro Book, $9.95
Everything® Games Book, 2nd Ed.
Everything® Giant Sudoku Book, $9.95
Everything® Kakuro Challenge Book, $9.95
Everything® Large-Print Crosswords Book
Everything® Lateral Thinking Puzzles Book, $9.95
Everything® Pencil Puzzles Book, $9.95
Everything® Poker Strategy Book
Everything® Pool & Billiards Book
Everything® Test Your IQ Book, $9.95
Everything® Texas Hold 'Em Book, $9.95
Everything® Travel Crosswords Book, $9.95
Everything® Word Games Challenge Book
Everything® Word Search Book

Bolded titles are new additions to the series.
All Everything® books are priced at $12.95 or $14.95, unless otherwise stated. Prices subject to change without notice.

HOBBIES

Everything® Candlemaking Book
Everything® Cartooning Book
Everything® Drawing Book
Everything® Family Tree Book, 2nd Ed.
Everything® Knitting Book
Everything® Knots Book
Everything® Photography Book
Everything® Quilting Book
Everything® Scrapbooking Book
Everything® Sewing Book
Everything® Woodworking Book

HOME IMPROVEMENT

Everything® Feng Shui Book
Everything® Feng Shui Decluttering Book, $9.95
Everything® Fix-It Book
Everything® Home Decorating Book
Everything® Homebuilding Book
Everything® Lawn Care Book
Everything® Organize Your Home Book

KIDS' BOOKS

All titles are $7.95

Everything® Kids' Animal Puzzle &
   Activity Book
Everything® Kids' Baseball Book, 4th Ed.
Everything® Kids' Bible Trivia Book
Everything® Kids' Bugs Book
Everything® Kids' Christmas Puzzle
   & Activity Book
Everything® Kids' Cookbook
Everything® Kids' Crazy Puzzles Book
Everything® Kids' Dinosaurs Book
**Everything® Kids' Gross Hidden Pictures
   Book**
Everything® Kids' Gross Jokes Book
Everything® Kids' Gross Mazes Book
Everything® Kids' Gross Puzzle and
   Activity Book
Everything® Kids' Halloween Puzzle
   & Activity Book
Everything® Kids' Hidden Pictures Book
Everything® Kids' Horses Book
Everything® Kids' Joke Book
Everything® Kids' Knock Knock Book
Everything® Kids' Math Puzzles Book
Everything® Kids' Mazes Book
Everything® Kids' Money Book
Everything® Kids' Nature Book

Everything® Kids' Pirates Puzzle and
   Activity Book
Everything® Kids' Puzzle Book
Everything® Kids' Riddles & Brain Teasers Book
Everything® Kids' Science Experiments Book
Everything® Kids' Sharks Book
Everything® Kids' Soccer Book
Everything® Kids' Travel Activity Book

KIDS' STORY BOOKS

Everything® Fairy Tales Book

LANGUAGE

Everything® Conversational Japanese Book
   (with CD), $19.95
Everything® French Grammar Book
Everything® French Phrase Book, $9.95
Everything® French Verb Book, $9.95
**Everything® German Practice Book with
   CD, $19.95**
Everything® Inglés Book
Everything® Learning French Book
Everything® Learning German Book
Everything® Learning Italian Book
Everything® Learning Latin Book
Everything® Learning Spanish Book
Everything® Sign Language Book
Everything® Spanish Grammar Book
Everything® Spanish Phrase Book, $9.95
Everything® Spanish Practice Book
   (with CD), $19.95
Everything® Spanish Verb Book, $9.95

MUSIC

Everything® Drums Book (with CD), $19.95
Everything® Guitar Book
**Everything® Guitar Chords Book with CD,
   $19.95**
Everything® Home Recording Book
Everything® Playing Piano and Keyboards
   Book
Everything® Reading Music Book (with CD),
   $19.95
Everything® Rock & Blues Guitar Book
   (with CD), $19.95
Everything® Songwriting Book

NEW AGE

Everything® Astrology Book, 2nd Ed.
Everything® Dreams Book, 2nd Ed.
Everything® Love Signs Book, $9.95

Everything® Numerology Book
Everything® Paganism Book
Everything® Palmistry Book
Everything® Psychic Book
Everything® Reiki Book
Everything® Tarot Book
Everything® Wicca and Witchcraft Book

PARENTING

Everything® Baby Names Book, 2nd Ed.
Everything® Baby Shower Book
Everything® Baby's First Food Book
Everything® Baby's First Year Book
Everything® Birthing Book
Everything® Breastfeeding Book
Everything® Father-to-Be Book
Everything® Father's First Year Book
Everything® Get Ready for Baby Book
Everything® Get Your Baby to Sleep Book,
   $9.95
Everything® Getting Pregnant Book
Everything® Homeschooling Book
Everything® Mother's First Year Book
Everything® Parent's Guide to Children
   and Divorce
Everything® Parent's Guide to Children
   with ADD/ADHD
Everything® Parent's Guide to Children
   with Asperger's Syndrome
Everything® Parent's Guide to Children
   with Autism
Everything® Parent's Guide to Children with
   Bipolar Disorder
Everything® Parent's Guide to Children
   with Dyslexia
Everything® Parent's Guide to Positive
   Discipline
Everything® Parent's Guide to Raising a
   Successful Child
**Everything® Parent's Guide to Raising
   Boys**
**Everything® Parent's Guide to Raising
   Siblings**
Everything® Parent's Guide to Tantrums
Everything® Parent's Guide to the Overweight
   Child
Everything® Parent's Guide to the Strong-
   Willed Child
Everything® Parenting a Teenager Book
Everything® Potty Training Book, $9.95
Everything® Pregnancy Book, 2nd Ed.

Bolded titles are new additions to the series.
All Everything® books are priced at $12.95 or $14.95, unless otherwise stated. Prices subject to change without notice.

Everything® Pregnancy Fitness Book
Everything® Pregnancy Nutrition Book
Everything® Pregnancy Organizer, $15.00
Everything® Toddler Book
Everything® Toddler Activities Book
Everything® Tween Book
Everything® Twins, Triplets, and More Book

PETS

Everything® Boxer Book
Everything® Cat Book, 2nd Ed.
Everything® Chihuahua Book
Everything® Dachshund Book
Everything® Dog Book
Everything® Dog Health Book
Everything® Dog Training and Tricks Book
Everything® German Shepherd Book
Everything® Golden Retriever Book
Everything® Horse Book
Everything® Horse Care Book
Everything® Horseback Riding Book
Everything® Labrador Retriever Book
Everything® Poodle Book
Everything® Pug Book
Everything® Puppy Book
Everything® Rottweiler Book
Everything® Small Dogs Book
Everything® Tropical Fish Book
Everything® Yorkshire Terrier Book

REFERENCE

Everything® Car Care Book
Everything® Classical Mythology Book
Everything® Computer Book
Everything® Divorce Book
Everything® Einstein Book
Everything® Etiquette Book, 2nd Ed.
Everything® Inventions and Patents Book
Everything® Mafia Book
Everything® Mary Magdalene Book
 Everything® Philosophy Book
Everything® Psychology Book
Everything® Shakespeare Book

RELIGION

Everything® Angels Book
Everything® Bible Book
Everything® Buddhism Book
Everything® Catholicism Book

Everything® Christianity Book
Everything® Freemasons Book
Everything® History of the Bible Book
Everything® Jewish History & Heritage Book
Everything® Judaism Book
Everything® Kabbalah Book
Everything® Koran Book
Everything® Prayer Book
Everything® Saints Book
Everything® Torah Book
Everything® Understanding Islam Book
Everything® World's Religions Book
Everything® Zen Book

SCHOOL & CAREERS

Everything® Alternative Careers Book
Everything® College Major Test Book
Everything® College Survival Book, 2nd Ed.
Everything® Cover Letter Book, 2nd Ed.
Everything® Get-a-Job Book
Everything® Guide to Being a Paralegal
Everything® Guide to Being a Real Estate
  Agent
Everything® Guide to Starting and Running
  a Restaurant
Everything® Job Interview Book
Everything® New Nurse Book
Everything® New Teacher Book
Everything® Paying for College Book
Everything® Practice Interview Book
Everything® Resume Book, 2nd Ed.
Everything® Study Book
Everything® Teacher's Organizer, $16.95

SELF-HELP

Everything® Dating Book, 2nd Ed.
Everything® Great Sex Book
Everything® Kama Sutra Book
Everything® Self-Esteem Book

SPORTS & FITNESS

Everything® Fishing Book
Everything® Golf Instruction Book
Everything® Pilates Book
Everything® Running Book
Everything® Total Fitness Book
Everything® Weight Training Book
Everything® Yoga Book

TRAVEL

Everything® Family Guide to Hawaii
Everything® Family Guide to Las Vegas,
  2nd Ed.
Everything® Family Guide to New York City,
  2nd Ed.
Everything® Family Guide to RV Travel &
  Campgrounds
Everything® Family Guide to the Walt Disney
  World Resort®, Universal Studios®,
  and Greater Orlando, 4th Ed.
Everything® Family Guide to Cruise Vacations
Everything® Family Guide to the Caribbean
Everything® Family Guide to Washington
  D.C., 2nd Ed.
Everything® Guide to New England
Everything® Travel Guide to the Disneyland
  Resort®, California Adventure®,
  Universal Studios®, and the
  Anaheim Area

WEDDINGS

Everything® Bachelorette Party Book, $9.95
Everything® Bridesmaid Book, $9.95
Everything® Elopement Book, $9.95
Everything® Father of the Bride Book, $9.95
Everything® Groom Book, $9.95
Everything® Mother of the Bride Book, $9.95
Everything® Outdoor Wedding Book
Everything® Wedding Book, 3rd Ed.
Everything® Wedding Checklist, $9.95
Everything® Wedding Etiquette Book, $9.95
Everything® Wedding Organizer, $15.00
Everything® Wedding Shower Book, $9.95
Everything® Wedding Vows Book, $9.95
Everything® Weddings on a Budget Book, $9.95

WRITING

Everything® Creative Writing Book
Everything® Get Published Book, 2nd Ed.
Everything® Grammar and Style Book
Everything® Guide to Writing a Book Proposal
Everything® Guide to Writing a Novel
Everything® Guide to Writing Children's Books
Everything® Guide to Writing Research Papers
Everything® Screenwriting Book
Everything® Writing Poetry Book
Everything® Writing Well Book